WORDS
STILL COUNT
WITH ME

Also by Herbert Mitgang

FICTION

The Return
Get These Men out of the Hot Sun
The Montauk Fault
Kings in the Counting House

BIOGRAPHY

Abraham Lincoln: A Press Portrait
The Fiery Trial: A Life of Lincoln
The Man Who Rode the Tiger: The Life and Times of Judge
    Samuel Seabury

REPORTAGE

Dangerous Dossiers: Exposing the Secret War against America's
    Greatest Authors
Freedom to See: Television and the First Amendment

CRITICISM

Working for the Reader: A Chronicle of Culture, Literature,
    War and Politics in Books

HISTORY (Editor)

Civilians under Arms: Stars & Stripes, Civil War to Korea
The Letters of Carl Sandburg
Washington, D.C. in Lincoln's Time
America at Random: Topics of the Times
Spectator of America

PLAYS

Mister Lincoln
Knight Errant

W . W . Norton & Company

New York / London

WORDS STILL COUNT WITH ME

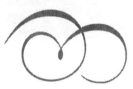

A Chronicle of Literary Conversations

HERBERT MITGANG

The text of this book is composed in Bembo
with the display set in Copperplate Gothic
Composition by the Haddon Craftsmen, Inc.
Book design by Jo Anne Metsch

Library of Congress Cataloging-in-Publication Data

Mitgang, Herbert.
Words still count with me : a chronicle of literary conversations
/ Herbert Mitgang.
p.   cm.
Includes index.
1. Authors, Modern—20th century—Interviews.   2. Literature,
Modern—20th century—History and criticism—Theory, etc.
I. Title.
PN452.M45   1995
809'.04—dc20   95-5392

ISBN 0-393-03880-7

W. W. Norton & Company, Inc., 500 Fifth Avenue, New York, N.Y. 10110
W. W. Norton & Company Ltd., 10 Coptic Street, London WC1A 1PU

1 2 3 4 5 6 7 8 9 0

For Lee D. Mitgang
No. 1 son, friend,
intrepid reporter

CONTENTS

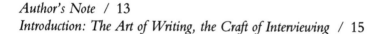

LITERARY LANDSCAPES

AUTHOR'S NOTE

These interviews with authors are not biographies but impressionistic portraits designed to reveal their creative lives. Some of the authors were caught on the fly; others expressed themselves more fully. Some lengths vary because of the exigencies of newspaper and magazine space. In some cases I have combined comments made to me by an author over several years. In other cases I have pared down their remarks because I found that much in little summed up their ideas instantly. For example, I asked Susan Sontag what were her big themes. She replied: "Literature and love. What else is there?" To the same question about his themes, John Cheever replied: "Love and death." What else need be said? Any serious author might say: Instead of trying to read me, read my books—find me there.

Most of these conversations and comments appeared in different form in the *New York Times, The New Yorker, International Herald Tribune, Chicago Tribune, San Francisco Chronicle,* the *Progressive,* the *Nation,* the *New Republic.* Several of the interviews and articles are published here for the first time. The final section of the book—"Literary Landscapes"—illustrates the commonality of literature in different corners of the world.

And for astute editorial guidance, a salute to a writer's and editor's editor, Donald S. Lamm, chairman of W. W. Norton, and his talented colleagues.

H. M.

INTRODUCTION

The Art of Writing,
the Craft of Interviewing

During the friendly typewriter age before the coming of the chilling electronic era, E. B. White, the finest literary stylist of our time, once told me: "Television has taken a big bite out of the written word. But words still count with me."

While searching my imagination for a title for this chronicle of conversations with scores of authors in the United States, Europe, and Asia during the past quarter of a century, Andy White's inspiriting comment came to mind. It perfectly expresses my own thoughts about writing, now and in the future. Despite dire electronic forebodings, written words, carpentered into telling sentences and paragraphs, will remain the building blocks of literature.

Not long ago, in describing the convenience of the computer as a word processor to Alfred Kazin, the literary critic and memoirist, I mentioned how easy it was to move a paragraph instantly without having to retype a whole page. "The problem isn't moving paragraphs," Kazin sagely replied; "it's writing paragraphs."

Over the years I've had an opportunity to talk with novelists,

historians, biographers, and poets in many places—and not by
E-mail, fax, Internet, or even cordless phone. While writing
daily and Sunday columns on the American publishing scene, I
decided to give myself the assignment of interviewing the authors I most respected in the world. Whenever possible, I initi-
ated the talks on my own, in the United States and abroad. To
be sure, I sometimes spoke with market-driven writers whose
names turned up on the best seller charts. But once is more than
enough; they are not among the authors included in this book.

Myself surprised, I found that my wanderings included a
number of magic-carpet datelines beyond New York and London: West Egg, Flat Rock, Santa Monica, Santa Fe, Dublin,
Paris, Lausanne, Milan, Rome, Palermo, Frankfurt, East and
West Berlin, Prague, Jerusalem, Saigon, Tokyo, and—not to
forget—Allen Cove, Maine.

Allen Cove can be found only on nautical maps. It's where
White lived—if you got there by sailboat. After I spent a long
morning and afternoon with him during the first of our encounters, we had a casual understanding that I would not mention
North Brooklin, his actual town, because he didn't want bus-
loads of tourists driving up to his house looking for Stuart Little
and Charlotte's Web. We had begun our friendship when I invited him to write an essay on anything he wanted to get off his
chest for the *New York Times* op-ed page. White replied that his
pen had run dry and he had stopped writing pieces, even for *The
New Yorker*. I sent him a dozen ball-point pens. Playing the
game, he replied that he had run out of paper; naturally I sent
him two reams and threw in a *Times* paperweight.

After calling me the most "active" editor (I chose to take it as
a compliment, not a gentle reprimand) he had known since Harold Wallace Ross, *The New Yorker*'s founding editor, White
came through with a half dozen brilliant essays. The fact that
Ross had been the managing editor of *Stars and Stripes* in Paris in
World War I and I had been the managing editor of *Stars and
Stripes* in Palermo in World War II made his remark all the more

appreciated because it brought our journalistic generations together.

One of White's delightful essays challenged an article by J. B.
Priestley, the British playwright, who had started a tempest in an
eggcup by finding the American preference for white eggs a sign
of national malaise. (White wrote: "Why is it, do you suppose,
that an Englishman is unhappy until he has explained America?
In New England, where I live and which is part of America, the
brown egg, far from being despised, is king. . . . A neighbor of
mine, a couple of miles up the road, is planning to go the brown
egg one better. He dreams of a green egg. And what's more, he
knows of a hen who will lay one.") White's defense from his
Maine henhouse, which I titled "Farmer White's Brown Eggs,"
somehow succeeded in telling his readers about nothing less
than the state of the human and animal worlds in New England.

I'm pleased to note that White and Priestley are among the
authors in this book I was privileged to interview.

In one of his lighthearted letters to me, White showed his
distrust of computers; it was inspired by the fact that the cashier's
computer at the *New York Times* didn't pay him on time and the
management was pretty cheap even when it did. He wrote, "I
figured out today that The Times was paying me thirteen and a
half cents a word, which is not as good as Calvin Coolidge was
getting for a column he wrote in the nineteen-twenties." In
another cheerful complaint he said, "Last Friday, my wife and I
visited the Brooklin Cemetery and bought a plot. I was amazed
to discover that it cost less than a year's subscription to The
Times."

When I visited White (by car, not sail) in Maine, I confessed
that every time I wrote about him I was nervous about my syn-
tax and split infinitives, among other shortcomings. I suspected
that I was violating half the good rules in his *Elements of Style*.
White's watchwords—clarity and simplicity—are easier to explain than achieve for authors or their interlocutors.

Over time a seasoned journalist meets presidents and prime

ministers, generals and admirals, and assorted dignitaries. I found many of the authors here, whose work I had read and admired, far more interesting in conversation than the high-and-mighty public officials and brass hats who had to speak cautiously in ghostwritten or measured words. By contrast, the most revered authors I met sounded as if they were thinking and talking and writing not for the record but for themselves: a demanding audience of one.

None of the authors was more forthcoming than Samuel Beckett. After some long-distance negotiating, we rendez-voused in a plain Parisian café that he had chosen near his apartment in the Fourteenth Arrondissement. I was in awe; after all, Beckett was Beckett as well as a direct link to James Joyce, who had cracked open the English sentence like a cryptanalyst breaking an enemy's code. Beckett's lined face seemed carved in polished granite, just as in his photographs; his blue eyes were more penetrating than I had imagined. But everything about his manner was softer and gentler.

Like the few geniuses that I had written about in the arts—Henry Moore, Frank Lloyd Wright, Alexander Calder—Beckett expressed himself with great directness about his work. (I believe that simplicity—the ability to cut through cant and get to the heart of a matter—is the common element of genius.) It was understood beforehand that Beckett did not grant formal interviews and there could be no direct quotations; all we were doing was having a couple of cups of coffee and cigarillos.

And so no conventional interview and no notes: *"Rien à faire"* ("Nothing to be done"), as the opening line of *Waiting for Godot* goes. For me, our ninety-minute talk turned out to be a pleasurable lesson in mental note-taking. Afterward, when I asked permission to photograph him because I thought he looked far less severe in person than in his pictures, he kindly consented.

With Vladimir Nabokov, I found myself similarly challenged, if not more so, before getting to see him in his residence hotel in Montreux, overlooking Lake Geneva. To protect the integrity of his words (above all, his words, written on small index cards, counted), he did not grant interviews, unless questions were submitted in advance in writing, answered by him in writing, and printed verbatim. My first attempt failed. Then I politely told him that I respected his conditions but that they amounted to censorship; that he was a professional novelist and that in my field I also considered myself a professional, who had covered wars and other calamities, and he would have to take his chances on my integrity, too. I knew it sounded pompous, but I thought, what the hell. Yet even that, I'm sure, isn't what made him relent; I had an ace up my sleeve.

Knowing that Nabokov was an avid lepidopterist, I made my final plea on stationery that was decorated with monarch butterflies on the wing. How could he resist?

When it came to Stephen Spender, Christopher Isherwood, and W. H. Auden, the trio who influenced a generation of British poets and essayists in the 1930s, I'm still chagrined that I never got to speak to Auden—surely in the front rank of great twentieth-century poets—except once or twice by telephone. I saw Spender several times in New York and at his home in St. John's Wood in London. For a book I wrote about J. Edgar Hoover's paranoid FBI files on authors, Spender helped me by disclosing that he had a secret mark on his passport which placed him on a "dangerous" list whenever he entered the United States.

With Isherwood, I shared a jug of California wine at his house in Santa Monica (his directions were wonderfully vague: "Turn left at the second palm tree"). Later I gave him a lift to Hollywood. Before jogging off, he casually delivered a memorable line that sent me to Andrew Marvell's "To His Coy Mistress" for part of the source: "If you have world enough and time, you can stay on Sunset Boulevard forever." But though Auden lived on St. Mark's Place in the East Village, a few miles from where I hung my hat, I failed to see him, and still regret it whenever I read one of his poems.

Some of the conversations were pure joy. Holding court in

his local restaurant on the Upper West Side of Manhattan, Isaac Bashevis Singer kept filling my breakfast plate with his leftover scrambled eggs, urging me, like a Jewish mother, to eat, eat. Singer could say more in a few enigmatic paragraphs about writing than others could at much greater length. On the decline of the Yiddish language, he spoke like a prophet: "Yiddish has been in trouble for the last five hundred years, and it will still be in trouble for the next thousand."

In the back room of Riccardo's, a funky newspaper hangout in Chicago, I couldn't keep up with Studs Terkel and Nelson Algren as they matched cognacs against martinis and their cigar smoke curled in lazy half Immelmanns overhead. Terkel, who pioneered oral history in book form, kept running to the phone, calling up "a reformed left-wing hooker" to join us for dinner, but she wasn't home. Terkel and Algren, closet intellectuals despite some of the streetwise characters who populated their books, were old friends. Adding to his famous aphorism— "Never eat at a place called Mom's. Never play cards with a man called Doc. Never go to bed with a woman whose troubles are greater than your own"—Algren said, "All the wisdom I acquired in the Orient can be summed up in one line: Never eat in a place with sliding doors unless you're crazy about raw fish."

It was an evening of laughs and one-liners as the two Chicago literary monuments tried to top each other with outrageous comments about various enemies of the Republic on the political right. Later I came to realize that at least half the time Studs and Nelson were really putting on a hick from Manhattan. The "reformed left-wing hooker" never showed up.

Among the twentieth-century authors who have left a strong mark on international literature is Rebecca West, author of *Black Lamb and Grey Falcon,* a prescient blueprint of the continuous ethnic identity crisis in divided Yugoslavia. Her early novels emphasized the independence of women, and her postwar reporting of the treason trials of Nazi sympathizers confirmed her great range as a writer. Before seeing Dame Rebecca in her apartment in Prince's Gate in Southwest London, I scooped up a big bunch of peonies at a corner florist. What else do you bring a Dame Commander of the British Empire? When she unlatched the door, I deposited them in her waiting arms. She graciously said that peonies were her—and her mother's—favorite flowers. As we talked across the teacups, Dame Rebecca gave me a *tour d'horizon* of her brilliant career.

Helen Wolff, whose "A Helen and Kurt Wolff Book" continued to be an impressive imprint even after her husband's death, was one of my essential sources for a number of these interviews. Kurt Wolff had been Franz Kafka's original publisher; after the Wolffs escaped from Hitler's Germany, they started Pantheon Books, then began publishing under their own names. Thanks to Mrs. Wolff, I was privileged to pursue her remarkable group of European authors: Günter Grass and Jurek Becker of Germany; Umberto Eco, Giorgio Bassani, and Italo Calvino of Italy; Leonardo Sciascia of Sicily (whom I had met before); Max Frisch and Georges Simenon of Switzerland; Stanislaw Lem of Poland; George Konrad of Hungary.

During the months I spent with Mrs. Wolff while writing a "Profile" about her for *The New Yorker,* she provided me with an unforgettable education in quality publishing. What is embedded in my mind is her conviction that given editorial attention and critical enthusiasm, serious books can find their audience in the United States.

Once in a while something that is written has a gratifying effect beyond the printed page. Probably the most important interview I ever conducted was with a German writer of no great fame named Hans Joachim Schaedlich who was in deep trouble in East Berlin. He had written a book that described the drab life in the German police state. It was published in West Germany, breaching the book curtain that was as dangerous to cross as the Berlin Wall. He then was branded an "enemy of the state." Schaedlich and his wife lost their jobs; even their child was not allowed to continue in nursery school by the cruel regime.

When I heard about the case in Frankfurt, I checked with

Günter Grass in West Berlin. Would I cause Schaedlich more harm if I, an American writer, visited him? Surprisingly, Grass encouraged me to try. I telephoned Schaedlich; his line had not been shut down by the Stasi, perhaps because it wanted to record his conversations and take down the names of his contacts. Schaedlich said that he was in such hot water already that a visit couldn't make things worse and might possibly help. I went through Checkpoint Charlie, past the humorless gray-uniformed women guards on the East German side of the border maze and the evil side of the Berlin Wall. Carbines sticking out of their car, the East German police trailed my taxi all the way to Köpenick on the outskirts of East Berlin. Good, Schaedlich told me, let them know I've got friends in the West.

After meeting Schaedlich, his wife and daughter and filing a story about them, I tried to see the East German cultural minister on three occasions to discuss the case. I stayed in West Berlin two extra days, went through Checkpoint Charlie again, and left a series of written questions with the minister's flunky, who naturally described himself as a poet. All the Iron Curtain covert agents I had ever met in the West, including the preglasnost Russians, always claimed to be poets—but I never had the wit to ask them to recite one of their poems.

I innocently inquired from the Cultural Ministry what activities qualified Schaedlich or any other writer or artist to be declared an "enemy of the state." My guess was correct; the "poet" said the minister wouldn't respond to any provocative questions by an American. That, of course, was the point. At least a housebound prisoner was aware that someone on the other side of the wall was concerned about one unimportant writer's freedom to publish—to exist, really, as a person. A few months later Grass and Helen Wolff told me that because of the embarrassing newspaper attention he had received, Schaedlich and his family were allowed to leave East Berlin and move to West Germany. Writer or not, it was wonderful to help spring one prisoner of a police state.

My talks with most writers were seldom that adventuresome. Two wealthy authors gave me excellent but conflicting advice about how I, too, could achieve fame and fortune. In his garden apartment in Lausanne, Georges Simenon, who made millions from his *policiers* and psychological novels, told me to follow his example and write hundreds of books. In his magnificent country house in Alveston, England, J. B. Priestley, who made millions from the theater, told me, "Young man, don't write books; write plays. Once you've had several going for you, you can live like this in your old age."

Right, gentlemen; but which should I write first?

Going over these conversations, I was happy to discover that no simple coda—other than a compelling desire to write truthfully and well—emerged from the work of the most dedicated authors. The worldly writers here range from the classical to the hortatory, from the realistic to the fabulist. But I detected no single school of writing. Such "schools" are arbitrary inventions of literary pedants, deconstructionists, and Nexis researchers—some brevetted as pretentious book critics by their publications—who are unaware of the bravura and subterranean instincts of a writer's creative process.

In many of these interviews I attempted to unearth the roots of an author's creativity. Writers of fact and fiction can nurture an idea in their minds for years. When you ask a writer how long it takes to write a book, the usual answer may be anywhere from one to five years. I always respond that a book takes ten years: two or three years to write and seven or eight years to think about. Imagine, cynics may well say, getting paid for doing nothing but thinking.

Of course, some writers whose work keeps them close to current events have to create almost instantly. I think of Garry Trudeau, creator of the brilliant *Doonesbury* comic strip, as fundamentally a writer who illustrates ideas. His familiar characters have been collected into dozens of books. "You have to care about your characters," he said, "because if you don't, the reader won't." One of the nicest things that can be said about Trudeau is that he's constantly in hot water with newspaper editors and government officials, proving he must be doing something right. In his book-lined studio in Manhattan, Trudeau told me that his ideas came from the past and present. He spends a good deal of time watching television, going to the movies, and reading newspapers, but he also keeps bound volumes of the comic book series *Classics Illustrated* on his bookshelves.

"One thing I don't do is walk around with a notebook," Trudeau said. "I let lightning strike."

Ours is a time of freewheeling individuality. Fictional characters are often created in mysterious ways. Graham Greene said that he found the main heroes in his books "working away far down in the dark cave of the unconscious while the world burned." The best writers follow their own stars, have something to declare, and say it with integrity and originality.

I liked what Leonardo Sciascia, the Sicilian author of metaphysical mysteries that exposed the hypocrisy of the Mafia and the long reach of the Vatican, told me at his country house deep in the interior of Pirandello's island. Crediting Ernest Hemingway for the aphorism, Sciascia said: "I don't write books; it's books that write me." Whenever I visited Sicily, I looked Sciascia up because he was one of Italy's major regional authors—at once traditional, literary, and political (on the left). His novels reflected the life of his city neighbors in Palermo and country peasants in Racalmuto. Historically both were oppressed and both were survivors—endless themes for any writer anywhere in the world.

Unlike so many American and European authors who made their reputations by placing their stories in a real or imagined small-town setting, Sciascia refused to move on to Rome or Milan or Paris or New York. I tried to persuade him to visit the United States, which he admired because of its literature and films, but he explained that his stories worked best close to home. Sciascia said that William Faulkner had intruded Greek tragedy into the detective story in a mythical region of Mississippi, and he wanted to achieve something similar on his native grounds. Once Sciascia said, "I'd so much like to have it said of me that I introduced Pirandellian drama into the detective story."

A few of the serious writers I encountered faced an unusual dilemma: After achieving critical success early in their careers, they later were condemned for following the marketplace and achieving popularity. Bitterness shadowed them all the way to the bank. One of the talks here took place in Southampton, Long Island, with an old army friend, Irwin Shaw, the short-story writer, novelist, and playwright. After *Bury the Dead* and *The Young Lions,* Shaw was troubled by accusations that he later played to the pit; that he had become a commercial writer who wrote down; that he no longer was "the old Irwin Shaw."

The new-old Shaw told me, "Now I'm considered a popular writer, but so were Tolstoy, Dickens, and Balzac and the ghost looking over all our shoulders, Shakespeare." Shaw, a onetime Brooklyn College ballplayer, insisted that he was still doing his best: "I used to watch Joe DiMaggio. He never made a hard catch. The hardest work for a writer is to make it look easy. You do the work, and if you do it right, you make the reader do the thinking."

For at least a hundred years (read, or reread, George Gissing's *New Grub Street,* 1891), the demands of literature and commerce have clashed. One of Gissing's characters spoke of "the glorious privilege of being independent." The struggle continues for writers trying to balance making a living and making literature. Scott Fitzgerald said that the beauty of literature was the discovery that your longings are universal longings, that you're not lonely and isolated from anyone. Half-apologetically Fitzgerald played both sides of the street, but even the stories he wrote for the popular magazines to stay afloat couldn't hide his literary talent.

When John Steinbeck received the Nobel Prize in literature,

he envisioned a high standard for authors in his acceptance speech: "The ancient commission of the writer hasn't changed. He is charged with exposing our many grievous faults and failures, with dredging up to the light our dark and dangerous dreams for the purposes of improvement." With less sentimentality, Graham Greene, who never got the Nobel he deserved, said something similar but in his own hard-edged way: "If only writers would maintain that one virtue of disloyalty—so much more important than chastity—unspotted from the world. That is a genuine duty we owe society, to be a piece of grit in the State machinery."

I suspect that several of the Nobel laureates with whom I had a chance to talk—Saul Bellow, Nadine Gordimer, William Golding, Octavio Paz, Czeslaw Milosz, Heinrich Böll, Eugenio Montale, Elias Canetti, Toni Morrison—would find Steinbeck's or Greene's sentiments agreeable. In novels, poetry, and plays, fiction writers indulge their dangerous dreams in the dark for unknown readers. Dante put it plainly for authors—and perhaps for interviewers who write about authors, too: *"Segui il tuo corso, e lascia dir le genti"* ("Follow your path, and let the people talk" or, more colloquially, "Do your own thing, no matter what the crowd says").

Interviewing is a craft; writing can be an art. After you've transcribed your notes and started to put the words that count together, art possibly follows. These are some thoughts about the methods behind many of the author interviews in this book and about interviewing in general.

The reader may discover what appear to be tricks of the trade here. But it has been my experience after talking with many people in the United States and abroad—from Nobel laureates in literature to presidents and prime ministers to untitled mortals—that the best trick isn't really a trick at all. It's to play fair with your subject, before, during, and after the interview. Surprisingly, trust works.

No American author was more trusted than John Hersey, an old friend and colleague in advocating the rights and freedoms of authors. Unlike many celebrated writers in our time who are captives of the New Journalism, metafiction, and other flavors of the month, he never aimed to betray those he interviewed or confused fiction and nonfiction in his writing. This is how Hersey expressed the difference:

> In fiction, the writer's voice matters; in reporting, the writer's authority matters. The writer of fiction must invent; the journalist must not invent. We read fiction to fortify our psyches, and in the pleasure that that fortification may give us, temperament holds sway. We read journalism to try to learn about the external world in which our psyches have to struggle along, and the quality we most need in our informant is some measure of trustworthiness. Good writers care about what words mean.

There are friendly and hostile interviews. Sometimes it's hard to distinguish between the two because the interview that is set up to promote an author (or a public official) may be more perilous than one arranged between the interviewer and subject directly. Of course, some publicists are perceptive and helpful to interviewers; eventually one learns to recognize those who dissemble and those who respect the boundaries of their occupation.

Yet more than ever we live in an age of so-called communications specialists, flacks, ghostwriters, and, worst of all, spin doctors, whose role is to put a happy face on a negative personality, statement, or event. Spinmeisters are the half-charming purveyors of half-truths who attempt to twist an interviewer's mind and words. Beware their blandishments.

Generally I have found it a distraction to have any third party—even a friend or one's own researcher—in the same room during an interview. When I was writing editorials during the Vietnam War, I would periodically go to the Pentagon and talk with some high-ranking officer to get information beyond the usual light-at-the-end-of-the-tunnel prevarications from Messrs. Nixon and Kissinger. (Robert Lowell exploded the tunnel light euphemism in verse: "If we see a light at the end of the tunnel, / It's the light of an oncoming train.") I usually found that I wasn't the only one in the Pentagon office to pull out a notebook. Invariably some lieutenant colonel or lieutenant commander would be writing down my questions and his superior's answers. There was an implied threat that I—or the general or admiral I was talking to—was not to be trusted alone.

A third party's presence often makes for a stiff exchange; what isn't needed is an audience that causes the subject to perform or speak only for the record. Of course, there are ways to overcome roadblocks erected by PR types. After you've put away your notebook and signaled that the formal interview is over, sometimes a casual conversation in parting can elicit previously denied facts. Another matter of craft: Late in the same day or early the following morning an interviewer can follow up with a phone call and speak with the subject directly in order to get a "clarification." Doing so offers a chance to zing in a few more questions and possibly get straight answers.

At one point I declined an offer to obtain a Pentagon press identification from an old Army Air Corps friend who worked as a civilian in the Department of Defense. Because of interservice rivalries, it made sense to approach sources in one of the military branches directly instead of getting clearance through the highest echelons in the corridors of power. The Pentagon was big enough to get lost in and avoid official channels. So are any number of smaller government and private institutions. For a journalist, breaking channels isn't the same as breaking your word.

I have observed wildly different styles to circumvent authority and arrive more closely at approximations of the truth. Homer Bigart and Seymour M. Hersh, two fervently admired reporters by their American colleagues, often broke through the deception of officialdom and showed how masters of the interviewing craft operated.

Bigart had several things going for him. Before attending a press conference, he would study the documents closely so that he could recognize holes in an official press release; he did not stay back at headquarters but risked his neck up front where the action was; he spoke with a stammer, which could be disarming.

I should add another characteristic that may be the most important of all for a journalist: a healthy cynicism and deep distrust of whatever might be an official, filtered version of a story. In Hemingway's phrase, "a built-in, shock-proof, shit detector." On the surface Bigart's polite demeanor looked deceiving, but he wasn't putting on an act. He could challenge headquarters briefing officers and see through military jargon better than any war correspondent I ever observed. It was an attitude thing: He did not enjoy being lied to.

Watching Hersh work the phone during interviews with his sources in competing intelligence agencies, I sometimes found it hard not to fall off my chair, laughing. We shared an office for several months in New York when he was already well known, and feared, for having exposed the My Lai atrocities in Vietnam and aspects of the Watergate atrocities in Washington. Hersh was the opposite of Bigart in style but no less effective. (A few times I had a spear carrier's part in Hersh's escapades; my role was to keep his bright young son, Matthew, reading in our office while his father sneaked out the back door to play tennis in the afternoon.) Whispering or shouting at his sources, Hersh seemed to use a carrot-and-stick technique, alternately cajoling and threatening to put their names in—or keep them out of—the newspaper.

Whichever, it regularly worked for him, but I wouldn't recommend Hershing or being Hershed to anyone who couldn't run as fast as he talked.

This may sound facetious, but I believe that the key to a good interview is not to conduct an interview. Ideally it's to have a conversation. The ideal may not always be possible; some interviews have to be done quickly, without warm-up time. In such cases it may be necessary to risk asking a few salient questions immediately, then checking out the answers against other sources familiar with the subject to obtain further elucidation. If there are blatant differences, interviewers can try to confront their subjects again—give them a second chance—for enlightenment. That's called fairness.

The interviews that worked best for me in this book dropped their me-against-thee confrontation and developed into conversations naturally. Both interviewer and subject felt each other out, lost their fear, established a sense of trust, and recognized that the interviewer was not out to ambush or trip up the subject. In a sense, interviewer and interviewee exchanged chairs. The aim was to converse freely and candidly. Only by doing so could the subject's true character and ideas emerge.

This is not to say that a conversation should be casual and meandering. After all, the subject is aware that you are coming into his or her life for a purpose and is primed for your questions. Obviously the interviewer should also be well armed with information about the background of the person being interviewed. Some expert interviewers are so versed in complex matters that to a certain extent they know what the answers to the questions they're asking will be beforehand—and when the subject is not delivering the real goods.

An interview shouldn't float all over the place. A semblance of control is a precondition to save time and to show the subject that you know your business—and perhaps the interviewee's business, too. The subject should be confident that the interviewer is pursuing an informed conversation. In a sense, it's a discussion with a script, but with a script that leaves plenty of room for purposeful improvisation. You're not engaged in one-upmanship but trying to establish the ambiance of a conversation. The discussion is driven, perforce, by your purpose: to accomplish what you've set out to do by obtaining information voluntarily.

I have seen interviews—and occasionally beem interviewed myself—where everything started off, and remained, on the wrong foot. Often the problem was an insensitive approach. The interviewer sits down with the subject, immediately pulls out pencil and notebook, then fusses with the tape recorder. (That's followed by the English major's lame joke about not being mechanical and distrusting machines.) Before the interview has even begun, a wall of resentment has been erected.

Another roadblock: The subject sits close enough to watch what the interviewer is writing and is aware that the tape is twirling. Everything is designed for the interviewer's benefit, nothing for the subject's sense of relaxation. In such a case the subject can't wait for the little red light to flicker off and the batteries to run down.

I have found it the better part of wisdom not to set down a word until a conversation gets rolling. I may miss a little, but with luck, I'm concentrating, even if I don't look it. After a while I hear the subject say something that stands out: an anecdote, a phrase, an insight. Only then do I pull out my notebook and ask, "Do you mind if I write that down? I want to get it just as you said it." I cannot recall anyone declining to allow me to get down his or her words of wisdom accurately.

Two things about the notebook: It's small enough to fit into my jacket pocket, and it isn't stamped "Reporter's Notebook," for heaven's sake. Even if it's visible, I try to sit where the notebook is not in the subject's direct line of sight. This way the subject is unable to observe what I'm writing—or wonder why I'm not writing—and become distracted. I'm not going to bother suggesting whether a pencil or pen is the better note-taking instrument. I'll leave that weighty problem to the interviewer's mother or journalism professor. Hemingway wrote with short pencils; I use a ball-point pen, which is another reason I'm no Hemingway.

As for tape recorders, I've used them for long articles but not during the usual interview. Once a subject has agreed in advance to hours and days of conversation, it's normal to use a tape recorder to get the exact quotes and tone of voice (you can hear a speaker "italicizing" words better on tape than in a notebook). A tape recorder can also be helpful if you're conducting an interview in a foreign language and can't make out every word; on replay, the taped words may be recognized or looked up. Like most interviewers who prefer not to use tape recorders but sometimes do, I also make handwritten notes as a backup.

The locale of an interview is important for atmosphere and privacy. Better on the subject's home ground than in a company office because conversation can be freer and with fewer interruptions. Restaurants are poor places to conduct interviews, unless you can find a quiet corner where the cutlery isn't rattling and the maître d' isn't coming over every few minutes to ask you if everything's all right so far, sir—on tape. I also happen to dislike what I think of as gastronomic interviews, where the interviewer tells the reader what the subject ate and food is used to break up quotations ("She ordered a second Perrier with a lime twist, nibbled on her shrimp salad with sesame seeds, then continued . . ."), as if some major character revelation were hidden on a lunch plate.

There are times when neither notes nor tapes are permitted and an interviewer's memory is truly challenged. It happened to me in Sicily when I interviewed Vittorio Orlando, former prime minister of Italy and last of the World War I Allied leaders. He was in his eighties but still vigorous when I met him at his son's house in Palermo. The first thing the canny old politician mentioned was that we could only talk as "friends," without formalities or, alas, written notes. I've forgotten his cutting remarks about Clemenceau of France and Lloyd George of Britain, but I recall with amusement what he said about himself: "President Wilson liked me best." After a half hour of listening and talking in Italian, French, and a smattering of English, I raced back to my trusty Remington portable, without talking to anyone, and wrote three or four pages of impressionistic notes.

If nothing can concentrate the mind like a hanging, the same can be said about an interview without note-taking. There's one rule that applies whether you use pencil, pen, or tape recorder: Transcribe your written notes (or mental notes) as soon as possible after the interview, while your impressions are still fresh.

Listening. If listening seems almost unnecessary to mention, why do I see it violated so often by interviewers? Some television interviewers, celebrities themselves, appear tone-deaf. They don't bother hearing the answers to their own questions. They're so busy checking off the long list of questions their researchers have prepared that they have lost the ability to follow up an answer containing a startling revelation. An interview of the absurd by a nonlistening interviewer goes something like this:

INTERVIEWER: Were you at the murder scene in Sag Harbor yourself that night?

SUBJECT: Of course I was. I'm the alleged perp. It happened right after the writer-artist softball game. The deceased made a wrong call at the plate. I used my old army forty-five, but it was purely in self-defense.

INTERVIEWER: So what's the last book you read, and are you writing a new one yourself?

SUBJECT: I said the old reprobate deserved what he got, Charles. If I didn't gun him down first, I wouldn't be here talking to you, do you get my drift?

INTERVIEWER: Couldn't agree with you more. Washington is sure one tough town. I speak from personal knowledge, but enough about me. Let's do it again soon. . . . Back in a moment, so keep it where it is.

All right, I exaggerate. But not listening, and trying to impress the subject of an interview with your own knowledge, go hand in hand. An interviewer must be open to surprise. It should be underscored that for the length of the interview the interviewer is not an equal; it's the interviewee who matters. Interviewers who answer their own questions and deliver sermons to prove their own importance exist in almost every field. I regard them as professional amateurs.

There is an ethical matter that remains troublesome because it is vague and unresolved. When interviews are not conducted face-to-face but by telephone, the interviewed party ought to be made aware that his words are being recorded. One journalist I know still uses a typewriter to take notes during a telephone interview; there's something honest about it because the other party can hear him banging away. Many journalists take silent notes on their computers during an interview; nothing wrong with that: Clearly the interviewer is writing down what the subject is saying.

It's the unseen telephone recording that, in my view, raises a moral issue. As a matter of courtesy, some publications do have a policy that writers should inform the person on the other end of the line that the conversation is being recorded; most publications that rely on outside as well as staff writers don't bother. Massachusetts, Pennsylvania, Florida, and California have laws requiring the consent of both parties to a recorded phone conversation, but it's not the law in New York State. What is universally prohibited is recording a conversation between two other parties without their consent. That, of course, is the crime of eavesdropping.

Although there are many styles of interviewing, all interviewers have unspoken ethical obligations to their subjects, to their craft, and to themselves—if for no other reason than to preserve their own reputations for truth and candor.

In *Writing Lives: Principia Biographica,* Leon Edel, the leading Henry James biographer, sums up the boundaries of a lifetime of research and writing: "A writer of lives is allowed the imagination of form but not of fact." This applies not only to biography but to interviews for any purpose. There's nothing wrong with rearranging the material in your notebook so that what the subject has told you makes sense and reads coherently. Neither presidents nor plebeians speak in sentences; they jump around and make additions and emendations. They aren't making speeches, they're talking—but without telling the interviewer where to put in the semicolons and periods. What the interviewer does is punctuate their remarks, pull the notebook scribbles together, and try to capture the essentials of a conversation, sometimes with direct quotes, sometimes not.

Does this violate the subject's spoken words? Of course not. After I interviewed Theodore H. White in his Manhattan brownstone, the author of the trailblazing *Making of the President* books urged me to do him a favor and fix up what he had said if it didn't hang together. (I had had one less drink than he did.) And after a talk with Saul Bellow in his apartment overlooking Lake Michigan, the Nobel laureate (who could speak in paragraphs) ended up by saying, "Do you think you can make anything out of this *tsimis?*"

The message from both authors was clear. Neither White nor Bellow expected me to twist their words, facts, or opinions. Without such an unwritten bond of trust, nothing could happen. Neither they, nor anybody else in this book, ever requested that I show what I wrote about them in advance of publication. (They probably knew that I would never accede to such a request.) Both distinguished authors recognized that an interviewer's job is to quote as much as possible of what the subject said verbatim. But they also realized that there is a need to reconstruct some elements of an interview carefully and honestly.

How different from the vainglorious pronunciamento by Janet Malcolm, an otherwise respected *New Yorker* writer, who wrote: "Every journalist who is not too stupid or too full of himself to notice what is going on knows that what he does is morally indefensible. He is a kind of confidence man, preying on people's vanity, ignorance or loneliness, gaining their trust and betraying them without remorse."

Among many others, I cannot imagine Joseph Mitchell, *The New Yorker* writer most revered by his peers, who made the

city's ordinary people extraordinary by the power of his elemen-
tal reporting, subtle insights, and polished prose, ever doing anything "morally indefensible" toward those he interviewed or
"betraying them without remorse."

Only one phrase in Ms. Malcolm's generalization did strike
home: "too full of himself," to which I would only add, "or
herself." In this respect she was on firm ground. Indeed, there
are celebrity and amateur journalists who are incapable of listening, except to themselves, and whose vanity stands in the way of
the interviewing and writing process.

After the interview is completed and transcribed, the work of
presenting the diverse facts accurately and attractively begins.
When I taught a seminar in narrative writing at Yale, I marveled
at the fact that some diligent students busily filled up their note-
books even when I thought I wasn't saying anything. At the end
of the school year I told the seniors who were interested in writing that they would probably forget nearly everything heard in
our classroom. But I suggested that if nothing else, they try to
remember two things:

The first: Before starting to write, forget all the overwhelming
research and reporting, stop for a few moments or more, then
ask yourself, What am I trying to say?

The second: How can I say what I really want to say wisely
and readably?

That's where the writer's art begins.

In one of his letters E. B. White described the writer's role
modestly and eloquently: "I have occasionally had the exquisite
thrill of putting my finger on a little capsule of truth, and heard
it give the faint squeak of mortality under my pressure."

What is the interplay between the reader and author, between
commerce and government?

Fresh threats to the public perception of creativity continue to
appear in awesome new technological forms. Writers and readers are expected to kneel before the latest hardware gods. But

fitting words cannot be machine-tooled; they will still have to be handcrafted by authors who last.

To be sure, computers can help to provide timely and utilitarian facts, magically pulled through wires; words can be repackaged, stored, and retrieved by an array of electronic wonders. Yet even the terms invented to describe these marvels—magnetic, digital and Floptical, silicon chips, on-line transmissions, and interactive systems—seem antilanguage, threatening. You can't kick the tires or look under the hood of Floptical words.

Electronic devices somehow seem to stand as a bulwark against original expression. Though undeniably useful as a writing and factual tool, the computer is hardly the key to creating literature. (Neither, in its time, was the quill pen.) Midway through life's journey, a writer can find himself in a dark wood, where the personal conflict between creativity and technology leads not to software but softwars.

By no means is this a call for modern Luddites to destroy laborsaving machinery, as English textile workers did in the early 1800s. Let's use them but not worship them as panaceas for the arts. The long-term effects of the new hardware are not yet known for printed books. There is the word, and there is the word processor. Although electronic hucksters maintain that the printed page is imperiled, familiar hand-held books offer what no small screen or portable disk carrier can ever provide: aesthetic and tactical pleasure and, above all, an intimate encounter between author and reader.

Far more alarming for literature are the great changes that have taken place in book publishing and bookselling in recent years. When I first began talking to authors and writing about the book world, dozens of viable publishing houses existed; some still bore the names of their nineteenth-century founders. A number of venerable houses have since winked out or become second-class citizens within large companies. Along the way many dedicated editors have been dismissed, and good books neglected or lost.

Some of the multimedia companies are more concerned

about delivering other forms of entertainment—from films to
theme parks—to the public. Their book-publishing divisions are
regarded as just another one of their "profit centers," subject to
the whims of bottom-line down-marketeers. Economic self-
censorship in the publishing houses, and a consequent lowering
of literary standards in editorial selection, have caused medioc-
rity to float to the top of the best seller lists. How many times
have I heard this apologia: It's necessary to publish trash in order
to publish poetry.

For several years two government agencies—the Federal
Trade Commission and the Department of Justice—were concerned about the gobbling up of publishing houses, of big fish
eating little fish. Antitrust suits were begun, and jawboning
helped to delay what were seen as possible monopolistic take-
overs. But the Reagan administration, with its penchant for dis-
mantling or destroying the regulatory agencies, ended such efforts, and planned cases were dropped. During these years chain
bookstores proliferated. While opening welcome new book
outlets where none had existed before, the chains had the same
effect as the publishing conglomerates on small publishing
houses: making life more difficult for independent bookstores to
survive.

The best seller charts printed in book review sections have
become part of the same big-player game, calling attention to
what is presold rather than listing what their own knowledge-
able editors may consider worthwhile. With notable exceptions,
the best seller lists, promoting the books that are stacked like
cordwood in the chain stores, are depressing. Ghostwritten
books by television and radio vulgarians, often as not right-wing
loudmouths, and sincerely tawdry novels by hacks with heaving
bosoms frequently head the lists.

Such lists, like those that rate television audiences, are ad-
juncts of commerce, not literature. They can be counterproduc-
tive because they hobble individual choice and discovery. The
best seller charts fail in a fundamental mission: to raise the educa-
ble tastes of American readers.

Despite the reported large advances for a small number of name writers, television personalities, and, yes, even their cooks, the great majority of authors in the United States struggle. According to surveys by the oldest writers' organization in the country, the Authors League of America, from their writing income alone professional authors exist below the poverty line. As Robert Anderson, the playwright and novelist, put it, "You can make a killing, but you can't make a living."

It is rarely noticed that only two occupations are specifically named and protected in the United States Constitution: authors and inventors. "To promote the Progress of Science and useful Arts," a clause reads, Congress is authorized to secure "for limited times to Authors and Inventors the exclusive right to their respective Writings and Discoveries." The foresight of the framers in the eighteenth century is at the core of copyright protection in the twentieth century.

Unfettered by censorship, the electronic era holds promise for the next century—if publishers, editors, and readers recognize that nothing counts on the printed page, or across the satellite heavens, without the author's words.

In his handwritten poem "Words," Auden put our theme in a few eloquent lines:

> A sentence uttered makes a world appear
> Where all things happen as it says they do;
> We doubt the speaker, not the tongue we hear:
> Words have no word for words that are not true.

THE
AUTHORS

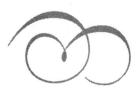

IGNAZIO SILONE

Rome

At the appointed hour, while Romans still rubbed sleep from afternoon eyes, I entered the terraced apartment house on the Via di Villa Ricotta, in the comfortably middle-class Piazza Bologna area, pushed out the toy flaps of the open-ceilinged elevator on a high floor, and immediately saw the neatly printed name in the slot above the doorbell: Ignazio Silone. It came as something of a shock; there seemed to be a missing element, perhaps an honorary title from the Italian Republic or, at least, a crest, emblazoned "Silone of Fontamara."

In title-conscious Italy, Silone has no title, but something all his own: an international reputation greater abroad than at home, a moral position that is respected by the neo-right and neo-left, though he is out of the current literary swim, an anti-Fascist past in exile preceding the partisan underground experience that is the common bond of so many Italian novelists, and a body of work that—curiously—is being revised.

He emerged from shadows into his shuttered drawing room, a figure of former crisis in a country that for the first time in decades was without any. He seemed solid, assured, with neither inner torment nor enthusiasm for lost causes. He looked more dignified and less embittered than expected—as if he, too, had undergone revisions in his nature. Beneath thinning gray hair and a high-domed forehead, his penetrating dark eyes seemed at once quizzical and melancholy, but from time to time the corners of his mouth lifted into a sweet smile.

He was born in 1900. Over twenty-five years ago—and what a quarter of a century it has been in the long downswing of world political change!—Silone's best-known novel, *Bread and Wine,* was published in the United States. This story of Pietro Spina, the underground leader who returns to his native Abruzzi from exile to try to organize the peasants and workers against the Fascist regime, became one of the landmarks of proletarian literature of the 1930s. For years it has been read in paperback editions.

Now we have a rewritten version of the 1937 *Bread and Wine,* translated from the Italian by Harvey Fergusson II, with a new preface by the author. It follows publication of a revised version of the 1934 *Fontamara,* Silone's first novel of good and evil in a Fascist-dominated town. Both books in the thirties belonged with Malraux's *Man's Fate* and Steinbeck's *The Grapes of Wrath* as tracts for the oppressed and idealistic all over the world.

I wondered about the morality involved in changing works of art after they had been accepted (even with possible flaws) by the public over a long, historic period of time.

"Those things I have changed do not concern the underlying morality of my books," Silone said. "The changes, rather, are designed to reinforce the ideas. My manner of thinking is the same as it was. It is the digressions, the superfluities, that I have changed."

Could he cite a specific example?

"Yes, in the new *Bread and Wine* I cut out the poisoning of the priest. Why? Because just at the time that I was writing the book, in the middle of the 1930s, an anti-Fascist priest had been poisoned. It was strongly in the news and in my mind, and I included this incident. Later, therefore, I decided to eliminate from the novel what was merely reportage."

Did he have a change of heart—of political sympathies—about his key character, Pietro Spina, the revolutionary?

"My views of religion and politics certainly have not changed since *Fontamara*. Where I have made revisions—and I consider them of a secondary nature—I have done so only for the sake of greater artistic unity. After the fall of fascism I had the opportunity to see my books printed in Italy for the first time. They had been published in your country and on the Continent, but not in my own. When I wrote the novels originally, I was more inclined to melodramatic methods than to calm narration. I therefore undertook to change the books, to deepen them, in all good conscience.

"Furthermore, I see nothing wrong if an author constantly rewrites the same book. One can think of Manzoni; he changed *I Promessi Sposi* [*The Betrothed*] again and again, writing the same book for twenty-five years. The same is true of certain composers and artists, polishing the same work all their lives. We all really have only one major story to tell. Spina in *Bread and Wine* is related to the Stranger who makes his first appearance at the end of *Fontamara,* and he crops up with other names in my postwar novels."

A critical reading of the original against the revised version of *Bread and Wine* discloses that essentially the story is the same. Pietro Spina, the underground leader, is still (to use a phrase popularized by the House Committee on Un-American Activities) a "premature anti-Fascist." The time is at the outbreak of the Abyssinian War, when Mussolini's legions moved across the Mediterranean, dreaming of empire for the corporate-military state.

There certainly is political updating—questionable, on the grounds that doing so revises not merely a novel but the picture of radical thought as it existed in fact in the 1930s. To cite a subtle change, at one point a friend of Spina's says: "I do not understand why Karl Marx did not introduce a similar costume for members of the Workers International to distinguish the functionary from the ordinary mortal." Now the same passage reads: "I don't understand why Lenin didn't introduce vestments like these among the personnel of the Kremlin to distinguish the functionary from the simple proletarian who carries his card and pays his dues." The first is a dig; the second a slap.

It should be quickly added that *Bread and Wine* is not all dead serious; that there are wonderful descriptive sections here and much peasant humor. Two funny names are still present, Carlo Campanella (who in New York became Mr. Charles Little-Bell, Ice & Coal), and Old Sciatàp (who got his name from the only phrase—"Shut up!"—he brought back from the United States to Italy). Although Mr. Silone lived in exile and is a long way from the Abruzzi villages, he conveys the rough peasants and the landscape with great authority.

The difference in tone that he hoped to achieve is best described by Silone himself. When *Bread and Wine* was published for the first time in Italy, he changed the title from *Pane e Vino* to *Vino e Pane*. He said he did so to distinguish the version published in exile from the version published after the downfall of fascism. In the American preface to the new book, he says, "I have the impression that in the new version wine plays a larger role than bread." And now, in his drawing room, he said with an enigmatic smile, "I believe that wine is more important than bread in our lives, too, don't you?"

I wondered how this attitude was reflected in his current work. "As for myself," he said, "I am more occupied with the human condition. Like Malraux. The form of the modern novel, for the moment, is not introspective. The destiny of a certain epoch is what interests me. It corresponds to the character in my novel—and by the way, the search for deeper meanings corresponds to the needs of the present epoch. The novelist's function is to place the individual within the state and to expose the state when it encroaches upon the individual's freedom.

"The writer is a member of society and must probe that relationship constantly. I do not mean that a novelist should compete with the psychoanalyst, who can surpass him in purely scientific analysis. But an author must know something about psychology. The larger literature must come to grips with the global man. What interests me is man: his same faults, his difficulties, his greatness. Men are in the end given over to themselves, left to themselves, faced with a failure of hope and moral crises. That is my story."

[OCTOBER 21, 1962]

CARL SANDBURG

Springfield, Illinois

Before Carl Sandburg is enshrined in marble, a handful of living memories may be relevant from an honored, occasional companion. In the last line of *Always the Young Strangers,* Carl writes: "If it can be done, it is not a bad practice for a man of many years to die with a boy heart." It was the boy heart that pumped bravely and freely through much of his life and writing. He was not as stiff-necked as some of his critics; he was willing to speak with candor though he wrote with great care; in a convivial mood he was one of the most joyous of men. He used that marvelous voice of his as an instrument—his friend Andrés Segovia recently told me that Carl's pitch was musically sound—and he was interested in how others expressed themselves. To Tallulah Bankhead he said, "I'd like to put your voice in my pocket."

We were walking around his *Prairie Years* country, and he relaxed by throwing out two-liners:

"Am I the first girl you ever kissed?"

"No, but I want you to know that I'm a lot more particular than I used to be."

"Have you a criminal lawyer in this burg?"

"We think so but we haven't been able to prove it on him yet."

In Springfield, we passed a Walgreen's, and he spotted a sign in the window saying $2.98 watches were reduced to $1.89. "Let's get us a couple of watches and clocks," he said. We also got some jackknives, which he loved. He used them to cut his cigars in half, and where some dudes carry handkerchiefs, he stuffed cigar butts. When he got to the end of the butt, he took out a pocketknife, jabbed it neatly into the tobacco, and used it as a handle for the last half inch. He called this, grinning, a hobo way of "sucking the nick-o-teen."

The commonplace in the streets he made uncommon, vulgar, and sometimes hilarious. A sign said: CARS LOVE SHELL. He expanded on this: CARS WORSHIP SHELL . . . CARS ARE JUST PASSIONATE ABOUT SHELL.

The language of advertising offended him, and he despised and mocked commercials on television. At dinner he used a gadget to cut them off. "Here comes a woman who *inhales,*" he said. "Click, click." As we ate, he parodied TV commercials with an old jingle before he swallowed: "Through the lips and over the tongue—look out, guts! Here I come!" That, he explained, came from the old fad of "Fletcherizing"—tasting all the food.

His system of bestowing autographs in restaurants and on the street had a certain logic. If a youngster came over with a napkin to sign, he usually did. If an adult male came, he would quiz him on how many of his books he had read; if the answer was satisfactory, he might sign or ask him to return with one of the books. If an adult female asked, chances would increase based on the degree of pulchritude. A well-thumbed Sandburg book always helped. Waitresses, shoeshine boys, and airline hostesses usually got his firm block signature, but respectable-looking stuffed shirts rarely.

He could blast politicians, especially Republicans. One evening after dinner we walked into the Illinois State Capitol building. He mentioned that he knew the governor's father when the latter served as a Chicago alderman. A Republican publicist handed Sandburg some political literature, which he accepted; but then the publicist added, "This literature is given to you courtesy of the secretary of state." Sandburg exploded, "You can tell the secretary of state to go to hell!" Later I asked him why he had jumped on the poor fellow, and Sandburg softly explained, "The statehouse is no place to give out political literature."

In his hometown of Galesburg, we stood in front of "Old Main" on the Knox College campus, where Lincoln had debated Douglas in 1858. As a youth delivering milk, Carl had cut across the campus many times and read the plaque with Lincoln's phrase that "they are blowing out the moral lights around us," referring to slaveowners. Here Sandburg could not resist striking out at some favorite targets. "I would say to those who are known in this hour in our country as Birchers," he said, sneering, "I would say that those who propose to impeach a chief justice of the Supreme Court of the United States, without saying what evidence they have—they are hoping that they blow out moral lights around us." And warming up in front of the Knox students, he continued: "The Birch Society is secret, like the Nazis. Those who want to impeach Chief Justice Warren don't know America. Richard Milhous Nixon," he added, sarcastically, somehow making the pronunciation sound evil. "General Eisenhower, he was silent during the McCarthy era. Why?" This was Adlai Stevenson territory, and Sandburg, as an old friend and campaigner for the governor and presidential candidate, was feeling his political oats.

An owl-eyed student from the college paper tried to get a rise out of Sandburg, and succeeded, by asking him what he thought of the poetry of Robert Frost. Sandburg snarled, "How many of my poems and his have you read?" The student mumbled in shock, mentioned a few, and then retreated. I was interested in the answer (many people asked him this) myself.

Later that night in his hotel room, we sat around drinking his favorite black-label Jack Daniel's. First we had some with soda. Then we drank it with water. Finally, when we got close to the bottom of the bottle, we found the proper formula—neat, over ice. At this point I felt emboldened to ask him the question, too:

"Carl, what *do* you think of Frost's stuff?"

"Robert Frost is a fine poet, but," he said, without a trace of malice and more in sorrow, "but what can you expect from him? He's a Re-pub-lican."

We headed the next day for 331 East Third Street, where he was born January 6, 1878. It is a three-room frame house, the second house east of the Chicago, Burlington & Quincy tracks. He began to sing: "Mama, mama, mama, have you heard the news? Daddy got killed on the C-B-and-Qs." The house is lovingly preserved by the Carl Sandburg Association. "My father swung a hammer and sledge at the railway blacksmith shop," Sandburg said. "He used an *X* to sign his name. There ought to be an organization made up of people whose fathers couldn't write their signature; it might tell a little bit more about this country than some of the so-called superpatriot organizations."

Here in this Swedish pioneer's cottage, with little more protection against the elements than a log cabin, Carl was born on a cornhusk mattress. One of his great prairie poems, from *Cornhuskers,* came to the surface:

> I was born on the prairie and the milk
>   of its wheat, the
> red of its clover, the eyes of its women,
>   gave me a song and a slogan.

Through Galesburg the trains of many railroads run: the CB&Q, the Burlington, the Santa Fe. Long ago the night whistles had summoned Sandburg on the road to Chicago and thence across America. Now, too, he heard Chicago calling. But first he checked in by phone with his wife, Paula, at the farm in Flat Rock, North Carolina, to tell her he was on his way home. He read her a newspaper editorial about his visit to Galesburg.

"Paula," he said, "did you know what you're married to? It says here that I'm a 'white-thatched octogenarian.' " And, perhaps recalling the days early in this century when both were Social Democratic party organizers, she said, "You've been called worse things, buddy."

No train was fast enough to get out of the hometown. Saying good-bye to an old friend, Max Goodsill of Knox College, he said, "Shake the hand that shook the hand of Elvis Presley." Then we caught a two-engine feeder plane on a one-slice-of-chewing-gum airline. Sandburg tried to settle back comfortably in the narrow seat. The plane shook and shuddered into the sky. When the chewing gum arrived, Carl opened his eyes, reached for a slice and put it in his jacket pocket next to the cut cigar butts, and asked the blushing hostess her name. "You're not what's wrong with this airline," he said, and settling back, he took out a bandanna, placed it across his eyes, and dreamed his way to Chicago.

[AUGUST 12, 1967]

NELSON ALGREN

AND

STUDS TERKEL

Chicago

Nelson Algren and Studs Terkel were sitting in the back room of Riccardo's one Friday evening matching cognac against martinis. This was awhile back, and they were putting on a hick from the First City, or maybe only testing the throwaway lines, but there they were, still showing a lot of stuff in their early sixties, two boys from Chicagah who are literary fixtures here as monumental as Mayor Daley and the Water Tower.

Algren said: "Never eat at a place called Mom's. Never play cards with a man called Doc. Never go to bed with a woman whose troubles are greater than your own."

Terkel said: "You've got to meet this wonderful woman, used to be a left-wing hooker. She remade her life, including naming herself after—are you ready?—an old friend of Chairman Mao's. She's now doing rehabilitation work, reforming the downtrodden sisters."

He walked to the phone booth near the boastful newspaper bar and returned a moment later. "Couldn't get an answer. I'll try her again later."

Terkel lit up another corona and twirled it like a baton, ordered another brandy, and followed it with a coffee chaser. Algren poured his coffee into the saucer and added brandy. He complained mockingly about the displacement caused by the olive in his martini.

"When I was in Saigon," Algren said, "I rented a place in Cholon, the Chinese quarter. You could always tell a Chinese because of a great desire to learn. If I was reading an English paper, a Chinese would ask me, 'What dat say?' Cholon was full of deserters and black marketeers."

Terkel cut in. "You're dead wrong, you didn't meet black marketeers, all you met was hookers. If you want to hear the real thing, I'll play you a tape of a South Vietnamese girl I recorded. She was from the Fellowship for Reconciliation and beautiful and intelligent."

"An Oriental woman, even a sixteen-year-old, knows she's a love object," Algren said. "American women don't."

"What about the French?" Terkel asked.

"Well, Simone de Beauvoir was just a French schoolteacher," Algren said. "Still, her book gave me a certain reputation. A Montreal thing who read one of my books came down and knocked at my door and checked in several years ago."

"He's felt a certain remorse ever since the poker game," Terkel said. "We were playing at Nelson's. There were two others in the game, a Moretti, one of the non-Mafia, unimportant ones, and an Indian from the Menominee tribe. They were cheating, but we couldn't prove it. Then the Canadian girl wanders in at two in the morning, and Nelson ordered her to go to bed."

"I've felt badly about it," Algren said. "The nerve to tell her to leave the poker room when all she wanted to do was watch us play."

Terkel got up again and said, "I'll try the left-wing ex-hooker."

Algren said, "There was a little hooker in Butte, Montana, who carried a picture of her high school graduating class from a little town out there. The town no longer existed because it had been shut down by Anaconda. She couldn't go back home. It was a terrible feeling. All she had left was a little picture of her graduating class."

"She doesn't answer the phone at the rehabilitation office," Terkel said, and ordered another brandy all around.

"All the sad women at writers' conferences," Algren said. "One time a woman said she was all set up for me in a motel across the road. I took off my undershirt when I got there, and she suddenly said, 'Who are you?' and I said, 'It's you who fixed this up,' and she said, 'What are you doing here?' and I said, 'I'm getting the hell out and calling the college psychiatrist,' and when I did, she was very rational with him. He called me the next day for information about the lady, but I didn't know her."

Terkel ragged Algren about their respective patrons and admirers. "We each have a millionaire crook who wants to turn legit by sponsoring our writing," Terkel said. "They're both Republicans," said Algren. "My millionaire has seventy million, yours only a lousy million," said Terkel. "Maybe they think it's good for Chicago to have writers instead of insurance agents," Algren said, extricating an alien olive from his martini with a golden arm.

"I think I'll try that number just one more time," Terkel said, blowing a confident corona ring.

"All the wisdom I acquired in nine months in the Orient can be summed up in one line," Algren said. "Never eat in a place with sliding doors unless you're crazy about raw fish."

Then everybody went where everybody knew they would end up when the evening began: back to their wives or typewriters. Somehow it sounded as if life were being lived here on the wild side, not made up, handcrafted, not just taped, by a couple of old pros showing the New Journalists early foot, fired by the hustle of the city with the big shoulders. Not long afterward it would turn up in sentences and stories in the telling and making.

[MARCH 24, 1974]

GIORGIO BASSANI

In novels, short stories, and vignettes, Giorgio Bassani makes readers aware of his corner of the world and concerned about the fate of his characters. We know that he is taking us upon an excursion into a dying time—the Fascist era—and into a place of his youth, Ferrara in northern Italy, among an ill-fated people, the Jewish families of the region. But we also know that an artistic intent lies behind the "plots" of his subtle tales. A reader can observe the author simultaneously unfolding his own reminiscences in a deliberate roman-fleuve style and recording his characters' passing adventures. Though we have foreknowledge of tragedy to come, we still care about what happens to this man, or that marriage—and especially if the trains carrying the people north to oblivion will ever return.

Bassani was walking down a New York street in the East Fifties, a fish out of Ferrara waters, when suddenly he spotted a life-size blowup of Fred Astaire and Ginger Rogers twirling cardboard memories for a dance studio one flight up, and he began to sing in English, "Top hat, putting on my top hat, tying up my white tie, brushing off my tails." He pointed to Astaire

and said in Italian, "What elegance!" and the window reflected
his own, his finely drawn features and carefully tailored jacket
and uncrinkled manners, something like his sentences, casual
and yet thought out.

We crossed Park Avenue, and he said, "That photograph reminds me of fascism. It is because during the Fascist era we saw
all the Fred Astaire-Ginger Rogers films at the cinema. Toward
the end no new films were allowed to come in from America, so
we went to the same ones again and again, memorizing the
songs." Unlike the movie made from his novel *The Garden of the
Finzi-Continis* (from which he insisted that his name be
removed), he had nothing but pleasant feelings for the Astaire-
Rogers confections.

Every few years Bassani visits the United States; every few
years one of his incandescent short novels is translated here. The
newest is *Behind the Door,* a story of adolescent discoveries set, of
course, in Ferrara, in 1930. We seem to be reading him back-
ward and forward in time as he himself reaches for his roots in
youth. His *Five Stories of Ferrara* encompasses the Fascist era up to
the turning point in 1943, when Ferrara's few hundred Jews are
rounded up and deported to Germany. His *The Heron* concerns
a survivor of the Holocaust symbolically trapped in guilt. And
even before, in *The Gold-Rimmed Spectacles,* we encounter a key
character (kin to Mann's in *Death in Venice*) who makes a brief
appearance in the *Finzi-Continis*. Bassani is not pursuing politics
or headlines in his books, which, woven together by place and
sometimes people growing up or projected out, become a flow-
ing tale. Hardly any American novelists lately have attempted
such an ambitious family and city chronicle—it demands closing
your mundane eyes but opening your pained heart—for standard editorial wisdom has it that best sellers require strong characters in conflict with major events. Bassani's characters are
wounded and in conflict with themselves.

Of several subtle literary remarks he has made in our encounters across the years, the most revealing was "I am Micol." The

narrator, who we can assume is the author in *Finzi-Continis,* first meets Micol as a child in the Ferrara synagogue and watches her grow into lovely womanhood. But fine novelists cross age and sex barriers to depict the ideas and longings of all their characters, living instead of merely inventing them, and then allowing the fictional lives to develop inevitable truths. Anyone from a president to an energetic poseur can manipulate facts and nonfiction, but poets and novelists aware of long literary traditions cannot be dishonest with their creations. They must be true to their Micols, *be* Micol.

Bassani, who is modest about himself but clearly interested in his own place in literature, talked about who really counted among dedicated novelists on both sides of the Atlantic. Bassani's phrase of approval—the test almost regardless of achievement and surely without the criterion of popularity—is being "a man of letters." He mentioned several of the Italian and translated American writers, lining them up against the wall and gunning them down unerringly. This one was a good writer, "fashionable and alert to trends," that one was "an interesting journalist," another "more of a professional man but not the literary profession." The names seemed unimportant; a reader in New York or Rome could fill in his own janissaries and candidates for obscurity.

It does not come out in his stories—at least, has not yet—but Bassani is linked in experience and involvement to a number of other Italian writers aware of the currents of political and social despair in their country. He was one of the founders of the Action party in 1942, spent nearly three months in prison in 1943, and was freed the day after Mussolini's fall. The anti-Fascist underground forged Italian politics and artistic life in that marvelous neorealistic time. Bassani became active in the left-wing Socialist party and, as a vocal representative of the idea of an "opening to the left," participated in the idealistic aspirations of his party.

In Italy artists and novelists from center to left, mostly the latter, participate in the national parliament. The contrast with creators in America is significant; California, to take a rude case, has been represented in the Statehouse by a minor actor (Ronald Reagan). Novelists have no place in Congress, Bassani is surprised to hear. His own involvement today is only peripherally political. He is president of Italia Nostra, an environmental group working to protect the country's natural and artistic resources.

Although the political scene beyond the door faintly echoes in the background of his stories, his Jewish upbringing and awareness in Ferrara are omnipresent. His family lived in Italy hundreds of years before that "Merchant of Venice." One of the main reasons Bassani disavowed the film version of *Finzi-Continis* is that it appears that the character of Giorgio is devoid of moral stature in the face of anti-Semitic persecution. "To have used my house in Ferrara for filming, attributing incidents there that did not involve me, and then to claim that I seemed capable of toying with the life of my beloved father added up to outrageous abuses of power," Bassani observed. "Had I suffered these without protesting, I would not be a writer, much less a man."

Vero, a man of letters.

[OCTOBER 19, 1975]

A M O S   O Z

Jerusalem

Amos Oz sits in a small studio on Jerusalem's Mount Scopus and
writes; shares his thoughts on Chekhov and Kafka in the summer with a group of Hebrew University students; returns home
on the weekend to his wife and two daughters at Kibbutz Hulda;
pulls guard duty or waits on tables or picks oranges for hours
under the sun. Oz remembers the sounds of World War II, of
the 1948 War of Independence, and of the recent wars in which
he has participated as soldier or reservist. He compares this to
living through his country's American Revolution and Civil
War.

With a tank unit on the Golan Heights a few years ago, Oz
saw an imaginative idea executed to confuse Syrian intelligence.
Instead of revealing locations by names and numbers, a soldier
familiar with the world before Hitler designated positions after
long-forgotten and destroyed shtetls in Poland. It was an un-
breakable code that might have been conceived by Isaac Bashevis Singer and fantasized by Chagall.

Oz is the only major novelist in Israel who lives on a kibbutz.
For a number of years he wrote in the hours before sunrise after

a long day of teaching and working the land. Since the publication of his novels—*Elsewhere, Perhaps; My Michael;* and *Touch the Water, Touch the Wind*—the kibbutz has given him greater time off for writing.

"I have the liberty to write, or *not* to write. My position on the kibbutz is the same as a carpenter or cobbler. In the beginning it was considered a little awkward when my books began to make money. But when I get a royalty check, I just endorse it and turn it over to the kibbutz treasurer. On the other hand, I don't have to live on advances, I don't fill out income tax forms, I have no mortgage, I don't have to write book reviews or lecture, and the only essays I do are for rage. My compensation is time; if I want to shut myself up or go off for a while, I can. It means a very modest standard of living, but I much prefer this life to existence in a literary aquarium.

"Kibbutz Hulda is a place where the elements are visible: It grows dark; there are sunsets. When I was younger, I could hear the howling of jackals. This can be a rather savage country, and of course, there is a basic Israeli sense of danger, an emotional sense of siege. The kibbutz life is quiet, but the material of fiction is here. You can listen to two elderly women talking of the old country in East Europe and you can also hear of elegant life in Vienna; there are nineteen different countries, including the United States, and nineteen different languages represented on our kibbutz."

Yet it is not an insulated life, culturally or socially. Oz is very much aware of transatlantic writers and writing. As he chainsmokes Europa cigarettes, he talks of John Donne and Allen Ginsberg, of Gogol and of his great respect for the late S. Y. Agnon, Israel's Nobel laureate in literature. "With the exception of Saul Bellow," he says, "I'm not terribly happy with the Jewish-American novelists. The others are too wise; their characters exchange punch lines instead of talking to each other; their books are just clever sociology. They don't have the echo of the universe; you don't see the stars in their writing."

His books have been somewhat better received in the United States than in Israel, where criticism is partly literary and partly political. And yet there is one major difference. Oz was recently advanced from staff sergeant to second lieutenant and now leads a little reserve unit that includes two lawyers, a painter, a group of kibbutzniks, and a literary critic. His blue-green eyes twinkling, Oz says, "It does give me a kind of pleasure to be in command of someone who criticizes my books."

Oz said that among American authors, his own writing had been influenced by Melville, Sherwood Anderson, and Faulkner.

Sherwood Anderson?

"I had a Hungarian teacher at Kibbutz Hulda who never set foot in America but who told me to read *Winesburg, Ohio* after it was translated into Hebrew. She knew I was a secret poet and wanted me to write prose. I had thought the real world was outside—in Jerusalem or New York or Paris. *Winesburg* showed me that the real world is everywhere, even in a small kibbutz. I discovered that all the secrets are the same—love, hatred, fear, loneliness—all the great and simple things of life and literature."

Of novel writing, he said: "There is no word in Hebrew for fiction; I boycott that word. It means the opposite of truth. Prose, yes, but not fiction. I write prose. I aim at truth, not facts, and I am old enough to know the difference between facts and truth.

"Writing a poem is like a short love affair; writing a short story like a long love affair; writing a novel is like a marriage," Oz said. "In a novel you have to make a half million decisions, from the choice of an adverb to where to place a comma. I can have a pang of self-indulgence over a single comma. I write my drafts in longhand; I need the sensual contact of paper, pen, ink, and my fingers. Then I fight it out on the typewriter."

Oz said he found an affinity between his writing, which is rooted in Israel no matter where he writes, and that of Central and South American novelists with their emotional tales about the extraordinariness of ordinary life. "The name of the game for me is shameless, gutsy storytelling," he said. "The Latin American novelists have the courage to tell a story as if nobody had ever told a story before and never had a story before."

On the horizon we saw the Judean hills, interrupted only by a line of sentinel trees. History is lived and written here simultaneously. Oz's wife works in the archives of the kibbutz movement. The kibbutz grows cotton, olives, avocados, and fruit and raises its own livestock. In the evening the generations get together to discuss the state of the world. "Debating is our local substitute for soccer," Oz said.

[OCTOBER 26, 1975]

CARLOS FUENTES

The diplomat is a writer; the writer is a diplomat.

Carlos Fuentes, one of the major novelists of Latin America, is Mexico's ambassador to France. Six days a week he represents his country's interests in Paris, with a strong emphasis on the cultural and economic independence of his government within the third world. On the seventh day he does not rest; instead he writes novels.

There is a venerable tradition of writer-diplomats in Europe and South America, but in the United States they are exceptions. Benjamin Franklin and Washington Irving in the long past and Claude Bowers and John Bartlow Martin in recent times come quickly to mind. More often it's the publishers rather than the writers who represent the United States abroad.

Speaking as Novelist Fuentes, Ambassador Fuentes said that diplomacy might be improved if more writers served their country and their muse at the same time.

"There's a cultural substratum beneath political and economic relationships," the writer said. "A novelist lives with his characters in a world of the imagination, where idealism and conscience and affairs of the heart dominate life. The might-have-been of human encounters and affairs of state can be imagined idealistically.

"In an imperfect world, a diplomat has to believe in the possibility of change just as a novelist causes his characters to reach for perfectability. If you can live with the imaginary, you can understand the other man's viewpoint and civilization—and these are central ideas of diplomacy today."

Some of these philosophical ideas are woven into Fuentes's novel *Terra Nostra*. The 778-page novel, translated by Margaret Sayers Peden, has received the Javier Villaurrutia Prize, Mexico's most important literary award.

Terra Nostra is a novel that breaks time barriers, reaching across the centuries from the Roman procurators of Judea to kingly Spain to a future vision of the earth in 1999, when "twelve o'clock did not toll in the church towers of Paris, but a cold sun shone."

Describing the ideas behind the novel, Fuentes said: "It's about the future imagined. Cervantes is one of the many characters. The novel asks, Who is more powerful, Felipe the Second of Spain or Don Quixote? The history of Spain is a story of feats and defeats. Spain was the only country where three civilizations—Christian, Jewish, and Moorish—thrived together for seven hundred years. Spain's greatness ended with the destruction of the Jewish and Moorish influence. Without the Jews, we would not be writing novels in Spanish today.

"The novel also moves across to the New World, where the destruction continued. There are parallels, if you look for them, between the treatment of Mexico and Vietnam by the United States. Even Lincoln was against the Mexican War when he was a congressman. The novel hopes to leave an impression that there should be a multiplicity of civilizations, a freedom to accept the ideas and cultures of all people everywhere."

As I strolled along Central Park South with Ambassador Fuentes, it was hard to imagine that only seven years ago he was branded an "undesirable alien" by the United States Immigration and Naturalization Service, that his visa was torn up, and that he could not come here because of suspected "leftist leanings." At the time he had been active in the defense of Fidel Castro's Cuban Revolution, a fact he never concealed, but no official explanation was ever given for barring him.

That incident touched off international protests in the intellectual community in the United States and the world. It embarrassed the Nixon administration and elements of the Justice and State departments and led to a reconsideration of the vague sections of the immigration laws that were used to ban artists, writers, scientists, and teachers.

During the Kennedy administration and before, Fuentes had also had visa troubles. "I was granted a five-day stay once by Bobby Kennedy when he was attorney general," he said, "but I was not allowed to leave Manhattan. One night Norman Mailer came over from Brooklyn, and a Humphrey Bogart-type character in trench coat tailed us through the streets. We thought we shook our gendarme that night, but the next morning, when I looked out the window of a friend's place in Manhattan, there was Bogart waiting for me."

Although he follows most of the modern writers on both sides of the Atlantic and Caribbean, Fuentes finds himself increasingly interested in the works of William Faulkner, Dashiell Hammett, and Raymond Chandler—for reasons peculiar to his own experience as a Mexican novelist.

"I think of Faulkner as a Caribbean writer," he explained, "because of his own baroque style and themes—a tragic novelist of loss and defeat in a country used to victories. Hammett is Hammett—a storyteller with an opaque quality that shines through his hard-boiled realism. I often reread his *Red Harvest*. And Chandler is the ultimate California writer, the state where territorial expansion ends—a subject we know a great deal about in Mexico—and extremes and extremism begins."

Intertwining fiction and personal history, as in *Terra Nostra*,

Ambassador Fuentes now strode along Manhattan's streets freely, without looking over his shoulder for Bogart, pondering the next theme for novelist Fuentes to write, always on Sunday.

[OCTOBER 28, 1976]

E. B. WHITE

Allen Cove, Maine

At six in the morning, E. B. White, one of the country's most precious literary resources, starts the wood fire in the black four-lidded kitchen stove, checks the action in the bird feeder dangling outside the living-room window of his nineteenth-century farmhouse, and peers with a Maineman's eyes at the autumn skies.

"Weather prediction: overcast," he has written ahead to a visiting acquaintance. "Yesterday I threw away in disgust a pencil you had once given me. It wasn't pulling its weight."

But wait a minute: The sun has broken through without advance notice. And the pencils, and pens and typewriters (the portable down at the writing boathouse, the upright Underwood with its old green signals on some of the keys in the workroom) are still in action, turning out some of the most moral, living prose produced by hand in the United States.

At seventy-seven, Andy White appears something like his sentences, at once elegant and straightforward. He acquired the nickname Andy at Cornell, after its first president, Andrew D. White. The nickname was commonly bestowed on Cornell students named White. Elwyn Brooks White was pleased with it since he disliked his given name.

His silver-haired wife, Katharine, sits on the living-room couch, whetting her keen mind on a newspaper jumble-word puzzle. There's a snap in the air, and he fiddles with a thick log in the fireplace. It flares up quickly—more a countryman's than an author's fire.

What's the secret of the fast ignition?

"Forty years of practice," he says, corresponding to the time the Whites have lived here, and then modestly explains that the kindling comes from old cedar telephone poles that have out-lived their wooden lives in the Maine winters.

The occasion for the visit is *Letters of E. B. White.* The book is collected and edited by Dorothy Lobrano Guth, his goddaughter, with an assist from Corona Machemer, from his publishing house, and with an affectionate salute to Katharine White, who "gazed steadily and skeptically at the whole mess with a patience born of her long years of dealing with unruly writers and untidy manuscripts."

The lighthearted tone of the book—and of its author—is set right from the start by White: "Ideally, a book of letters should be published posthumously. The advantages are obvious: The editor enjoys a free hand, and the author enjoys a perfect hiding place—the grave, where he is impervious to embarrassments and beyond the reach of libel. I have failed to cooperate in this ideal arrangement. Through some typical bit of mismanagement, I am still alive, and the book has had to adjust to that awkward fact."

Actually, the letters add up to a series of love affairs: with Cornell and old campus friends; with the glorious plainness of the English language that he dignified in revising *The Elements of Style* by his former professor William Strunk, Jr.; with the state of Maine and its fishing and sailing waters; with the animal world, domestic and foreign, that led to *Stuart Little, Charlotte's Web,* and *The Trumpet of the Swan;* with *The New Yorker* magazine and especially its founding editor, Harold W. Ross; with

Katharine Sergeant Angell, *The New Yorker* editor who became his wife.

Sipping a vermouth cassis, which he called a French taxi driver's drink, White noted a few lines about their literary courtship, part of the autobiographical text between the letters: "I soon realized I had made no mistake in my choice of a wife. I was helping her pack an overnight bag one afternoon when she said, 'Put in some tooth twine.' I knew then that a girl who called dental floss tooth twine was the girl for me."

While Mrs. White took her afternoon rest, farmer White drove to the village library to donate a few books and to borrow one that he wanted to read, Saul Bellow's *Henderson the Rain King*. Matter-of-factly he pointed to the row of wooden shelves that he had himself built for the library.

Then he walked over to the general store, bought a bottle of orange juice, and took it up to the counter.

"Hi, Al," he said to the proprietor.

"Hi, Andy," Al Ormondroyd said, at the same time selling a copy of the Ellsworth *American* to a city slicker.

Driving on a few miles, he stopped at the boatyard run by his son, Joel, a naval architect from Massachusetts Institute of Technology, and studied the small boats jiggling on the windy waters. In a cavernous boatshed, he climbed aboard the nineteen-foot centerboard sloop *Martha,* named after his granddaughter, which his son built for him. He has sailed these waters, alone and with friends and family, most of his life.

He pointed to the carved dolphins, four on each side of the bow, that he designed and decorated in gold. Sailors need dolphins around for good luck. Like Louis the trumpeter swan in his book, "who thought how lucky he was to inhabit such a beautiful earth," E. B. White is on the side of good luck and the angels.

Back at Allen Cove, he spotted his geese on the pond below the farmhouse and barn. He picked up some apples and waved them aloft, inviting the geese to have a snack before dinner.

"Hey, want an apple?" he shouted. The geese honked back that they certainly did, but in their own good time because they had other business to attend to first.

"Geese are the greatest clowns in the world," he said. "I wouldn't be without them."

To followers of White's work, this is historic literary territory. The barn has inspired many of the characters in his stories for children. In a corner of a cellar window a spider had spun a web but, he noted, it was a different species from the large gray spider that lived here with Wilbur the pig in *Charlotte's Web*.

In his small gray boathouse facing the cove, he wrote *One Man's Meat,* most of *Charlotte's Web,* and, he says, "ten thousand newsbreaks." These are the satirical and humorous observations that round off the columns in just about every issue of *The New Yorker*. They are unsigned, but they bear the White imprint. Their headings have become part of the language: "Neatest Trick of the Week"; "Go Climb a Tree Department"; "Letters We Never Finished Reading"; "Our Forgetful Authors"; "Funny Coincidence Department"; "Wind on Capitol Hill."

"The New Yorker sends me a package of news items every week, and I mail them back with the heading or footnote," he said. "I like doing the breaks because it gives me a feeling of holding down a job and affords me a fine glimpse of newspapers all over the country. I turned in my first one just fifty years ago. Everybody in the shop used to do them. One day I got a call from Ross asking where I was. I said I was home with the chicken pox. And he said, 'I finally get someone who can do these breaks, and he gets the chicken pox.' "

The *Letters of E. B. White* underscores that the author, when aroused by some major imperfection in the state of the world and its literary freedom, can muster all the weapons in the arsenal of language.

A fascinating exchange in the book recalls his dispute with the editorial page of the New York *Herald Tribune,* which approved the blacklisting of Hollywood writers who refused to answer questions about their politics before the House Committee on Un-American Activities. Because White was on the side of privacy of political beliefs, he was personally attacked by the *Herald Tribune*'s editors. His letters to the editor are part of the mined old gold in the book.

The same consistent instinct for freedom of expression caused him to write a letter to the editor of the Ellsworth *American* early in 1976, questioning an article in *Esquire* magazine by Harrison E. Salisbury that was "sponsored" by Xerox as part of an advertising message. The corporation planned two more such author-underwritten articles but dropped them when White's internationally reprinted views convinced Xerox that such editorial intrusion would be disastrous for freedom of the press. White's reasoned letters were added to the text of this book.

"That's the kind of thing that would have sent Ross up the wall," White said. "The shadow of advertising was not allowed in the editorial department. He was a nut on the matter of separation of ads and text. He had an almost Victorian sense of morality."

Did words still count in this country?

They did here on the farmhouse bookshelves—the words of Charles Lamb, Thomas Hardy, Jane Austen, George Meredith, the Russian novelists, and any number of *New Yorker* book writers. Nothing clashed with what he had written in *The Elements of Style:* "No one can write decently who is distrustful of the reader's intelligence."

Sipping his Boodles martini, Andy White replied, "TV has taken a big bite out of the written word. But words still count with me."

[NOVEMBER 17, 1976]

NORMAN MAILER

"There is a fancy wistfulness about writers in their fifties," Norman Mailer says. "They wonder, 'Do I still have enough skill left to bring it off?' "

After being away from fiction for a decade, he says that he is working steadily and well now on his *big* novel—the biggest for him and one of the longest planned by any American writer, past or present.

He is still surprisingly youthful. As always, he appears almost elegant: an old rifleman in an officer's trench coat. His stance remains open. He hesitates for a modest moment between sentences, then comes out of a neutral corner with an uppercut to the mind. "This is a tricky business," he says of the challenge of writing like a heavyweight again. "The trick is to go beyond one's reach."

Most of the time he is in Provincetown, Massachusetts, putting in two and a half hours in the morning and another two and a half in the evening. When he completes the work, it could go between 550,000 and 800,000 words.

Ned Bradford, his editor at Little, Brown in Boston, says that

Mailer seems to be going along systematically on the novel and has written more than 175,000 words. He also stressed that the one million dollars were not just for one book but for "the work"—which could be for anywhere from two to four novels, depending on natural breaks.

"I'm writing about Egypt in the twentieth dynasty, 1130 B.C." Mailer said. "Why? Because I fell through a novelistic hole. I thought I would dip into the period, and then it began to absorb me. I went to Egypt once, but didn't get much out of the trip. Both Cairo and the pyramids were impossibly crowded.

"Actually, the first third of the book takes place in Egypt, the second third on a spaceship; the last third is contemporary."

The Egyptian dynasty comes from research, the space world is not unfamiliar to him since he wrote *Of a Fire on the Moon,* and the contemporary life he has lived fully.

"I've been possessed with the conundrum of time ever since I started writing novels," Mailer continued. "But I'm not doing this mechanically. There have been some mistaken reports that I was going to follow a Jewish family from the time of the pharaohs, but the characters and events are still evolving.

"I know it's dangerous to characterize what I'm trying to do, but I want the novel to be a consistent explanation of time. What I'm trying to do is more abstract than realistic—and endlessly more pompous.

"I've done eleven hundred pages, double-spaced. I hope it doesn't get much longer. I'm perhaps two-thirds through, and it should be done in a year. The only Jew in it is a guy named Moses, that revolutionary character. I hope he didn't look like Yasir Arafat."

Mailer said that he had a secret scheme to tie the trilogy together but that he wasn't telling anybody.

He contends that writing is a dangerous occupation, especially if your situation is such that "you have to keep the bread coming in." With more charm than despair, he notes that he has had more publishers than ex-wives: six to five. He has seven children, five daughters and two sons, ranging in age from twenty-seven to five. And he lives with, he says, parodying the gossip columnists, a "CC—Constant Companion."

Because of his various obligations, as well as his wide-ranging interests, he still finds himself taking time out every now and again to make the bread and pay the taxes. He takes side trips in books, such as the one on Marilyn Monroe and the latest on Henry Miller, and in magazine articles, covering conventions, candidates, the Central Intelligence Agency, and Watergate.

He was in New York celebrating the publication of *Genius and Lust: A Journey through the Major Writings of Henry Miller.* He considers Miller, at his best, the greatest living American writer, worthy of comparison to Hemingway and Faulkner.

He also is an admirer of Saul Bellow, who will receive the Nobel Prize in literature in Stockholm. "To my surprise, I felt good about Saul getting it," he said, "because he deserved it. I sent him a telegram of congratulations."

Mailer, of course, had been mentioned as a candidate for the Nobel, and his future chances will probably ride on the big novel.

"I've had a few false alarms about the Nobel," he said. "After *Armies of the Night* in 1969, an Associated Press reporter called me early in the morning of the day of the announcements because he had picked up a rumor that I would get it. I learned later that he had mixed me up with another M—Malraux."

He says that he could have used the prize when he wrote *The Deer Park,* his novel with a Hollywood background, because everybody jumped on him then. In those days there was his frequent talk about defending his writing title—the boxing analogy. "But I'm no longer talking about defending it. Well . . . maybe against Tolstoy. I was more on the order of Ezzard Charles than Joe Louis, anyway."

He still thinks that the boxing metaphor is useful because there is a resemblance between a fighter and a writer. Both, he believes, are engaged in cool and controversial acts, both make their own moves, and any good fighter and writer become aware that the main bout is with themselves. "Knowing that," Mailer says, "you become a wiser man."

[DECEMBER 10, 1976]

GEORGES SIMENON

Lausanne, Switzerland

"When I turned seventy three years ago, I decided it was time to stop living in the skin of Inspector Maigret and my other characters. I said to myself, 'I have written two hundred twenty novels under my own name and one hundred and fifty with pseudonyms. From now on, I am going to live only in my own skin.' "

Georges Simenon, the most prolific and most translated living author, master of the *roman policier* that has made him wealthy without losing him the respect of his friends in the community of letters, is shedding not only his characters but the excess baggage of life. Hereafter his writing will consist only of memoirs, set down at his own pace.

The Belgian-born author, who has lived in France, the United States, and, for many years, Switzerland, sat in his small garden apartment on the outskirts of Lausanne, puffing on his perennial pipe, watching the finches and doves dining on the bird food he had sprinkled under the 250-year-old cedar tree outside the garden doorway, and talking in English and French about the freedom of simplicity.

Watching over him and hanging on to his words were Teresa,

a charming North Italian woman who has been his companion for a number of years, and Joyce Aitken, a British woman who runs the "Secretariat de Georges Simenon," keeping track of his many contracts, typing his manuscripts, and fending off his reading public.

"I've given up living at my château. It sits in the countryside near here, unoccupied. I sold my cars: the Rolls-Royce we called Grandma, the Jaguar, the Rover, and the two Volvos. I once had eleven servants. I no longer bother to give interviews every week on the state of the world's affairs. I prefer living my little life.

"Not having to play the role of a writer, I can even talk more freely. I am not a member of any political party. I am a peaceful anarchist, more radical than liberal. If Maigret were still living now, I think he would be an anarchist and a leftist.

"I am against the literary world. No cocktail parties, nothing. In France they say I have written too much. The critics don't matter to me. There are two countries where you can interchange critics—Russia and the United States—because they are not serious analysts of a man's work. Anyway, I'm a lone wolf and always have been."

He now reveals that Inspector Maigret had always been a critic of the system, but between the lines. When Maigret allowed his criminals to escape, it was because he was an anarchist in revolt himself. There are no criminals, Simenon says, only men.

"All the problems today are caused by people who think they are superior. I don't believe in great men. I call them phantoms. We saw what a little man, truly, Richard Nixon was. Politicians are merely puppets in the hands of the big corporations. What I am trying to do is understand and distinguish among men.

"I'm not an activist myself. I am bashful and don't like to give advice, but I think that people who take to the streets are sometimes necessary. Nowadays I stroll around here every afternoon, looking at each man, this one's smile, that one's scowl. I know something about psychiatry. My best friends are not writers but psychiatrists from around Lausanne. We talk about motivations. I don't consider any man responsible for his acts any more than those birds outside the window."

Although Simenon has ceased writing fiction, his books will continue to be translated for years to come. As usual, the latest Simenons touched off conjecture about whether he is a novelist of Parisian manners writing mysteries or a mysterious man of hidden dimensions disguised behind the Maigret mask.

But there is a new series of Simenon works coming out of his skin that engages him and places punctuation marks around his present life. He has never been more excited about any project. "I am now letting off *vapeur*—steam," he says. "I am speaking plain words. No more electric typewriter for me. Instead I play with my little tape recorder when the spirit moves me. For my own pleasure, I dictate what comes into my mind, and then it is typed into manuscripts that are becoming books.

"It's a mixed grill—memories of my childhood, the color of the day, the faces encountered on my walks, the small world around me. No, this is not autobiography; I don't believe in that. I live in the present, not the past. Still, I believe that these books will last longer than my fiction because they concern real life and real people. Curiously, I am getting more letters about them from French readers who have read these books than from my regular Maigret readers."

He relit his pipe, inscribed a book in French for a visitor with the words "In a little rose house where I have encountered another man," and set forth on his afternoon stroll in search of others, and himself.

[DECEMBER 13, 1976]

REBECCA WEST

London

There is nothing like a Dame—especially if she is Rebecca West, Dame Commander, Order of the British Empire, and uncrowned queen of British letters.

Somehow it seemed right to bring her a bunch of chrysanthemums for her birthday and also as a homage to the comprehensive collection of six decades of her writing, *Rebecca West: A Celebration.*

Across the teacups in her flat at Prince's Gate in Southwest London, she took a visitor on a *tour d'horizon* of her literary and journalistic world. Despite a few bodily ailments, Dame Rebecca continues to write fiction and book reviews and to offer witty observations on the contemporary scene.

Few writers are better able to do so. She started out as a book reviewer for the *Freewoman* in 1911 and later put some of the theories of freedom and equality into her personal life. She worked for women's suffrage and was a member of the Fabian Society, the English organization that favored socialism by peaceful means.

Celebration includes all or parts of her books, some new articles and a long story, and sections of a novel in progress, *This Real Night*. Her famous trial reporting on crime and treason, which ran in *The New Yorker,* is of course in the collection. These covered such war traitors as William Joyce (Lord Haw-Haw) and Klaus Fuchs as well as the Nuremberg Trials.

"Treachery was once very chic and idealistic," Dame Rebecca said. "It's now so professional."

And the collection naturally includes a part of her *Black Lamb and Grey Falcon.* She has put together a two-hundred-page sampling of that major twelve-hundred-page history and travel book, still a definitive work on Yugoslavia.

"I'm two-thirds through the new novel," she said, "and I'll finish it if old age doesn't carry me off. I have so many interruptions—book reviews once a month for the *Sunday Telegraph,* which I enjoy doing because it enables me to keep up with new writing, and occasional appearances at official functions."

She was pleased to be named a Dame in 1959. It was the first such honor given to a woman journalist, though she still considers it a funny title for a writer. But the burdens of office are not heavy enough to prevent her from making outspoken remarks about the government and other writers, past and present.

"The Labor party today is full of bumblers saying, 'Rhubarb, rhubarb,' she said. "They are a different lot from many of the early socialists. I go back to the time of Kerensky and the Mensheviks. Do you know that the stage director Peter Brook is the child of two Mensheviks?

"I've always enjoyed visiting America. The awful thing about your Vietnam War was that you had to learn about losing power in the world. There's no way of learning that except by defeat. We learned it, the Russians learned it, and you finally did in Vietnam. And now Africa is getting out of hand. Nothing new: Look up Cleopatra's edicts on foreign policy. It's all there.

"The lesson of Watergate was also important. But I wish people wouldn't roll their tongues over what happened in your country so. In a lot of ways Nixon was not stupid. He was an example of bad form combined with original sin."

Dame Rebecca is equally blunt on literary affairs and person-ages:

"We have a lot of eccentrics in this country, like Malcolm Muggeridge. He's a nice old donkey. I always feel that his reli-gion comes first. He is always trying to put Christ on the map.

"Graham Greene? Heavy weather. I thought *Our Man in Havana* was good, but his places are so unlike the real locales. Iris Murdoch does go on writing about freaks. She's an example of university being a bad influence upon a writer.

"Muriel Spark is a very strange and isolated character. Her *Ballad of Peckham Rye* and *Mandelbaum Gate* were fine. Living in Italy is probably good for her. Honor Tracy? A great comic writer and journalist."

Among current American writers, Dame Rebecca admires Saul Bellow, John Cheever, and Peter De Vries. As for the past, "I loved Thornton Wilder's plays," she said. "Hemingway was drunk at the time that I met him. But he did a revolutionary thing for style; dialogue in American novels was awful until he came along and realized the importance for a writer of leaving out.

"James Thurber was all wrong about Harold Ross of *The New Yorker*. When Ross wrote 'Who he?' on your manuscript, he didn't mean that he didn't know about a person you wrote about, but that you had not explained him clearly for the reader, and he, as well as his successor, Bill Shawn, was usually right. I loved Shawn's way of raising questions. 'And now for a few indelicacies,' he would say."

A recent cataract operation prevents her from "banging it out on the typewriter," she said, "but you get to be very clever about writing in longhand." Which is just what she started to do, after another cup of tea, there being nothing like a writer who's a Dame—with something to declare.

[DECEMBER 25, 1976]

VLADIMIR NABOKOV

Montreux, Switzerland

Presidents of the United States are not supposed to be quoted directly without their consent. Why shouldn't a distinguished international author enjoy the same privilege? If you are not quoted, you cannot be misquoted.

To protect what he regards as the integrity of his words, Vladimir Nabokov has not given interviews in recent years unless questions were submitted in advance in writing, answered by him in writing, and reproduced verbatim. But he did tell a reporter that he would be delighted to make his acquaintance without a formal interview—without those tripping quotes. Nabokov and his wife, Véra, are at home in the Montreux-Palace et Cygne, a grand dame of a hotel with a modern face-lift, overlooking Lake Geneva. They have lived here for many years. According to the novelist-lepidopterist, if you are there in the right season, a butterfly will glide past the eaves and balustrades. But butterflies are not now on the wing. At least, none are visible in the elegant salon of the hotel's interior bar, where glasses are filled by hovering attendants.

Nabokov likes having an apartment in this caravansary be-

cause it frees him from everyday cares. A cook comes in to pre-
pare dinner. The concierge keeps an eye on the mail and brushes
off intruders without appointments who want to see the great
writer they have read about, if not read. Or perhaps they have
read *Lolita,* but not *Ada* or *Pnin* or his critical biography of
Gogol. And here he can be served his favorite port—the one, he
observes, with the man wearing a black cape on the label.

Nabokov continues to write steadily and casts a cold eye on
the literary fashions of the moment. He follows the American
scene by closely reading the magazines and newsmagazines. *The
New Yorker* is still *The New Yorker,* he finds, but its short stories
are not of consistently high quality because there aren't enough
good short stories around generally. *Playboy,* which has also run
his stories, is seen, if not studied. He enjoys the *New York Review
of Books* because of its scholarly controversies. International literary and scholarly news of books is provided by the *Times Literary
Supplement.*

His list of admired contemporary writers is apparently quite
short. Nabokov mentions several he does not like on what
might be called the New York–Chicago axis, but requests that
their names go unmentioned because he regards some as friends.
But he rather likes the nickname conferred upon him in this
cygnelike setting: "The black swan of Montreux."

In recent years memories of his family and upbringing as an
aristocrat in czarist Russia have occupied his attention. In the
future there is a second volume of his memoirs. Of the Soviet
Union, the less said the better. His work is not published there,
but he is aware that his books are smuggled into the land of his
birth.

The final volume of stories from his émigré period in Berlin
and Paris period came out early in 1976, as *Details of a Sunset.*
Some had been published in *The New Yorker* and *Playboy.* People
familiar with his literary activity have been urging him to publish
his correspondence with Edmund Wilson, the late critic, because many letters that are said to be brilliant were exchanged
between them.

Frederic W. Hills, his editor, discloses that Nabokov has completed his next novel in his head. It's all there: the characters, the scenes, the details. He is about to do the actual writing on three-by-five-inch cards. The cards are then filled with words, shuffled, and, in his editor's phrase, Nabokov will deal himself a novel.

Its reference title is "Tool," presumably an anagram, somehow based on a character named Laura. But it is idle to speculate about the title or the meaning, his editor says, because Nabokov likes to play games with words, ideas, and publishers, and it is impossible to tell until those shuffled cards are typed into a manuscript.

And what is the new novel about? this interviewer asked.

"If I told you," Nabokov replied, "that would be an interview."

[JANUARY 5, 1977]

WALKER PERCY

"I lived a hundred miles from William Faulkner but he meant less to me than Albert Camus," said Walker Percy. "I may have been lucky that way."

Talking of his novel *Lancelot,* the writer offered a few clues to his thought and work. None is more telling than his admiration for the French and Russian novelists—Camus and Sartre, Gogol, Tolstoy, and Dostoyevsky. With a chivalric touch, he thought it best not to mention (and possibly offend by omission) his favorite American authors.

"The French have something that is rare for our fiction writers—a philosophical conviction with novelistic art," Percy said. "The combination is usually fatal, but the French seem to achieve it. Sartre solved the problem of joining art and philosophy in his best work, *Nausea,* and Camus did so in several of his books.

"I worked on *Lancelot* for three years, and I owe a debt to Camus. In his novel *The Fall,* one man talked to another man, and that's the way it goes in mine. It's an interesting form and a difficult one, something like a dramatic morality play.

"In constructing *Lancelot,* I thought: Why not have the silence serve as a sort of dialogue? One of the ideas that I try to get across is the failure of communication between people. Lancelot is not altogether unhappy in his cell in the prison hospital. He feels better than his doctors in the so-called sane world on the outside. And the girl in the next cell is mute. Lancelot tries to reach out to her. Why not communicate by tapping on the wall? Words do get worn out. Maybe the purpose of language is to revive itself—including through the novel.

"In the novel I try to balance the hero between the normal and the pathological," Percy said. "Who is worse off, the patient or the doctor, the inmates or the outside world? The Lancelot character represents an honor code. If he had lived in the twelfth century, he would have been a Crusader who believed in an idea, just as the Israelis in modern times have a noble idea. The only difference between the Crusaders and the Israelis is that the Crusaders lost. Sometime I'd like to see Israel.

"The novel also aims to remind us about three revolutions: the first one in Virginia, when the British were kicked out by the framers of the Declaration and Constitution; the second one in the South, which was lost because of the wrongs of slavery; the final one entering the third century for the United States— where else but in Virginia, where much of it all began?

The idea for this novel took hold in Covington, the New Orleans suburban town of ten thousand where he lives with his wife, Mary, in a miniature French château. It is in bayou and pine-road country. Mrs. Percy and one of their two daughters started a bookstore-gift-antique shop called The Kumquat six months ago. With two grandsons in the vicinity, it is a comfortable and happy life for the Percys.

But New Orleans is not the South of the popular image, and Percy is far from being a lord of the manor. In the 1960s he helped to form a biracial group, the Greater Covington Community Relations Council, which had its scrapes with the Ku Klux Klan. He voted for Jimmy Carter, "with fingers crossed," aware that the president is also an atypical southerner.

It is the collision of cultures, the melting pot of New Orleans, that keeps Percy there. The only other city he would live in, except that it's not in his native South (he was born in Birmingham, Alabama), is San Francisco, because of its many voices and races. What he deplores is the growth of the "southern Sun Belt" as a political idea, stretching from the Carolinas to Los Angeles, "dominated by such figures as Billy Graham and Oral Roberts, John Connally and Richard Nixon."

Behind the character of Lancelot, something of a failed NAACP lawyer, is what Percy calls "the Roman Stoic," and in the background of the novel is the changing face of the United States.

Hollywood holds a special fascination for Percy. Unlike Faulkner, he never wrote for the screen and never intends to. But in his first novel, *The Moviegoer,* which received the National Book Award in 1962, the neighborhood movie houses became oases of reality in an unreal world.

Here Percy the New Yorker flicks across the magic lantern of his life. His uncle William Alexander Percy, author of *Lanterns on the Levee,* had sent him to Columbia University's College of Physicians and Surgeons to become a doctor. He received his M.D. in 1941.

"I led a misspent youth while going to medical school," Percy said, laughing. "To get away from the grind, I'd go to the Loew's State on One Hundred Eighty-first Street and the RKO Coliseum on One Hundred Eighty-third Street. My uncle would try to get me to come downtown to the opera house, but I spent four years in the movies in Washington Heights. Did you know that June Allyson is from Washington Heights?

"Then I interned at Bellevue Hospital. I performed autopsies on more than a hundred twenty-five corpses, mostly alcoholics who had contracted tuberculosis. I got TB and was sent to Saranac Lake in the Adirondacks. It took me two years to recuperate. I read the French and the Russian storytellers. After that experience I decided to do what I had always wanted—write. If you want to be a novelist, I sometimes tell students at Loyola or Louisiana State University, where I occasionally take a class, work in the wards."

The author of *Lancelot* was in New York before going up to Cornell to speak at a Chekhov festival. "He was a doctor, like me, who also didn't particularly like medicine," Percy said.

But before doing so, he had a free evening while his wife was hunting down gifts and antiques for the bookstore. "If *Dr. Strangelove* is playing somewhere, I'm going to see it again. It's the great American movie. I'd even go to a neighborhood movie in Brooklyn," Percy the moviegoer said.

[FEBRUARY 20, 1977]

JAMES JONES

James Jones, the tough-faced author who fought as a welter-weight in the army, punched his way to the top of the postwar literary scene in 1951 with the publication of *From Here to Eternity*.

"I write about war," Jones said in his middle years, "because it's the only métier I've ever had."

From Here to Eternity won the National Book Award for fiction, a feat Jones never again matched in the counterpunching world of literary criticism. His success continued financially, and so did his reputation as an author who could command advances and attention as a celebrity from Paris to Long Island. Dauntlessly he kept turning out books and living as a public figure.

His first novel is usually ranked with the handful of World War II books that, in the phrase of the time, told it like it was. A mistaken belief exists that it was a "war" novel when, in fact, it was a prewar novel.

The great strength of *From Here to Eternity* was that it revealed what life was like in the "Regulars," the army that existed at the end of the Depression as a refuge for the jobless, the misfits, and the adventurers, commanded by officers waiting to be promoted quickly in the next war. The novel ended with Pearl Harbor.

It was an army that Jones knew firsthand. He was born November 6, 1921, in Robinson, Illinois, the son of a dentist, Ramon Jones. His education ended after high school, when he enlisted in the army, serving from 1939 to 1944. He became a sergeant and received a Purple Heart.

Not long after enlisting in the army that he later said he disliked, but that provided him with continuing material for his books, he read Thomas Wolfe's *Look Homeward, Angel.*

The young man in that novel reminded him of himself and his own small-town background. Jones began writing in the army. Making up for his lack of higher education, he studied at the University of Hawaii in 1942 and at New York University in 1945.

Even so, he said: "I'm no intellectual, I'm no intellectual radical. But I've always been a rebel. A writer should be everything. He should be able to be everybody. I mean there is a good deal of pessimism around. If the world were to be blown up, I mean that I could even enjoy the spectacle—though I wouldn't be able to write about it."

After the war he worked on his first novel, in Illinois, after Lowney Handy, a housewife, and her husband "adopted" him and encouraged him to write. "Without Lowney around to crack the whip, I wouldn't do anything," he said. "She can be pretty tough on me and cuss me out about everything from women to being conceited, but when I get disgusted, she tells me I'm the best damn writer in the world."

Following the acclaim of *From Here to Eternity,* Jones lived in a writers' colony founded by Mrs. Handy and built around him, which he helped to support. Then he moved into an eighty-five-thousand-dollar four-room bachelor house in Marshall, Illinois, filled with a collection of rifles, pistols, French-made toy soldiers, bowie knives, Meissen figurines, and several dozen chess sets.

His second novel, *Some Came Running,* came out in 1958. It was three hundred thousand words longer than the 861-page *From Here to Eternity.* Jones told the story of nine people in a small Illinois town who were "running for eternity." The contrast between the hard-living army characters of *From Here to Eternity* and the beer-swilling civilians of the new work failed to please the critics, who said that the author had taken on an American theme beyond his reach.

The Pistol, in 1959, and *The Thin Red Line,* in 1962, were fairly well received. These war stories also drew upon upon his own experiences. *The Thin Red Line* was an account of an infantry company on Guadalcanal. Like the company of men in *From Here to Eternity,* Jones individualized his characters and documented his scenes of war.

To those who called him only a "war novelist" who appeared to glorify combat, Jones said that his books were actually antiwar in scope. He maintained that any accurate account of war had to show "the regimentation of souls, the systemized reduction of men to animal level, the horrors of pointless death, the exhaustion of living in constant fear." Moreover, he said that a true antiwar work revealed that "modern war destroys human character." Jones said that the dehumanizing institutions of war symbolized the corrupting tendency of contemporary institutions.

Jones and his wife, Gloria Mosolino, a former actress whom he married in 1957, moved in 1958 to Paris, where they became part of a new expatriate group of writers. Their elaborate house on the Quai d'Orléans on the Île St. Louis required an increased income. The Jones ménage included an English woman and an Indian gentleman as a couple around the house.

Next to the Purple Heart and Bronze Star, a Calder mobile twirled overhead. The boy from Illinois and Guadalcanal had become an international celebrity living in another world.

"I rarely go to the Right Bank except to work on films," Jones said. "I don't like writing movie scripts, but the pay is high, and so is the price of Paris. Paris has become our home. I wouldn't live anywhere else."

"It has nothing to do with my work," he said. "When I'm at my typewriter, I could just as well be living in New York. But when the day's stint is done, I walk the streets with Stendhal, Proust, Rousseau, and Voltaire. I feel lost in a primeval forest among the columns of Notre Dame. I get goose pimples just looking at this scene."

Jones said that Stendhal was his favorite writer because "he sustained his enlightened cynicism." He also described his new surroundings as "Hemingway country." However, Jones balked at comparing himself to the Hemingway persona.

"One has to be an egomaniac to be a writer, but you've got to hide it," he said. "Hemingway was more concerned with being an international celebrity than in writing great books. He worked harder on his image than on his integrity. He was a swashbuckler who didn't swash his buckle, or who didn't buckle his swash."

Unlike Hemingway, however, Jones continued to be criticized as a writer, regardless of his themes. Unlike Hemingway, he did not avoid writing for films and turning out books clearly designed for the commercial market. And unlike Hemingway, he had gone to Paris not in his youth but in his flourishing mature years.

In *Go to the Widow-Maker,* in 1967, Jones again made an effort at a long work, this one nearly seven hundred pages. It included a variety of characters, among them a playwright hero who indulged in skindiving, a sport that Jones had taken up seriously. The novel also included patches of his philosophy: "All these guys. All over the world. It doesn't matter what they call it: Communism; Americanism; the Empire. They're small boys standing in the men's room watching their daddies make peepee. . . . So they take refuge in bravery. That proves they're men. So they make up games. The harder the game, the braver the man. Politics, war, football, polo, explorers. Skindiving. Shark-shooting. All to be brave. All to be men."

In 1975 Jones, his wife, and their children, Kaylie and Jamie, established a new beachhead, in Sagaponack, on the eastern end of Long Island. After spending sixteen years in Paris, he found it a congenial place to work and live. "It's so beautiful out here," he said. "I'm getting older. I've still got a lot to do. And I got the feeling that the only real cultural excitement is happening in the U.S."

[MAY 10, 1977]

FRANK SWINNERTON

Cranleigh, Surrey, England

People keep asking Frank Swinnerton for his reminiscences of Charles Dickens, who died in 1870. But he cannot help them because Frank Swinnerton is only ninety-two.

And so here he stands in his own right, the oldest practicing novelist in the English-speaking world and maybe any other, greeting you at the swinging wooden gate of Old Tokefield, his sixteenth-century stone cottage in Surrey, looking, come to think of it, Dickensian, or, more precisely, Pickwickian.

At evensong Frank Swinnerton fits the description of a Man of Letters. A literary critic, essayist, and editor, he has dignified the publishing world and its writers in nonfiction. In his novels, which hover between London and its surrounding counties, his characterizations of the middle class are done with affection and perception.

His fifty-sixth novel, *Some Achieve Greatness,* has been issued by his American publisher. The theme is rediscovered love and the possibility of another chance for people in their middle years—the early fifties.

"We have been married for fifty-two years," Swinnerton

says, walking down the garden path with his wife, Mary. "I think I am the only English author who observed his golden wedding anniversary." Both seemed as pleased with this land-mark as with any of his literary achievements. They live mod-estly by the labor of his pen.

"Arnold Bennett liked our cottage because he said it didn't matter here where you put your spent matches," he said. "But he could not stand the solitude of the country for himself. Ben-nett and H. G. Wells praised my short novel *Nocturne* when it came out in 1917, and we all became friends.

"I also met George Bernard Shaw about the same time. He told me, 'Swinnerton, you're only a wretched artist, but I think you're worth insulting.' Of course, he also told the story on himself of going into the bookstore and demanding, 'Have you any works by that great buffoon Shaw?' "

Swinnerton chuckled; Mrs. Swinnerton smiled.

"After years in London, we made a deliberate decision to live here in the village," he said. "The moment a writer attracts at-tention, he is invited into society, becomes better known than his characters, joins the West End clique, and craves publicity. We prefer the country, work unwillingly very hard, and have few intolerances."

There are certain other advantages for a novelist away from the seductions of the city. "I take a constitutional in the morning after breakfast, saying hello to neighbors, stopping at the green-grocer's and the other shops. I am on very good terms with all the villagers. People tell me about themselves. If a young woman is acting moodily, another whispers to me, 'Boy trouble.' I hear a lot of confidences that are background for stories."

He lights up when recalling many of his friends who are gone but whose works live. "I knew Sinclair Lewis, crossed the At-lantic once with Willa Cather—an honest woman, and I thought her books very good, too—and met F. Scott Fitzgerald. In fact, I was responsible for publication of *The Great Gatsby* in England, recommending it to Chatto & Windus. Fitzgerald came around to the office and sat there, very brisk, with his hat on. I told him I had enjoyed *Gatsby*. He took his hat off. He asked me my name. Swinnerton? 'Oh, my God,' he said. '*Nocturne* is one of my favorite books.' "

Swinnerton believes that his own best novel is *Death of a Highbrow,* published in 1961. Given the chance, he also wanted to correct the rumor that whenever he completed a book, he ate a hot plum pudding to celebrate. "I only have a plum pudding regularly at Christmas," he says, which may be about the same thing since he writes a book a year.

Between shopping and doing his own gardening ("Trimming hedges and digging ditches enables you to work and think out stories at the same time"), he is preparing his next three books. The first is a novel *The Three Daughters,* the second a book of literary appreciations, *Share My Delight,* the third a biography of Arnold Bennett, which may be called *The Last Word.*

Although the *New Grub Street* of George Gissing's 1890s literary world is different today, the struggle for survival still goes on for the serious novelist in England. Swinnerton's readers on both sides of the Atlantic are limited but devoted. There have been some paperback editions of his work, but he does not attain film or television sales, living only off his books. It's still a struggle.

During one negotiation, he recalled, Stewart Richardson, Doubleday's editor in chief, informed him of a possible paperback reprint. Is the fish on the hook yet? Swinnerton inquired. On the hook and in the net, Richardson replied across the Atlantic. In that case, Swinnerton said, I can put a new roof on the cottage.

It is half past four in the afternoon, and time for a cuppa. "I should imagine that my writing is dated," he says, "but I can't see how it could be otherwise at my age." He sips his tea, says his good-byes, and then walks behind the cottage to his studio, determined to get in a little more writing before supper.

[AUGUST 10, 1977]

KURT VONNEGUT, JR.

Frankfurt, Germany

Private Kurt Vonnegut, Jr., a rifleman during the Battle of the Bulge, was captured in Luxembourg, sent on a long train ride to Saxony, put in a prisoner of war camp in the Sudetenland, and, under the Geneva Convention rules of war, worked for his keep until the end of World War II. For further details, read his novel *Slaughterhouse-Five*.

Vonnegut returned to Germany, staying at a castle outside Frankfurt, under somewhat different conditions. He was working again—but this time for his latest novel, *Slapstick*. Vonnegut's visit was part of a European publishing tour that included Holland, Norway, Sweden, Finland, and the Soviet Union.

At a private luncheon the author met his new German publisher, Klaus Piper of R. Piper Verlag of Munich, for the first time.

Piper said, "I like *Slapstick* very much because it is not too narrow. You have a large vision."

Vonnegut smiled and replied, "Obviously, you're the publisher for me."

Piper said, "I don't publish books; I publish authors."

The statement pleased everybody present—Seymour Lawrence, Vonnegut's U.S. publisher; Walter Fritzsche, Piper's editor in chief; and Michael Schulte, his translator, who had once been an exchange student in Philadelphia. They talked about why Vonnegut's books crossed international borders.

"I hit it off with the young people, the blue jeans and guitar set," the author said. "They are the ones who turned up at the universities and bookstores while we were touring Scandinavia and the other countries. Like *Catch-22* and the books by Tolkien, there is a responsive chord."

Piper said, "I have a prejudice against science fiction." Lawrence said, "Kurt isn't a science fiction writer; he is a moralist." Fritzsche said, "Yes, the key word is moralist."

I wondered how you give meaning to Vonnegut's throwaway line "So it goes" in *Slaughterhouse-Five,* or to the latest, "Hi ho," in *Slapstick.*

Schulte, the translator, said, " 'So it goes' has an equivalent in German, and you can probably find it in any other language. In southern German dialect there is a phrase that is very close, *So ist das holt* a kind of term of resignation, like the American, 'That's the way it is.' "

The "Hi ho" in *Slapstick* is a little more difficult. The translator and editor thought of making it "Hee ho" because the *i* was pronounced in German like an *e* and then thought of simplifying it into a more jocular phrase, "Ho ho," but that distorted the meaning slightly and made it into a joke instead of a sardonic comment. In the end the translator decided to leave it just as it appeared in English.

While Lawrence felt that Vonnegut's *Cat's Cradle* was a breakthrough book for the author, Fritzsche said that he believed the absurdity of war in *Slaughterhouse-Five* was even more of what he called "a seminal experience." The Piper editor said, "Reading it, you suffer with the human race. As for *Slapstick,* despite all the mockeries, it is a serious book. Like Buster Keaton, there is a human quality about it that makes you cry."

Vonnegut listened to this analysis, without putting in his own meanings. He was not displeased. Not when Fritzsche added, "Vonnegut uses science fiction to tell us about ourselves. And in *Slapstick*, laughter itself is the message."

The conversation swung to World War II. Piper, who was said to have been in the Catholic anti-Hitler movement, remarked that he had not been in uniform because of health reasons and that no one in his family, not an uncle or a nephew or a cousin, had ever had anything to do with Hitler. "We were not heroes," he said, "but we had nothing to do with them."

Vonnegut said that he certainly was no expert on World War II. "I was only a bit player," he said, "I didn't get a big view of things as a prisoner of war. Asking me about the big picture is like asking a clown to play Hamlet."

Nevertheless, after three decades the former rifleman who had lived through the irony of being bombed while a prisoner, was now back in Germany, discussing literature and other matters. Lawrence later noted that Vonnegut's books in hard-cover, quality, and mass paperback editions exceeded sales of a million copies a year.

On German television a few nights afterward, Vonnegut, rather formally dressed for an old infantryman, was asked about the state of the world.

"I am a very happy capitalist," he said, possibly surprising this interviewer and the audience. "The greatest problem is loneliness and a lack of dreams. I grew up dreaming of the future, and I am very sorry that people don't have too many dreams any more."

[OCTOBER 28, 1977]

JAMES T. FARRELL

Young Lonigan first appeared in 1932. *Olive and Mary Anne* has just been published—a Christmas gift of five tales from one of the country's old literary pros, James T. Farrell. The new book is his fifty-first.

"I start writing between eight and nine in the morning," Farrell said the other day, "and I continue until I get tired. I worked until four in the morning twice in a row this week. It was going very well."

Olive and Mary Anne ranges across the main Farrell landscape—Chicago and New York—places where he began and where he went to, with many stopovers in the world of books and human affairs. The book includes five stories about love and human relationships.

Farrell has been working on a big series—*The Universe of Time*. The story of *Olive* is part of it but also stands as an independent work within *Olive and Mary Anne*. The stories in the book, he said, are derived from certain persons he has encountered across the years but are "completely imagined."

Olive tells about a troubled heiress in New York, one of the seemingly normal people you pass on the street who are carrying a burden of invisible inner turmoil. In her marriage, "love did not come," and between efforts at painting, she took "a fling at sex and booze." The series of psychiatrists became another routine in her life. And her downspin continued.

"People are always looking for Studs Lonigan in my stories," Farrell said. "I suspect that readers wouldn't know that Olive is a character I've created if my name wasn't on the book."

Chicago was the background for his education, and he still finds it an exciting city—including the White Sox, though he says good things about the New York Yankees, the home team now. The streets of Chicago and the University of Chicago provided the education. He recalls the ten As and three Bs he got in the two years he attended the university, but he left the classroom because he had too much writing on his horizon.

"I always have more manuscripts on hand than I can publish," he said. "I started writing knowing that I'd have to write about what I knew. Carl Sandburg was a great influence upon me; his books gave me my first ideas about Chicago. I first interviewed him way back in 1929. He deserved a Nobel.

"I continued my education by reading and writing. I've moved around the country and spoken on many campuses. Once a year I try to get to Paris. And I visit my son, who's a physician and a very good one, out West."

The *Studs Lonigan* trilogy was published in paperback, and a new edition will come out in hard-cover from the original publisher, Vanguard Press. The Franklin Library is issuing 12,500 copies in one of its handsome editions of *Young Lonigan,* each signed by the author. He's writing various essays and articles—and there's always the next baseball season.

"I don't look back, and I don't like to reread my books," Farrell said. "I'm always interested in the next book that I'm working on."

[DECEMBER 16, 1977]

MARILYN FRENCH

I caught up with Marilyn French where all authors dream of going when all's well: the Fiji Islands in the South Pacific. It was 3:30 P.M. our time and 8:30 A.M. hers, with an International Date Line somewhere in between, and she sounded a little sleepy. But she was looking at a palm tree and we were being brushed by a snowflake, so there were no apologies. Besides, it was our nickel, and since it was halfway around the world, we decided to dispense with the formalities and talk fast to the author of *The Women's Room.*

As readers of her novel know, Marilyn French is a person with strong views. First off, she said she did not want to be called Miss or Mrs. but Ms., and if that was forbidden by the *Times* style manual, she had a fallback title: Dr. The doctorate was earned in English literature at Harvard, which figures in the novel, and seemed appropriate, since it was her book, her palm tree, and her personality.

"I just finished a promotional tour of Australia and New Zealand and decided to come here for a rest," Dr. French said. She is divorced, with two grown children, and lives in the Boston area. She still has links to Harvard, which provides her a library card, contacts with students, and an opportunity to observe the scene for future literary projects.

"The Women's Room is not about the women's movement," Dr. French said, "but about women's lives today. I take the reader into my confidence in the book—in the tradition of the naïve narrator speaking directly in the fourteenth-century poem *Piers Plowman."*

Dr. French began her novel in 1972, found the form not right for what she was trying to say, tried it again a year later, and still it was wrong. Then in March 1975 the idea occurred to use a split narration—the first-person author and the third-person character called Mira. Dr. French described Mira as "a major character that ordinary women would feel compatible with." With this formula, she started the book in May and finished it in October, creating a fictional chronicle of two wives of the 1950s turned into the women of the 1970s.

Dr. French wrote two novels in the 1960s, *The Island* and *The Carving of the Stone.* Her Ph.D. thesis grew into her one previously published work, *The Book as World: James Joyce's Ulysses.*

We wondered: Might the cover of the next printing read, "By the author of *The Women's Room?"*

Across the South Pacific Dr. French replied: "I have a feeling that Harvard wouldn't go for that."

How *The Women's Room* came to be published is something of a Cinderella story (if the comparison is not considered too antifeminist and pro-prince). James H. Silberman, president and editor in chief of Summit Books, left Random House a little over a year ago to start his own company at Simon and Schuster. Eventually the first book published by Summit would turn out to be this hardcover best seller, with paperback rights acquired by Jove/HBJ for a sum that could reach a million dollars. But it didn't start out as a sure thing.

Charlotte Sheedy, Dr. French's literary agent, was Jim Silberman's secretary at the Dial Press years ago. He called her and said he needed a big novel for his new house. Miss Sheedy said she had one, but she felt it wasn't "a Jim Silberman book."

Silberman then sent a messenger around for the big manuscript, read it over the weekend, and found that *The Women's Room* fit like a glass slipper.

[DECEMBER 29, 1977]

J. B. PRIESTLEY

Alveston, England

Looking out upon his thirty acres of greensward from the nine-teenth-century mansion he calls Kissing Tree House, near Strat-ford-on-Avon in Warwickshire, J. B. Priestley offered a word of advice to writers who dream of being as famous and prosperous as, say, J. B. Priestley.

"Young man," he told me, "don't write books; write plays. Once you've had several going for you, you can live like this in your old age." His arm motioned around the elegant rooms of his country home. He puffed on his pipe and stared hard at his listener, letting the point sink in.

John Boynton Priestley is heavy with honors and royalties. After turning down a knighthood and a peerage, he consented to receive the Order of Merit from Queen Elizabeth—an honor limited to twenty-four great Britons, such as Henry Moore, the sculptor, and Sir Frederick Ashton, the choreographer.

Priestley's three-act comedy *Laburnum Grove,* which he wrote in the early 1930's and was produced at the Booth Theater on Broadway in 1935 with Edmund Gwenn as its star, is attracting crowds in a revival at the Duke of York's Theater in the West

End. The *Times* of London critic, Ned Chaillet, noted the anti–
big-business tone of the play, saying that "Mr. Priestley's glee in
unmasking hypocrisy is as lively now as ever."

The playwright-novelist-essayist seemed as lively in person as
his work appears onstage and on the printed page. He could
even be called combative, at least on the surface, until he had
warmed up and had a chance to expound on the state of writing
and the world.

"To hell with Broadway," Priestley said. "You're either marvelous or your play is gone Saturday night." His strong views are
not without echoes in the offices of the Dramatists Guild in
New York. "I've had thirty plays produced, profitably, all
around the world. My work has been on and off Broadway—
including *Dangerous Corner, Eden End, Time and the Conways,*
and *When We Are Married.* I'd as soon have my plays done at the
universities."

(His *The Inspector Calls* turned out to be a hit in London *and*
on Broadway in 1994.)

His novels and essays and autobiographical works make an
even longer list than his plays. Anthony Burgess recently wrote,
"His last big novel, *The Image Men,* is his best." *Instead of the
Trees,* a third volume of his autobiography, was published in the
United States. It was set among the giant redwood trees of Cali-
fornia, just as his first volume of autobiography, *Midnight on the
Desert,* used another American locale—a ranch in Arizona.

"I lived and wrote happily in the American Southwest,"
Priestley recalled. "I liked Arizona, New Mexico, and Nevada
in the 1930s. But I avoided Southern California. I would not
mind going to Boston again—a civilized city. But I'll never go
to New York again. I was there about six years ago. It's turned
sour. Still, despite what the reporters say—I'm usually misquoted in the press—I like America."

Priestley said he also liked a number of American authors and
playwrights, past and present. "I read Rex Stout's mysteries because they're such good novels. I wish that I could have met

him. I would also have liked to know F. Scott Fitzgerald, but not necessarily Ernest Hemingway.

"Among the playwrights, I have an interest in Tom Stoppard—an original. I respect Tennessee Williams. Arthur Miller is all right but not a natural dramatist, merely an intelligent man. But I don't go to the theater in London. I spent forty years writing and directing plays. That's enough."

Politically, Priestley said that for many years his sympathies were on the left. He wrote frequently for the *New Statesman*. He was one of the founders of the Committee for Nuclear Disarmament. Now he finds some excesses among Britain's working class—"overpaid and underworked," he put it. He regards himself as an independent but, clearly, an opinionated independent.

On one subject he is outspoken: the tendency of some highly paid writers and performers to abandon England and seek tax havens. "I'm an Englishman and live in England," he said, "I want to be near my family and friends. If the tax collector decides where you should live, then he's won."

Priestley's son, Tom, is a film editor, and a very good one, he said. He has four daughters, fifteen grandchildren, and one great-grandchild, from his first two marriages. Most of his family lives in and around London, and there are visits back and forth to Kissing Tree House.

His third wife, Jacquetta Hawkes, the archaeologist and author, joined him and a visitor in the living room. Hawkes had spent the morning writing, in her office upstairs, and Priestley spoke of her archaeological forays and books with admiration.

"Hundreds of people have told me what a wonderful life I must have," Priestley said, but quickly spoke of the hard writing life. He considers himself a professional writer, a laborer with words. Although he has been compared with Dickens because of his great output, he says that no comparisons are valid—except that a writer must write, and entertain, and write again.

"Most writers enjoy only two brief periods of happiness," he has written. "First, when what seems a glorious idea comes flashing into mind and, secondly, when a last page has been written and you have not yet had time to consider how much better it all ought to have been.

"Much of the rest might be described as mental pregnancy with successive difficult deliveries, and all without smiles from Mother Nature, for we are of no use to *her*. Have you ever met a really happy writer, a Corot or Renoir of paper and print? I never have."

Priestley relit his pipe and sipped an afternoon drink.

"I am not writing anything at the moment—and I don't intend to," he said. "Why should I? I've been going steadily since 1910. My income is considerable. I don't have to struggle anymore."

But didn't he have more to say in writing—if for no other reason than out of habit?

"Well, I'm thinking of writing one last piece called 'Doing Nothing.' It's not easy to do nothing. You have to spend an hour or two dictating letters. You have to read the newspapers and answer the telephone. It's almost as hard as writing, doing nothing. Only certain gifted individuals know how to do nothing. Women can't," he said, his eyes twinkling.

Jacquetta Hawkes listened, smiling.

"It's an art I'm trying to perfect," said Priestley, unconvincingly.

[JANUARY 2, 1978]

HERMAN WOUK

Washington, D.C.

Relaxing in the second-floor workroom of his comfortable house in the Georgetown district of Washington, D.C., Herman Wouk talks about the long literary journey that has culminated in *War and Remembrance*.

He regards *War and Remembrance* as his most important and mature work, for it combines his own moral and religious feelings with the mighty events of the Second World War—the Holocaust and the battles—that challenged civilized men and governments.

To the right of his desk and running around into the next room are a thousand volumes of war books—his research and sources. In front of his desk is a wall of books on Judaica—his ethical values, which he once described in *This Is My God*. Eventually the war books will be removed, but the religious books will remain as frontlets between his eyes.

"Writing this book was the most fun I've ever had in my life," he says, "but at the same time I feared that I wouldn't live to complete it." The genesis of this book goes back at least sixteen years. "I was fortunate enough to have a theme so big that either you say to yourself, 'Quit, boy,' or you say, 'Go on.' I couldn't help going on."

He opens up his work journal. The entry for May 17, 1962, handwritten in English and Hebrew, reads: "I may as well start my task. . . . I am entering on a work that can hardly take me less than three years." And then he turns to the final entry, dated June 4, 1978: "But I can say that, with God's help, I did it. That was the assigned task."

Wouk has been his own taskmaster ever since he graduated from Columbia University in 1934 and went on to write weekly radio scripts for Fred Allen, the comedian's comedian. "Allen was the best of the writers on his staff," Wouk says. Several of Wouk's own novels—*Aurora Dawn,* his first, published in 1947, *Marjorie Morningstar,* 1955, and *Don't Stop the Carnival,* 1965— display Wouk's humorous streak.

But the telling event of his life was his wartime experiences, as a deck officer aboard a destroyer-minesweeper for three years in the Pacific theater. (One of his winning campaigns was a wartime romance with Betty Sarah Brown, whom he met when she was a navy personnel executive in San Pedro. They were married in 1945 and have two sons; *War and Remembrance* is dedicated to their firstborn son, Abe, who died accidentally at the age of five.) Wouk's novel *The Caine Mutiny,* received the Pulitzer Prize in 1952 and brought to life a character who became part of the American language—Captain Queeg.

"When I started writing *Caine Mutiny,*" Wouk recalls, "I thought I was writing *War and Remembrance.* My original idea was that the *Caine* characters would have families and branch out into a big war story, moving through the main theaters. But I didn't have a grasp of the history then, so I abandoned that scheme. I remember writing in my journal in 1950 that *The Caine Mutiny* was a realistic novel about war but not my major 'war' book.

"And so I wrote *The Winds of War,* an eight-hundred-and-eighty-five-page novel that came out in 1971, as a historical lead into *War and Remembrance*. It stands on its own as a quiet prologue to what I hope is a more profound book. *Winds of War* tells of the events in the world leading up to Pearl Harbor, while *War and Remembrance,* which includes many of the same main characters, opens a week after Pearl Harbor and is a story about America at war. Why did we go to war? What happened to the Jews? What happened during the great sea battles? What were the world's leaders saying and doing? These questions are part of *War and Remembrance.''*

To grapple with these themes, Wouk moved to Washington in 1964 so that he would be near the Library of Congress, the National Archives, and experts with firsthand experiences and memories. In addition, he visited some of the major places in the novel—Berlin, Stalingrad, Moscow, Yalta, Teheran, Auschwitz, Theresienstadt (the so-called Paradise Ghetto, run as a showplace concentration camp by the Nazis). One place he did not have to revisit, for his Leyte Gulf and Midway battle scenes, was the wide Pacific; he had earned four battle stars there and knew the territory.

But *War and Remembrance* is a historical romance about real and imaginary people. Paraphrasing and updating Joseph Conrad, the author says he has tried to "throw a rope around World War II." He turns to a volume next to his desk for the right definition of historical romance: "a prose narrative dealing with imaginary characters involved in events remote in time or place and usually heroic or adventurous." Then he hefts his big war novel. "That definition suits me fine," Wouk says.

[MARCH 23, 1978]

GORE VIDAL

When I called Gore Vidal's editor, Jason Epstein, he said that at the moment the author was having dinner at a restaurant in Amalfi but would probably return soon to his villa in Ravello. That seemed right. If you have written *Kalki,* a novel about apocalypse and the brave new world to come, living along the Amalfi coast in Italy seemed the only way to go.

"Gore is a compulsive worker," Epstein said. "He gets up very early, writes on legal pads until late in the morning, does his mail, and then gets back to work again. He goes through a number of drafts till he gets it right. I don't think he can type; at least I've never seen a typewriter in his house. But he turns over his draft to a typist, insists on giving me a clean copy, and revises his manuscript several times over.

"He started writing *Kalki* about a year and a half ago while living in Beverly Hills. Right now he's working on a historical novel, which is all I'm allowed to say. Maybe he'd be willing to tell you more about it."

A voice at the villa said, *"Pronto,"* and asked who was speaking. I replied, *"Il New York Time-es."* A cheerful Signor Vidal got on the line. We had not talked since the anti–Vietnam War days, when he had written his devastating play *An Evening with Richard Nixon,* which came to Broadway in 1972.

"I've been here for seven years," he said. "Ravello is below Naples. It was discovered by the Bloomsbury group—D. H. Lawrence, Lytton Strachey, and friends—and then forgotten. I find it a wonderful place to work. Yes, the first draft of *Kalki* was done in Los Angeles. Jason very tactfully said that it was not quite right. The second version was written here. I've done other books here, too, including *Burr* and my essays."

He explained that the Italians had changed their tax laws for a while, taking some 93 percent of his income for world rights. The New Yorker went into exile in Los Angeles, but the laws have since been made more reasonable. He pays his full taxes to Washington and "what they demand" to Rome, where he also maintains an apartment. "But where I live and work," he says, "is in my skull."

Vidal, whose range of subjects in sixteen novels, five plays, and six books of essays is wider than that of any other American writer, says that the theme of *Kalki* was never fully explained in the comments about his book. "Critics were too busy reviewing me instead of the book and saying that I was the female narrator."

Was he aware that one of his favorite targets, Nixon, shared the best seller list with him?

"It's all my fault," Vidal said, laughing across the Mediterranean. "I regard him as entirely my own invention. I created him in *The Best Man,* first with Frank Lovejoy on stage in 1960 and then with Cliff Robertson playing him in the movie four years later. And, later, in the Nixon play.

"I now insist that the best seller list run the Nixon memoirs on its fiction side. I'd even be willing to have *Kalki* listed as nonfiction to make room.

"The book that I am working on will be the last of my ventures into history. It takes place in the fifth century B.C. One man could have come across Zoroaster, Confucius, Socrates, and the Buddha. They all lived at about the same time. I now write the books that keep the author himself interested. The brain that doesn't feed itself eats itself."

[JUNE 7, 1978]

S E A N   O ' F A O L A I N

A N D

M A R Y   L A V I N

Dublin, Eire

James Joyce casts a long shadow here, over the "gentes and laity-men, fullstoppers and semicolonials, hybreds and lubberds"— including the young and veteran writers. The language of *Finnegans Wake* is still mother's milk that can be drunk on both sides of the rail in the pubs, pouring forth along with the stout and ale.

A chance came to enjoy a doubleheader: talks with Sean O'-Faolain and Mary Lavin, two of the most respected of the veteran writers who have stayed put. They are talking writers and writing talkers, and the conversation kept returning to the influence of Joyce and the state of letters in Ireland today.

First, O'Faolain:

"This is Joyce territory," he said, relaxing with a light whiskey in his modest attached house in Rosmeen Park, a short bus hop from Dublin center. He pointed toward the front window. "About a quarter mile from here is Martello Tower, where the great man lived.

"Joyce was the most ungregarious of men. Yeats, too. Yeats never had a conversation in his life; he had monologues. I knew Yeats as much as anyone can know a man who is up there. His personality kept changing, depending on the year. He finally did create a personality for himself: the grand seigneur. Gogarty said he was like one of the titled butlers—evicting imaginary tenants."

From memory the writer suddenly began to recite the opening line of *Ulysses:* "Stately, plump Buck Mulligan came from the stairhead, bearing a bowl of lather on which a mirror and a razor lay crossed. . . ." He added, "Mulligan was Oliver Gogarty, and I knew him, too."

O'Faolain's *Selected Stories* have appeared in various American magazines, and his travel writings from Italy are classics. He prefers writing to talking.

"All Irish writers are Irish talkers," he said. "A babbling brook, they are. I used to see them in the Irish Academy of Letters. But I thought that once Yeats died, the academy had no function. Sean O'Casey turned his back on it, too.

"Irish literature in my younger years had a big job to accomplish: to cut out the politics. Yeats was of the age of poetry in Ireland, but he became self-exiled to himself. Joyce was from another tradition; he made his own literary revival. Yeats was the least Irish of the poets. He wanted a poetic theater in Dublin, but he kept breaking in with realism.

"I'm more of a prose man. I did one play, a comedy, *She Had to Do Something,* and had the honor of being booed. The realism took over, but I wasn't a realist, I was too dreamy. Some of us tried to be Zola, but we all came out of Turgenev—a mixture of realism and romanticism.

O'Faolain said that realism is a dead end for the modern Irish writer.

"Nobody here is doing political novels; you don't get the feel of the present in the stories. Yeats once said about the new writers, when I was young, 'They don't play with their material.' I have played, but I'm not a natural writer."

His wife, Eileen, author of *Irish Sagas and Folk Tales,* entered the room, with refills. "The folksy Irish story is gone, too," she said.

"My ambition all along has been to write a novel," O'-

Faolain, the short-story writer, said. "I've written three and destroyed three. So now's the time for me to write one. I'm officially retired. Which means that I'm secretly writing."

Next, Mary Lavin:

"I revere Sean O'Faolain as a writer," she said. Lavin (who is Mrs. Michael Scott) had seen O'Faolain the night before in the residence of United States Ambassador William V. Shannon, journalist-turned-diplomat. "Sean O'Faolain knows more about the short story than anyone living. Me, I'm a compulsive storyteller and story talker. Dublin in this respect helps."

She was at home in her mews house behind Fitzwilliam Place in Dublin town, surrounded by manuscripts and memories.

"Every time I step out the door, something sidesplitting happens. It's quite different in the States. I was born in Walpole, Massachusetts, but I've lived in Ireland since my early teens. I never stop foisting off my adventures to my unfortunate listeners. But what they get is only the waste product of my written stories.

"I started writing for fun when I did my master's at University College here, but it was never fun after that. I got hooked on writing. The short story is an addiction. You can spend more time on a short story than on a novel. I work all the time. It's a little easier now that I'm older and my daughters are grown. Sometimes I write in bed in the morning and stay there all day until it's time to peel the potatoes for dinner.

"You see, I have very long hair and can't get into the streets. I also get terribly involved with people I meet, so I have to keep secretive. I write in longhand and have lots of typewriters around for moral support, but I don't use them. I give my manuscripts out to a typist and correct the typescript.

"I've won a lot of prizes and scholarships, but I make nearly nothing from my writing. I am both vague and with my feet on the ground. But somehow I've put out a body of work. I've been mentioned for doctorates, but I struggled so long to be Mary Lavin, novelist, that I would not want to be Dr. Lavin and have people think I can take out their appendixes. I was once president of the Irish Academy of Letters."

Lavin's work occasionally appears in *The New Yorker. A Memory* is a recent short-story collection.

"I don't care if there's a new style of writing today," she went on. "I started reading the French and Russians and the Americans: George Sand, Racine, Sarah Orne Jewett, Edith Wharton's short stories—not her novels—and Henry James. I came to the Irish writers last."

What is the central Lavin theme?

"Only one: the greatness of man's time on this earth. That has preoccupied me, and from it other things stem. What I say may have a religious undertone. I'm a born critic, and I've never stopped questioning the Catholic Church's rules. Yet no other religion would make me ponder the things that are associated with Catholicism, such as celibacy and divorce.

"Now that I'm old, I really love the church. It can destroy people but if you survive it and assert yourself, you come out with a stronger character, like the church itself. I emerged with a stronger belief in the right of man to a private conscience."

That brought the talk back to the great writers of the Irish renaissance in this century, from Yeats to Synge, Gregory, O'-Casey, O'Connor, not forgetting Joyce.

"We carry a heavy tradition of greatness," Lavin said. "Most of the present novelists have carved out their own little places. I don't think Irish writers today are affected by Joyce—more's the pity."

[OCTOBER 10, 1978]

GÜNTER GRASS

Günter Grass's novel *The Flounder* is not about fish but about women, men, and the state of the world. Because women, men, and the state of the world are all controversial, suddenly his book has stirred up strong feelings, especially in the feminist community.

"Most women who read the book all the way through like it," Grass said. "Those in the women's liberation movement who say there is no difference between men and women don't like it. I like the difference. I hate those who don't like the difference between men and women."

"*Vive la différence*," Helen Wolff, his publisher, added.

Grass, who with Heinrich Böll, the Nobel laureate, symbolizes the free literary and political commitment of the postwar generation of writers in West Germany, was sitting in Mrs. Wolff's office, talking about his novel.

Most critics have found that the theme of *The Flounder* defies easy summary. In the book the narrator tells his wife throughout her nine months of pregnancy of his many lives as a husband or lover of eleven female cooks.

Although the author sometimes explains that the book is about the importance of nutrition through the ages, some feminists have noted it was really about the war between the sexes—with the narrator leaning toward cooking and childbearing as the proper, if not only, role for women in the world.

Below Grass's thick mustache was a rainbow of color: blue shirt, green trousers, red socks, and tan sport shoes. It seemed like the proper attire for the novelist, who is also a graphic artist, poet, and political activist.

It was the combination of his writings—*The Tin Drum, Dog Years* and other books—and activities on behalf of the Social Democrats that put him on the cover of *Time* magazine a few years ago as the novelist who could speak to the new generation of Germans and yet would not allow the Nazi past of its fathers to be forgotten.

"The Flounder is about women and food, but it is also about women and war," Grass said, "including what women have done against war—unfortunately, mostly silence."

"Remember *Lysistrata,"* Mrs. Wolff reminded him.

"Things of a literary nature are less important," he replied.

Grass defended his book against charges of antifeminism by pointing out that there were nine chapters—deliberately so, to pay homage to the nine months of pregnancy. Yet he conceded he had satirized some female radicals in the novel: "I am critical of the small group of women who try to speak for all. I have invented the word *womenal* for those militant women who serve as hanging judges of men. They react like men instead of retaining their femininity."

Underlying his novel is the fairy tale "The Fisherman and His Wife" by the brothers Grimm. The author's talking fish and characters move through the centuries together, from the Stone Age to the present. The fisherman and the flounder are immortal, and so, too, are the women who bear different names but strike some readers as female chauvinists.

"My novel isn't just a little snack," Grass said. "There is too much drugstore literature today, which people read on the run. Too many books that are junk food. I like to think of *The Flounder* as a big, hearty dinner, which readers can savor."

Grass said he was lucky to have made contact with younger generations in his novels: "The youngsters in Germany read *The Flounder,* and that has turned them back to *Tin Drum,* I'm glad to say. Our young generations see the need for a book like *The Flounder* because it gives more than reality. It is an invitation to the reader to use my and his own fantasy. And we need a sense of fantasy in today's world."

Grass participates in today's world a little less these days than when he campaigned for the election of his friend former Chancellor Willy Brandt a decade ago, writing pamphlets and giving more than a hundred speeches in his behalf.

"Even though I am not as politically active now as in the 1960s," Grass said, "I am still devoted to the causes of freedom. Heinrich Böll, Carola Stern, and I edit a quarterly magazine called *L-76*—the *L* stands for literature, the *76* stands for the year we started it. We use a lot of authors from East Europe and from the two Germanys.

"The magazine is a platform for the non-Communist opposition in Europe. I don't mean just the right-wingers—like Solzhenitsyn, who has given those strange antifreedom speeches since he went to live in the United States—but writers who are rarely suppressed. It is published in Cologne, where Böll lives, by a trade union publishing house, Europea Verlag. We try to include both cultural and political articles in it that could not be printed elsewhere. Literature is the one connection we have between East and West Germany."

Grass, who lives in Berlin and also in the Schleswig-Holstein area of northern Germany, has been to New York ten times. He said that he loved the "concentration, the destruction, the constant growing" and that someday would like to live in Manhattan.

[NOVEMBER 25, 1978]

BARBARA TUCHMAN

When she was fifteen, Barbara Wertheim was ill for three months and had to remain at home. Her French governess, Mlle. Thouvenel, read Racine and Corneille aloud to her between drills in the conjugation of verbs. Thanks in part to those long-ago lessons, hundreds of thousands of Americans are reading Barbara W. Tuchman's adventure in history, *A Distant Mirror: The Calamitous 14th Century,* a book requiring intensive research in French documents.

Those who have admired Tuchman's histories—*The Guns of August, The Proud Tower, Stilwell and the American Experience in China*—are aware that in addition to going to books and documents, she visits the scenes of her stories. Eventually she synthesizes her facts into splendid prose.

For *The Guns of August,* for example, she visited some of the World War I battlefields. How did she achieve that same feeling of presence about events that occurred six centuries ago?

"I made two trips to the places that are central to the narrative," Tuchman said. "I followed the routes of the main figure in the book, Enguerrand de Coucy, who was the most skilled of all the knights of France. I drove all around Picardy and Nor-

mandy and other areas where he lived and fought. I copied in-
scriptions off stone monuments. I saw a monastery where he
once stopped.

"To understand the Swiss campaign in the book, I decided to
take the route across the Alps that Coucy took. But it was
blocked by snow. So I drove as far as I could on the Swiss side,
took the tunnel through, then drove back from the Italian side.
In our mechanical age, somehow we can't cope as well as they
did with horses.

"Then, two years later, I decided to follow the route of the
Crusaders. With a friend of mine, Natasha Deakin, who speaks
the Slavic languages, I went down the Danube, visited Sofia and
examined documents at the Institute of Balkan Studies, and continued on from there to Istanbul and to Brusa, where Coucy
died. I think I covered most of the important places in my narrative."

Tuchman's seven-year research and writing project was
sparked by a tantalizing question: What was the effect on society
of the most lethal disaster of recorded history, the Black Death,
and what happened in the next half century of wars, schisms in
the church, Crusades, and other misfortunes?

Behind that question, the author felt, was a message for our
time: the possibilities for modern disaster and war in this age of
"collapsing assumptions." And so she assigned herself the difficult task of discovering and rediscovering the past—in documents, chronicles, and on the scene.

Tuchman, who lives with her physician husband in New
York, first began reporting in 1937 as a correspondent for the
Nation, during the Spanish Civil War. She served as an editor at
the Office of War Information during World War II. Her writings have since spanned military and diplomatic history in this
century, ranging from Israel to China.

During the long journey of *A Distant Mirror,* her editor, Robert Gottlieb, offered some editorial suggestions but mainly provided encouragement. At one point he told her that she was

showing too much concern with money, but she said that it was as central to the life of the fourteenth century as it is to the twentieth. A special "Note on Money" appears in the book.

I asked Tuchman what her next subject—or century—would be.

"I'm trying not to think." She laughed. "I told Bob Gottlieb that the next time I'd cover some historical episode that only lasted two weeks—and whose sources were all in English."

[NOVEMBER 25, 1978]

MARY RENAULT

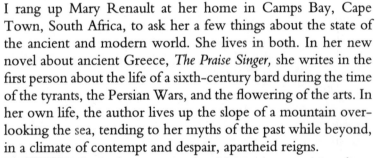

I rang up Mary Renault at her home in Camps Bay, Cape Town, South Africa, to ask her a few things about the state of the ancient and modern world. She lives in both. In her new novel about ancient Greece, *The Praise Singer,* she writes in the first person about the life of a sixth-century bard during the time of the tyrants, the Persian Wars, and the flowering of the arts. In her own life, the author lives up the slope of a mountain overlooking the sea, tending to her myths of the past while beyond, in a climate of contempt and despair, apartheid reigns.

I wondered why her name and writings—in contrast to those of fellow South Africans Alan Paton, Nadine Gordimer, and Donald Woods—were not associated with the cause of racial justice.

"I have never had the urge to write about apartheid. If you were born here and are a part of the generations that have lived with it for a long time, it is natural. But I have never had that experience, I have never profited from apartheid, and I have never been segregated. I write what is normal for me."

What about the world outside her door?

"I have been involved in political stuff, which is actually a cottage industry among the English. I have protested against apartheid and signed petitions. But I don't pass myself off as a heroine. You don't get locked up for writing protests." Renault has been a president of the South African chapter of PEN, which is dedicated to the writing freedoms.

She said that she chose Cape Town thirty years ago in the great wave of immigration following World War II. Everyone at that time felt claustrophic on the tight little war-devastated island. After hard years as a wartime nurse she decided to settle permanently in a sterling country. It seemed the right place for a historical novelist; Cape Town was an early settlement. She has never returned to England or visited the United States.

"Mary Renault is a pseudonym. My real name is Mary Challans. My father was a physician. I studied at Oxford, intending to teach, but decided to become a writer instead. I turned to nursing to help out during the war. That background has helped me in my novels because I learned about human existence and how people react to illness and crises."

Why did she turn to Greece in such novels as *The Last of the Wine, The King Must Die, The Bull from the Sea, The Persian Boy* and *The Praise Singer?*

"Greece has always interested me. There was a large library at my high school in Bristol. I was riveted by Plato. I asked myself and still do in my books: What was life really like then? That's the whole point of writing. I visited Greece after the civil war there. I was inspired. It was the landscape I wanted for my books."

Why do her novels emphasize homosexuality and lesbianism?

"In writing about Alexander, I was careful not to judge him by twentieth-century standards. He was a revolutionary force, and he was a homosexual, there was no doubt about that. There are historical descriptions about 'youths of remarkable beauty' who remained with Alexander. Lesbianism was not as well documented, but it was there, too, in the poetry of Sappho."

Renault, who is unmarried, says she would have liked to know what the ancient Greeks thought about the authenticity of her work. Modern Greeks accept her books as fact. She believes that when she writes about the past, she can shed light on the present; her next novel will probably again be set in ancient Greece and again be written from modern South Africa.

[JANUARY 21, 1979]

JOHN CHEEVER

In the last of the sixty-one stories in *The Stories of John Cheever,* the narrator says: "My real work these days is to write an edition of *The New York Times* that will bring gladness to the hearts of men. How better could I occupy myself? The *Times* is a critical if rusty link in my ties to reality, but in these last years its tidings have been monotonous. The prophets of doom are out of work."

The tidings are that Cheever's stories have brought gladness to the hearts and minds of readers without necessarily changing the headlines that drive us all mad. A little of the world and what a writer can—or cannot—do about it crept into our conversation the other morning.

"I don't put politics into my stories. I don't possess an estimable political sense. Of course I vote carefully. As a writer I think there is a difference between politics and literature. It seems to me that literature is a broader concern.

"I was not interested in prison reform when I wrote *Falconer;* all I wanted to stress was the mysterious quality of one group of people imprisoning another group. Prison reform, anyway, is too complex and begins with the judiciary.

"In my stories, I also avoid anything that's primarily historical, such as wars and depressions. In *The Wapshot Chronicle,* which spanned forty years, I managed to skip two wars."

Didn't his own involvement in war get into his stories?

"I served with a line rifle company, Twenty-second Infantry, Fourth Division, mostly in the South, then the Pacific, but never in combat. I did write some army stories; they appeared in my first collection, *The Way Some People Live.* But they were embarrassingly immature, and I have never gone back to wartime themes. None of those stories appears in this book."

The stories in this book, he notes in a preface, "seem at times to be stories of a long-lost world when the city of New York was still filled with a river life, when you heard the Benny Goodman Quartets from a radio in the corner stationery store, and when almost everybody wore a hat."

We talked about the fact that Cheever—like F. Scott Fitzgerald during the turbulent 1930s—has been criticized for not having characters engagé. Fitzgerald's high-hatted lovers did not bounce off the page one headlines; nor do Cheever's.

"I seldom go looking for a story. I don't research them. Journalism and literature are very different. I would rather be thought of as writing about men and women. The soul of man doesn't need a locale. I'm fond of the degree of free will within an environment."

How do Cheever stories originate?

"I often try to put my experience in the form of a story that seems to illuminate. If people find it familiar, then there is illumination. Light is an image that I am very fond of. I literally try to put some of my characters in a strong light. Another image that I use a great deal is water. I come from a seafaring family. I went fishing yesterday out of New Rochelle, past the Narrows. You can catch a lot of fish out there, but not yesterday."

Both you and John Updike are longtime *New Yorker* writers. What is the difference between John Cheever and John Updike?

"Well, I'm twenty years older than John. Updike writes far more explicitly about sex, for one thing. Explicit sexual scenes don't particularly interest me. Everybody knows what's going on. I can't think, in the whole history of literature, of an explicit sex scene that was memorable, can you?"

What were the big Cheever themes?

"Love and death," he said, softly.

[JANUARY 28, 1979]

CHRISTOPHER ISHERWOOD

Santa Monica, California

At an age (seventy-five) when even writers relax, Christopher Isherwood has more works by and about him being published than in any previous season. That seemed a good enough excuse to call him up to get the directions from Los Angeles to his house in Santa Monica. His final caution was so California: "Turn left at the second palm tree."

"Once," he told me, "I received even more memorable directions from an Indian woman near a reservation. She told me, 'Go north of the Little Hill and beware of the Great Sands.' And of course she was being very specific, because one could sink into those Great Sands."

There is no name on the mailbox of the house in which Isherwood has lived for the last twenty years, longer than in any one place in his life. He walked around the modest and comfortable cantilevered house that overlooks a valley of small homes, trees, and telephone lines. From the porch, as well as from a reflecting mirror in the dining room, you could see a patch of water and a headland a mile or so away defying the Pacific Ocean.

The author-playwright-scenarist appeared relaxed and, like

"Herr Issyvoo" in his *Berlin Stories* or his other autobiographical characters, the still-youthful subject of one of his books. His hair was unfashionably close-cropped and his clothing unconventional—jeans, polo shirt, moccasins, Lee denim jacket—as if he felt no need to impress anyone with anything but what he wrote. The only decoration he wore was a brass button in his lapel that read: "Stunts Unlimited."

"A friend of mine who is a stunt man in pictures gave it to me," he said, smiling. The button looked like some sort of tribal Croix de Cinéma peculiar to Hollywood, which has long captivated the dreams and skills of Isherwood.

Pouring drinks from a jug of California wine, he mentioned some of the recent and forthcoming writings by and about him:

All the Conspirators, his first novel, written in 1926, has just been reissued by New Directions in a paperback edition. It is a portrait of decaying middle-class English life after the world war.

Avon Books is bringing out his novels and memoirs in paperback editions, most recently, *A Meeting by the River,* and *A Single Man,* and already published, *Christopher and His Kind, Down There on a Visit, Memorial: Portrait of a Family, Prater Violet,* and *World in the Evening.*

Two biographies: *Christopher Isherwood: A Critical Biography,* by Brian Finney, Oxford University Press, and *Isherwood: A Biography,* by Jonathan Fryer, Doubleday.

A play, *A Meeting by the River,* based on his novel and written with his friend and coresident here, Don Bachardy, opened and closed quickly in March at the Palace Theater in New York. He explained that it worked better in a small theater, such as the Mark Taper Forum in Los Angeles or on campus in Knoxville, Tennessee, and he expects it to be done again for college and high school audiences.

My Guru and His Disciple will be published by Farrar, Straus & Giroux. He spoke about the book, meaning that he spoke about himself:

"I first met Swami Prabhavananda, a Hindu monk, in 1939,

soon after leaving England and settling in California. I last saw him in 1976, just before he died. I became one of his followers, aware of a Presence within him. He helped to bring out the sacred side of me." He paused, as if to cancel seriousness from the conversation, and then added, amused, "Next, I am doing the profane side of my life—the show biz stuff, the screenwriting, all sorts of things from the time I arrived here."

He had come to the United States to fulfill a long-held desire—"As a youth, I had literally dreamed of palm trees"—after a notable career writing in England and Europe. In his workroom, he showed a visitor the bookshelves that add up to a history of modern English literature in the 1930s, written by his friends and himself. Behind his desk, one of the shelves, measuring eighty-five inches, was filled with nothing but books written by W. H. Auden, Stephen Spender, and, snugly between them, Christopher Isherwood.

I picked off the shelves a copy of *Prater Violet,* one of the finest novels ever written about filmmaking, and asked the author to find one particularly beautiful sentence about London that stuck in my mind so that it could be quoted exactly. Without missing a beat, Isherwood turned to it and read: "The little houses had shut their doors against all strangers and were still, waiting for dawn, bad news and the milk."

The library shelves also held books by the romantics—"I'm a great Byron freak"—and all the stories by Dickens and Chekhov. "I admire many of the American writers," he continued, mentioning, among others, Tennessee Williams and Gore Vidal. What about Hemingway? He laughed.

"I once told a mutual friend that I liked all the parts about Venice in *Across the River and into the Trees.* When this got back to him, Hemingway said, 'Tell Isherwood I like all the parts about Berlin in his books.' "

Isherwood asked for a lift back to Los Angeles, where he was to meet Bachardy, the artist he lives with who has done the drawings of him that appear on the Avon editions of his books.

While navigating for a frightened driver on the freeway, the author said that he still spent most of his working time writing and his free time speaking for the rights of homosexuals and other civil rights causes.

At an intersection, I acted confused behind the wheel about homebound directions; Sunset Boulevard seemed to be in the wrong place. With a twinkle behind his glasses, Isherwood said: "If you have world enough and time, you can stay on Sunset Boulevard forever."

Then he buttoned up his leather jacket, shook hands, and jogged off to his destination, a small figure whose life and characters have made a large mark on a generation of writers.

[AUGUST 2, 1979]

COLLEEN McCULLOUGH

When last I spoke to Colleen McCullough—several millions of dollars ago—she was still talking about the possibility of going to nursing school in England. The other day, the statuesque auburn-haired author of *The Thorn Birds* said that she had changed her plans for now, if not for the rest of her life.

"I don't believe a patient would appreciate the idea of having a millionaire nurse carrying the bedpan," she said.

The people with the adding machines estimate that McCullough may make $5 million including all sorts of rights, for this, her second novel. It began with a $5,000 advance from the hardcover publisher and, as word of its story spread, was acquired for a phenomenal $1.9 million for paperback.

Her first novel, *Tim,* was well received critically, but it did not get her on the cover of the newsweeklies. "It was on a completely different subject," she said. "About the relationship between a hard-bitten spinster and a retarded youngster." It is being reprinted with a cover that makes it loud and clear that the author wrote *The Thorn Birds*.

If there are any readers in the English-speaking world who do not know the general outlines of the book by now, the blame cannot be placed on McCullough, who has hit the road for half a year. Australia; Great Britain; Germany, at the Frankfurt Book Fair.

The Thorn Birds is a 530-page saga of a singular family, the Clearys, which begins in the early 1900s in Australia and then moves around the world, almost up to the present. The romance includes a charming priest, which helps to account for the book's success.

Robert D. Hale, general manager of Hathaway House, a bookshop in Wellesley, Massachusetts, informed the publisher that the character of the priest was "the most fascinating fictional male since Rhett Butler." Next thing, the quotation was misquoted into a selling line: "An Australian *Gone with the Wind.*"

"I did not make the comparison," McCullough remarked.

She did not have to; everyone else did.

"When I visited Australia two years ago, I wasn't the, quote, famous novelist and could spend more time with my mother and friends. This time, for eight weeks there and in New Zealand, too, I was on the run as a celebrity: Local girl makes good. The average Australian reader seemed to enjoy the book. It sold forty-three thousand hard-cover copies in Australia, which is unusual because the country's population is smaller than that of metropolitan New York."

The author was born in Wellington, New South Wales, scene of part of her story. After working as a teacher in the Australian outback and as a librarian and journalist, she came to the United States. She was "a master technician, a teacher, and also the chief maker of pots of tea" while serving for ten years as a neurophysiologist at Yale University's School of Medicine.

And she was, at the same time, writing. Although the first two drafts of *The Thorn Birds* were written in some three months, the characters and places were nursed for years. Now she has several other novels in mind, including a war novel and a contemporary novel. She is fascinated by the role of the Australian and British forces and the role they played from North Africa onward in the Second World War.

"I haven't had time to start working on the next book," Mc-Cullough says, "and luckily I don't have to yet."

She still hasn't read *Gone with the Wind*.

[AUGUST 10, 1979]

NADINE GORDIMER

Nadine Gordimer won the 1991 Nobel Prize in literature. Hers had been a long journey—from censorship in South Africa to Stockholm. For nearly twenty years before her deserved award, we had spoken periodically about her books and about the difficult circumstances encountered by authors in her country. Because Gordimer's themes often touched on race relations, she often found her works questioned. In time her fiction and essays—and those of other authors and artists in different fields—exposed apartheid and helped to bring the system down.

What a difference between the time she received the prize and when I interviewed Gordimer after her novel *Burger's Daughter* was banned in 1979. Eventually it was allowed back on the bookshelves—"thanks to international pressure," she told me. Gordimer underscored the fact that protest can embarrass and move the authorities to take the printed word out of prison.

Here is how our talk went while *Burger's Daughter* was still in prison:

"I'm angry and sad," Gordimer said. "If you compare the novel I wrote to the version mentioned by the censors, you would not believe that they were describing the same book. My books have been banned before, and the public hears about it, but I am particularly saddened for the beginning writers here who are less known. Their banned books do not receive much attention, and they can be discouraged from undertaking strong themes."

Gordimer's novel was first published by Jonathan Cape in London. The British edition was then shipped to South Africa. After three weeks, it was ordered removed from the bookshelves by the Directorate of Publications of the Republic of South Africa. The case is being appealed, but if a South African wants to read *Burger's Daughter,* he will have to do so in another country.

"All it takes is violation of one clause under the Publications Act for a book to be declared 'undesirable,' " Gordimer said. "This novel is banned under five of the six clauses. I can tell you, it's incredible."

Before we talked, she had mailed me a copy of the banning order. The document, signed by E. G. Malan, director of publications, referred to Gordimer as "the authoress" (a condescending form of address if there ever was one) and declared that "the committee"—unnamed—found her treatment of the theme "undesirable." And what is her theme? "Black consciousness and organizing for the coming black revolution. . . . The authoress uses Rosa's story as a pad from which to launch a full-scale attack on the Republic of South Africa. The whites are the baddies, the blacks the goodies."

The banning order also claims that the novel is "indecent" and harmful to "public morals," citing a few street words that undoubtedly are known to seven-year-olds, baddies or goodies. Page after page is cited to prove that "the book is prejudicial to the safety of the state" and that "characters in her book are used to propagate Communism."

But what can you expect from an authoress?

[AUGUST 19, 1979]

TOM WOLFE

Tom Wolfe used to be a newspaperman himself, so the right place to talk to him about *The Right Stuff* seemed to be the Artists and Writers restaurant-bar on West Fortieth Street, once the *Herald Tribune* hangout, equidistant between Times Square and the Garment Center. The fashion plate of American letters—not only does he wear a vest, but it's double-breasted—honed his sentences at the *Trib* in the early 1960s, but the official identification from his publisher omits any mention of his background as an ink-stained wretch.

To describe the early astronauts and what made them, as well as their instruments, tick, Wolfe adopted a style different from that of his earlier books. "I relaxed," he explained. "I wanted the book to have the voice of a Chuck Yeager rather than a Ken Kesey. I presented the story in a straightforward way. I very seldom use the first person anymore. That can work only if you are a participant. I decided to do it the hard way—as a group portrait—because there is no central character. The biggest challenge was organization and structure, which is why writing the book stretched out over six years."

When we talked about Norman Mailer's book about the astronauts, *Of a Fire on the Moon,* in which Mailer called himself Aquarius, Wolfe said, "I enjoyed his *Armies of the Night* because he was a part of the story, a celebrity arrested in the march on the Pentagon, but as Aquarius he put himself between the reader and the astronauts."

Inevitably we got around to discussing the New Journalism, a term Wolfe wishes had not been invented. "When I explained it, it always came out as being half fact, half fiction, subjective writing, instead of what it really is: very thorough reporting using every effective device known to prose, including what is usually associated with the novel."

What about all that fancy punctuation that once characterized Wolfe's style?

"I came along and saw all those punctuation marks lying dormant and decided to use them—exclamation points, dots, dashes, multiple parentheses, and multiple colons. They were quite tolerant about them at the *Herald Tribune.*" Above his white waistcoat and polka-dot tie, Wolfe smiled a semicolon half-smile.

[SEPTEMBER 23, 1979]

HANS JOACHIM
SCHAEDLICH

East Berlin

I walked through the maze of Checkpoint Charlie. On Unter den Linden I found a taxi that stood some distance away from the omnipresent carbine-slug *Polizei*. Without revealing the exact address, I asked the driver to take me to a certain street on the outskirts of East Berlin, German Democratic Republic. I wondered if he recognized the Yiddish accent in my German. After a long ride the driver dropped me off on a street corner in Köpenick, a pleasant residential district of two-story row houses. I waited until the taxi was out of sight before finding the right house at the end of the street. I acted as if I didn't see the police car that tailed us all the way.

Hans Joachim Schaedlich was not hiding. He stood in the doorway and welcomed me. I was afraid for him, but it was too late for him to be afraid for himself.

Schaedlich had been declared "an enemy of the state." I wanted to see what the face of an enemy of a police state looked like. It looked like any other face. Schaedlich was a man in his early forties, staring resignedly behind dark horn-rimmed glasses, with a half-smile around his mouth, a man you would pass on the street. We spoke in four languages: English, German, French, and dictionary. Whenever an exact word was found, he looked pleased. As a man who had made his living as a translator, precision counted with him. His wife, a well-turned-out woman in her early thirties, served tea, as if nothing had happened to them.

What had happened was that he had written a book, *Versuchte Nähe*, fictionalized vignettes and parables that revealed the drab, alienated quality of life in the German Democratic Republic. It had been turned down by the authorities who control publishing in one way or another—through the Ministry of Culture, or the writers' union, or the publishing houses themselves, which sometimes conveniently run out of paper. Then it was published by Rowohlt of Hamburg, in West Germany, breaching the Book Curtain.

Before visiting him that autumn, not wishing to exacerbate his troubles, I checked with some of his fellow writers in the West, including Günter Grass. They encouraged me to see him; so did he, when I phoned him from Frankfurt. In his living room he described how the authorities had pressured him and his family. He lost his steady job as a translator. His wife, who had been working on a doctorate at the university in East Berlin, had her stipend taken away. Then catch-22: Because she no longer had to be away from home while studying, their child was not allowed to continue in nursery school.

If Schaedlich denounced his own book, the authorities told him, the benefits would be restored. He declined to do so. With no possibility of making a living, he applied for a visa to move to the West. It was denied. As we talked freely, I asked if it would harm him if I went around to the Ministry of Culture and simply made an inquiry about his case. Schaedlich and his wife laughed. How could they be harmed more than they already had been? They said that when he was awarded a prize for his book in Austria, the attention there and moral support of prominent writers in West Germany had helped keep his name—indeed, his personhood—alive.

Before returning to West Berlin, I went around to the Ministry of Culture. After a half hour an assistant came down from an office on a high floor and said that the minister was too busy to see me. As we chatted in the waiting room, the assistant, an affable young man, said that he was a poet. With a straight face I said that I would like to read his poems some time. Then I wrote out some questions in longhand for him to deliver to the minister. The questions, without special pleading, were fairly simple ones: What were the criteria for publishing a book in East Germany? What were the official objections to Schaedlich's book? What could make a writer an enemy of the state?

The young poet said that perhaps the cultural minister would see me tomorrow. The next morning I went through Checkpoint Charlie again, rather more openly this time. The assistant looked a little embarrassed; now the cultural minister was out of the city. However, he assured me that my questions had been delivered to the minister himself, but he hinted that the questions were "difficult." A few weeks later I wrote to the minister again, repeating my questions. I never received a reply.

But a few months after my story about him appeared, Hans Joachim Schaedlich and his family were permitted to leave East Berlin. The former enemy of the state now lives in Hamburg.

[DECEMBER 16, 1979]

JORGE LUIS BORGES

In Manhattan for one day before going to Indiana University for a series of *charlas* ("chats"), Jorge Luis Borges, the internationally revered Argentinian poet and storyteller, sat in a restaurant only two blocks from where *Evita,* the musical about the Argentinian dictator Perón's mistress and wife, was playing.

I asked him (guessing his reply but wanting to hear his own inimitable ironic-humorous response) if he planned to attend it.

"Why should I? We never mention her in Argentina today. At least, I hope people don't. Evita was one of the ladies in the brothel, you know."

Borges knows about the Perón dictatorship from personal experience. "Perón did not like my family because we despised his regime. He arrested my mother. I was removed from my post in 1965 as director of the National Library and appointed an inspector of fish and fowl—a chicken inspector," he said, only half amused.

Borges smiled sweetly, innocently. An ever-present smile composes the features of the silver-haired poet's face, an inner serenity that perhaps comes from the fact that he has been blind for a quarter of a century—and an inner vision that has enabled him to dictate some of his finest writings during these years.

Most of his works—including *The Book of Imaginary Beings* and *The Aleph and Other Stories*—have been translated by Norman Thomas di Giovanni. His own English is excellent and has enabled him to lecture at universities from Japan to America.

Borges said, "I'm still writing poetry. What else can I do? I'm eighty and blind. But poetry has a way of its own that overtakes you. If you are blind, you can remember things better. You must. My mind is full of quotations. I can remember works that I care about. Some of my poems are haiku. They are difficult in Spanish because of the longer words than in Japanese or English. And I can also dream.

"New York is a good place to dream," Borges said. "I love Buenos Aires, where I live, and London and Paris, but New York is like ancient Rome, the capital of the world. I also like Texas, which has a feeling of Argentina about it. The cowboys are like gauchos, but the Indians in your country and mine are even better. A gaucho can be cruel, but an Indian rides bareback, without a whip, because there is a friendly relationship between horse and rider."

He said that his writings had never been banned in Argentina by the dictatorship "because I wasn't important enough." During World War II he spoke out against the Axis and anti-Semitism. Today he regards himself as primarily a poet who is apolitical. He regrets that he personally cannot correct injustices. "I am a warlike pacifist," he said. "I blame wars on weapons, not people." He is an admirer of Israel and has received the Jerusalem Prize there. "All my life" he once told a colleague, "I've been trying to be a Jew, and perhaps, with my Spanish and Portuguese ancestry, I come from that heritage."

I asked Borges why he had never received the Nobel Prize.

"I'll never get it," Borges said amiably, "because I think someone there has read my books—and that's very dangerous."

[MARCH 20, 1980]

SAUL BELLOW

Chicago

Saul Bellow laughed and said, "Do you think you can make anything out of this *tsimis?*"

I had my doubts, because we were taking what diplomats call a *tour d'horizon* and ballplayers call touching all bases. Talking about presidential politics, writers without the touch of the poet, Henry Kissinger as a Metternich manqué, New York and Chicago and Jerusalem, the *tummlers* in the world of letters.

A tough man to interview is Saul Bellow, who usually avoids ink-stained wretches. Your pencil can't keep ahead of his mind; even in conversation, his sentences are enlivened with a quote from Rousseau here, a reference to a Beethoven symphony there.

Feet up, we were sitting on the terrace of his apartment thirteen floors above Lake Michigan, somewhere between Evanston and Chicago. He wore a relaxed air and clothes to match, slightly elegant even when casual, a blue polo shirt with white collar, brown loafers and inflammatory red socks, a man of at least two tones. Bellow looked as youthful as when we had last talked in New York, one eye peering intently, the other skeptical or twinkling, wisdom showing more than age.

A storm was rising over the lake below us. The novelist's wife, Alexandra, a mathematician who teaches at Northwestern, asked us if we wanted a drink, perhaps some tea, but we decided to remain outside and watch the lowering sky. "She's a wonderful woman," Bellow said. "I'm used to looking at pieces of paper I've written and understanding them, but when I look at her mathematical papers, I'm puzzled."

Unlike Mr. Sammler of Manhattan, Bellow said he didn't get to New York very often these days. "It depresses me; there's such a sense of malignancy and despair." He sounded like Augie March: "I am an American, Chicago born—Chicago, that somber city—and go at things as I have taught myself, free style, and will make the record in my own way." At nine Bellow came to Chicago from Lachine, Quebec, his birthplace. He has lived here most of his life, keeping up his professorial affiliation—"my camouflage"—with the University of Chicago. He belongs to an arts club where he is served good lunches and to an athletic club where he plays racquetball, but somehow manages to stay out of the city's cultural reach.

"I started to write a book about Chicago like my book on Israel, *To Jerusalem and Back,* but I found it much harder to do. I knew the Chicago that was, but not the Chicago that is. The Chicago of the twenties and thirties was pretty much wiped out." He visited the jails and hospitals, spoke to labor union leaders, company heads, politicians. "But I got the polite shutout; they handed me an éclair, especially baked. Still, we don't have plastic politics here. The people of Chicago are very proud of their wickedness. This is good old vulgar politics, despite the pretensions. I came up against the mask during my research, so I decided to put the book aside. I was not accustomed to taking so much time away from fiction."

He is writing a novel, as he has been doing since his first, *Dangling Man,* appeared in 1944. Of course, the subject is not one to talk about. "But I don't lay a glove on New York this time," he said, smiling. His electric typewriter is set on a table in the living room, and he sits on a secretary's chair, with his back to Chicago and a view toward the lake. Around him are such magazines as *Encounter* and the *Middle East Review,* a stereo, and rows of bookshelves; he is, arguably, the most scholarly novelist-playwright writing now. One would have to go back to Thornton Wilder for comparable erudition.

"I try reading other people, and occasionally I come across a book that has something in it. But I don't see much that moves wonder in my soul. Only once in a while is there a glint of the real thing." A glint? "With a novelist, like a surgeon, you have to get a feeling that you've fallen into good hands—someone from whom you can accept the anesthetic with confidence."

As for his own writing, he said: "The business of the writer as witness is to pass all the things he sees and knows through his own soul." He quoted from Rousseau's *Confessions: "Je sens mon coeur et je connais les hommes"*—meaning that he feels what is in his own heart and understands mankind. "Someone once asked Mandelstam whom he writes for, and he replied that he wouldn't dream of writing for anyone he knew, that he wrote for those he didn't know in expectation of making some discovery with them. If you write for people you know, you find yourself limited. God knows, we're limited enough without new limitations on ourselves."

The thunderstorm swept in over Lake Michigan; even Bellow the Rain King couldn't part these waters. As we went inside, he said reassuringly, "It's like the storm in Beethoven's Sixth Symphony. It only lasts twenty minutes."

[JULY 6, 1980]

EUGENIO MONTALE

Milan

Eugenio Montale, Italy's Nobel laureate in literature, lives in an apartment between the Duomo and La Scala in Milan. As a journalist and essayist for many years on the *Corriere della Sera,* he was a literary activist, going back to his years as an anti-Fascist writer and editor. Now he stands above the political turbulence in his country, a symbol of the continuity and individuality of the serious poet in the land of Dante who goes it alone, outlasting styles and governments.

A hard man to get to, in his writing and in person. When he received the Nobel Prize in 1975, few people in the United States had ever heard of him, and fewer still had read his poetry. James Laughlin had never met him but put out a few volumes of his poetry under the New Directions imprint that sold perhaps a thousand copies in a good year. The award was a recognition of steadfastness by author and publisher, underscoring the need for small houses unpressured by conglomerates.

Now the deadlines are behind him; the tone of disenchantment in his work is replaced by a kind of humorous resignation in his conversation. If his poetry is considered hermetic and distant, he is not, given the right moment and mood.

Montale summed up some of the high points of his life: born
in Genoa, studied to be a singer, went off to the First World War
as an infantry officer, returned to an Italy of disillusionment and
incipient fascism. In the 1920s he joined with the philosopher
Benedetto Croce in a famous "Intellectuals' Manifesto against
Fascism," then worked for one of the anti-Fascist journals, *Il
Baretti,* until it was suppressed by the Mussolini dictatorship.

Then in the quasi underground: For ten years he served as
curator of the Vieusseux Library in Florence. In 1938 he was
forced to give up this post because he refused to join the Fascist
party. Later he affiliated himself with such literary-political partisans as Elio Vittorini, author of *Conversation in Sicily,* and others
in the resistance movement centered on Florence. Nevertheless,
he was able to separate his poetry from his political instincts.

In one of his books, *Ossi di Seppia* ("Cuttlefish Bones"),
Montale reveals his style and attitude toward life: a seeker rather
than a declarer:

> Do not ask us for the formula apt to open up
> the world to you,
> but only for some crooked syllable, dry like
> a withered branch.
> Only this can we say to you today,
> what we are *not,* what we want *not.*

How do you define your own poetry?

"I'm not a romantic or a symbolist or a hermetic—all names
assigned to me by critics. I am past the stage of trying to put
myself in a category. Let the critics have the fun and the honor.
I myself can't decide what to call my poetry, and I don't want
to."

Why did you turn to poetry in the first place?

"My real hope was to become a great baritone. That was the
wish of my voice but not of my talent. [A moment of laughter.]
Then I found that I had a greater desire—to become a writer. So

eventually I combined the two. I wrote a lot of music criticism for the *Corriere*. Now I'm retired, but I still go to La Scala as often as I can. My favorite opera? *The Magic Flute*."

Which poets influenced your own writing?

"I don't know if the right word is *influenced*. But I certainly schooled myself in the poets and writers of the past—Cervantes, Manzoni, Baudelaire, Mallarmé, Henry James. And of course, I translated many writers—eight plays by Shakespeare, Herman Melville's *Billy Budd,* Nathaniel Hawthorne, William Faulkner, Ernest Hemingway, John Steinbeck, F. Scott Fitzgerald, Dorothy Parker. For a long time I earned my living by translating English and American writers."

What are you writing these days?

"*Poco poco*—very little. I've written a few short poems."

How long does it take to write a short poem?

"One month. I would describe my poems now as philosophical reflections."

How do you spend your time these days?

"I live alone in Milano, without family; my wife is dead. In the summer I rent a garden apartment in Forte dei Marmi, along the Ligurian coast. I have some good friends and neighbors there, like Henry Moore, the sculptor. Living alone, I'm like Robinson Crusoe. [Laughing.] By the way, *Robinson Crusoe* is one of my favorite books."

Living near the Duomo, do you consider yourself or your poetry religious?

"Some people and readers say yes; others no. I don't say."

How do you feel about yourself?

"I find life amusing. I'm just a ship that is berthed. For a long time I was a man lost at sea, but now I feel that I've been rescued. Why? Because I'm alive and still on earth."

How did the Nobel Prize change your life?

"I'm still the same man. I'm not a grand poet. I'm just a man of the streets."

[JULY 10, 1980]

SUSAN SONTAG

Susan Sontag said, "I'm not a Renaissance woman."

If the social critic and author of a new book of essays, *Under the Sign of Saturn,* says she is not capable of trying everything in the arts, followers of her work must take her word for it. But that still leaves a little room for what she is: literary critic, novelist, essayist-journalist, film scenarist and director, theater director, and (she said at home in New York) someone who would "love to direct an opera."

The essays, most of which first appeared in the *New York Review of Books,* include Sontag's observations on the work of Paul Goodman, Leni Riefenstahl, Antonin Artaud, Elias Canetti, Walter Benjamin, and Roland Barthes. None is a household name in the popular journals, but all provide Miss Sontag with a forum for her views on literature, philosophy, culture, politics, the arts, film, feminism, and fascism.

"What's a Renaissance woman?" Sontag wondered. "It's not a particularly useful phrase. I think there are many writers who have had my range of interests. It's quite common in Europe, but not in the United States, to have writers who are involved in many activities. Chekhov went to Sakhalin Island to investigate prison conditions there. There are many problems for a concerned modern writer without turning back to the Renaissance."

Is there a general theme underlying her work in all its forms? She replied, in one of her offhand conversational remarks that somehow, even at breakfast, come out as large statements: "Literature and society—what else is there?"

As an example of someone whom she admired and who had influenced her because of his large vision, Sontag named Paul Goodman. She said he had put himself at the service of literature, looking for its human possibilities, written honestly about his homosexuality, had been "a connoisseur of freedom" and had gifts that neither Sartre nor Cocteau had: "an intrepid feeling for what human life is about, a fastidiousness and breadth of moral passion."

She notes in *Under the Sign of Saturn* that in every apartment where she has lived, most of Goodman's books could be found on the shelves. In her two-story apartment in an 1850s brownstone not far from Union Square, the walls are lined with thousands of books—arranged by literary periods, by countries, by Romance languages. But there is no television set.

"I like reading," she said. "It's my television."

Sontag is generous in her judgments of writers who are reaching for something other than the marketplace.

"Norman Mailer is not a model," she said. Although at one point she was moved by his writing, she does not now appreciate his subjects, such as his book on Marilyn Monroe, *Of Women and Their Elegance.*

Sontag admires E. L. Doctorow and his *Loon Lake* because "he is one of the few contemporary writers who is playing for the real stakes. The fact that he is also a commercial success is a fluke. He's still different because he is trying to write books that are first-rate."

There are not many American writers in the "international

class," she said, although there are any number who "know how to make narratives." Among those who are playing for the real stakes, in her opinion, are Donald Barthelme, Elizabeth Hardwick, William Gass, and Harold Brodkey. "They are involved," she said, "in the enterprise of literature." On the international level, she mentioned Italo Calvino of Italy, Danilo Kis of Yugoslavia, George Konrad of Hungary, and Luisa Valenzuela of Argentina.

Sontag will soon be off to Italy to redirect Pirandello's *As You Desire Me* for the National Theater. It was a big hit last summer in several cities, and she is breaking in new actors in preparation for opening in Florence. She likes directing because "it's wonderful to work with people."

She is writing a novel and short stories, but avoiding what she is famous for: essays and criticism. "I've been to Poland and Japan recently without writing about either country, so I think my resistance is strong."

[OCTOBER 10, 1980]

WILLIAM GOLDING

There are two reasons to ring William Golding at his home in Bower Chalke, near Salisbury, England. First, his new novel, *Rites of Passage,* and second . . . well, because he is William Golding, of whom the late critic Stanley Edgar Hyman once said, in an appropriate and lovely metaphor, "He baits his hook for Leviathan."

Not many contemporary novelists who have gained popularity set their hooks for whales; many seem to angle only for minnows and suckers. But Golding has continued to explore the depths of men and mankind. Fishing in the treacherous waters of life, he has found more evil than good. The sea, in fact, has never been far from Golding. It figures in several of his novels and his own experiences.

"I spent five years in the Royal Navy during the war against the Nazis. What did I do? I survived. I worked my way down, starting out on cruisers in the North Atlantic as an ordinary seaman and ending up in command of a rocket ship on D Day. The war didn't last long enough for me to get a big promotion, like Admiral Nelson, who had the advantage of a longer war. All I ever rose to was *left-tenant.*

"What was my feeling about that war? Well, I suppose it was one of the few wars in history about which one can say that once it became inevitable, it was a just war. No, I don't go sailing about any more. Just the car ferry over the Channel or crossing the Mediterranean. But I suppose the sea has had an influence on my writing."

I asked him why he had reached back to medieval England to write what may be his finest novel, *The Spire,* about an obsessive clergyman's determination to build a spire upon his church at the cost of other men's lives. Golding would not respond directly—just as he declined to talk about the motivations behind his 1979 novel *Darkness Visible*—because, I surmised, he did not care to explain his symbols in fiction. But a hint of the reason behind his reluctance came in his reply: "The reader always knows better what a book is about than the writer."

Of *The Spire,* he did say, "Of course, one's experiences find their way into one's work, even if only in a general way. If you live nine miles from Salisbury Cathedral, it is natural to take something away for your writing. But the story in that novel could have taken place elsewhere; the spire could have been anywhere. I was writing about a cathedral of the mind."

Speaking of *Rites of Passage,* he offered a similar comment: "It is true that the novel is set aboard a ship in the late Napoleonic Wars, but it could be a ship any time." Did its passengers bear any kinship to those of Katherine Anne Porter's *Ship of Fools*? "Well," he replied, in a slight transatlantic huff, "it clearly isn't a Chinese ship, and they're not fools. I think I move more characters around here than in any of my other novels. I would say they have certain, ahem, call it comic overtones of the Anglo-Saxon."

On the book jacket, the foretopman in the ship's crew is described as "Budd-like Billy Rogers," and I asked him if there was any resemblance to Herman Melville's *Billy Budd*.

With gale force, Golding said, "I don't write the blurbs. Nothing in common to *Budd* at all, nothing. No possible similarity ever occurred to me. Anyway, this chap in my novel doesn't get hanged." In the background Golding's wife, Ann, an analytical chemist whom he married in 1939, could be heard prompting him. "My wife points out with great acuity that the name Billy is fairly common in this neck of the woods."

Might, then, his character Billy derive from his own attitudes and name? "I've been called a lot of things in my time. . . . [Again, an interruption.] My wife reminds me that they used to call me not Billy but Schoolie in my navy days—because I had been a schoolmaster before becoming a writer."

At the moment, Golding said, he was "empty-headed," not doing much except gardening, walking, playing chess, and (off-stage laughter) "answering phone calls from New York." But he said he feels "a curious kind of subterranean rumbling" which could indicate the formation of another novel in this, "the autumn of my life." He sticks pretty close to home, with his family and books. There are several other writers in the neighborhood, such as Lord David Cecil, but he finds that there is a certain companionship in the company of past novelists who have worked this terrain, among them Anthony Trollope, whose *Barchester Towers* and *Cathedral* novels were set around Salisbury.

"An excellent friend, Trollope," Golding said.

Lord of the Flies, William Golding's first published novel, is in its ninety-seventh printing and has just passed the remarkable figure of seven million copies in a trade paperback edition since it first came out. Its popularity enabled him to leave teaching at the age of fifty and devote himself fully to writing. Among high school and college students it has become something of a classic. "The students first told their professors about *Lord of the Flies,*" Golding said, amused, "and now the children are the professors."

[NOVEMBER 2, 1980]

JAMES A. MICHENER

James A. Michener, one of America's and the world's most popular writers, can poke fun at his own popularity.

"In recent years, I have received an extraordinary amount of praise for my 'other books.' At a party some enthusiastic woman who obviously finds much enjoyment in books rushes up and cries, 'Mr. Michener. I can't thank you enough for your great novel about Hawaii. Tell me, how did you have the energy to write *From Here to Eternity*?' . . . I must confess, however, that the public at large seems to feel that as good as *Eternity* was, first place has got to go to my hilarious novel of the Pacific *Mister Roberts.*"

In fact, Michener expresses surprise about his wide appeal. He had just returned from Poland—which could be the scene of a future novel—when I spoke to him. "I think it's remarkable that a man could write the kind of thing I do," he said, "lengthy, intricate, not dependent on sex or violence, and acquire the readership I have.

"There may be some reasons. Through long apprenticeship, I learned about sentences and paragraphs. The only talent I have is that if I described a chair in a paragraph, I think I could make the reader stay to the end of that paragraph.

"From an intellectual viewpoint, I have a terrific compulsion to communicate. I'm very careful about the construction of a narrative. I've pondered this a good deal. I'm never easy until the structure falls into place. That is a matter of art—something I learned from music and painting and good literature.

"Then there is the choice of subject matter. I had a very good education: Swarthmore, the University of Northern Colorado, St. Andrews in Scotland, Harvard, and other colleges where I studied and taught. Some people have said I have a good sense of timing, but I don't think it works that way. Computers couldn't do it. You couldn't do *The Source* in the abstract. Education interests me. I think I have a didactic streak and probably would have been a good lawyer or college professor. The opening of *Hawaii* is widely used in geology courses in some schools."

Michener remains America's most popular *serious* novelist; I emphasize the word *serious* to distinguish him from the trash-masters and trash-mistresses grinding out what the book trade calls "popcorn for the eyes."

Readers have to work harder at his novels than at many other best sellers. Michener presents what he conceives would help the reading public to understand a subject, a lifestyle, or a country. He would not be offended at being called an educator in his novels. Many other best-selling novelists have less desire to educate than to entertain—and to have room left over for their next entertainment.

But most of all, other best-selling novelists often seem to take dead aim at the marketplace, at what the public wants. This does not appear to be Michener's aim. He seems to be offering what *he* wants to do, to be exploring locales and histories that intrigue *him*. In this respect, he most resembles Herman Wouk, whose big novels also grapple with war, prejudice, courage, and morality without the internalizing, subjective writing, and emphasis on ambiguous character of, say, two American Nobel laureates,

Saul Bellow and Isaac Bashevis Singer. Yet despite Michener's apparent determination to write first of all for himself, his novels have attained as loyal a following among a wide cross section of readers as did the stories of Charles Dickens in the last century.

This much is certain: People read a Michener novel because he is the author, not necessarily because of its locale or particular theme. *The Covenant* is set in South Africa. *The Source* had its roots in Israel. *Hawaii, Caravans, Iberia, Sayonara, Centennial,* and *Chesapeake* took place in various parts of the globe, including the United States. Each bears the Michener benchmark: material researched on the scene, not merely in libraries, blending real and fictional characters, delivering romance, adventure, and history, often at length. His new novel is 878 pages.

The Covenant is in the epic tradition that Michener has set for himself. It begins in the mists of South African history, fifteen thousand years ago, and comes up to the present; it does not evade such issues as apartheid, though the author, a Quaker of enormous goodwill, has an inclination to ameliorate and present all sides. Michener is well aware of the meaning of prejudice and tolerance. He has been married for twenty-five years to Mari Yoriko Sabusawa, an American of Japanese descent, who spent time in a California internment camp after Pearl Harbor. Researching *The Covenant,* Michener spoke to every sector of South African society: black, colored, Indian, Afrikaner, and English.

Michener said that for *The Covenant* he made three extended trips to South Africa. He was treated courteously by every segment of the country, and his phone rang constantly with offers for assistance and untrammeled discussions. In Soweto he spent five days speaking to black leaders, for and against the government; three days were spent under government supervision and two days on his own. He had forthright discussions with Afrikaners who believed in apartheid and with banned persons, black and white.

I asked him if he expected that *The Covenant* would encounter trouble in South Africa? "When it is read as a whole," he replied, "it will be seen as an ecumenical treatment. Some die-hards may resent the book. But for a novelist, the people must come first. One idea predominated as I began the novel. I had respect and affection for the country, and I wished it well. I prayed that it would negotiate successfully the dangerous years ahead."

But the mere mention of apartheid—even in fiction—can result in censorship in South Africa. After suppressing *The Covenant,* the South African censors reversed themselves and lifted their ban.

The irony is that for all his success, Michener lives quietly at home in Pipersville, Pennsylvania, and in a cottage in St. Michaels, Maryland. He and his wife have established scholarships for many college students, and they frequently aid poets, novelists, and dramatists in distress through generous donations to the Authors League Fund. The Micheners have given millions of dollars to institutions and individuals. The compassion Michener expresses for his fellow authors is a mark of the man, and perhaps the secret of his popularity is that the compassionate touch carries over into his novels. To his fellow authors, he is known as the First Citizen of the Republic of Letters.

[NOVEMBER 1980]

JOHN HERSEY

This year and next year and perhaps the year after, John Hersey, who has written some of the lasting books of reportage and fiction of our time (going back to *Hiroshima*, about the human devastation caused by the first atomic bomb, and *The Wall*, an imaginative story rooted in fact about the Warsaw Ghetto), will be working on a large novel that reaches back into his own past. It is set in China and written in the form of biography. The author was born in Tientsin (now Tainjin) in 1914, the son of American missionaries, and spoke Chinese in his youth.

"I've got a long way to go," he said cheerfully, sounding like an author living in that wonderful creative time when research leads to discoveries that match your own instincts. [*The Call* was published in 1985.]

"One of the things I'm trying to do is get the background of the missionary impulse. The missionary record was somewhat mixed but probably more valuable in China. It bears a kinship to such later efforts as the Marshall Plan, the Peace Corps, and the more recent human rights policies.

"In China there was a period beginning around 1900 when a

second wave of missionaries arrived, not just evangelizing but concerned with the quality of life. They did a lot to open the way for the revolution against the Manchu dynasty and, in some respects, for the later Communist Revolution, by suggesting ways for China to modernize and still stay Chinese. The contribution in education was most spectacular. A lot of the people educated in missionary colleges later played roles in government.

"My father was with the YMCA, and my parents were very much involved as Social Gospel missionaries. In the tradition of Jacob Riis and Helen Hull, they saw injustices in society that could be corrected. In a sense, it was something like the mood of Teddy Roosevelt's trust-busting and Franklin Roosevelt's New Deal—looking out for the welfare of the little man."

Hersey, who lived in China until he was ten, has vivid memories of a happy childhood there, where he met children from different lands in the international concessions—sovereign enclaves granted by the Chinese government to foreign powers. "You could go by rickshaw from France to England to the United States," he recalled. In 1946 he returned for a visit; he has not been back since then but hopes to return soon. Some of his books, including *A Bell for Adano* and *Hiroshima,* have been translated there.

Hersey still teaches one term a year at Yale, which he attended and where he was once master of Pierson College, and devotes a good deal of time to the Authors League and Authors Guild, helping to improve the lot of writers in this country.

[JANUARY 4, 1981]

[A PERSONAL NOTE]

Here it's necessary to get personal and, for once, drop the interviewer's guise. Hersey was a reticent man when it came to talking about himself or his books; not for him huckstering and author tours. He allowed his work to speak for itself. Still, he told friends that the one personal trait he regretted was his reserve. But his reserve was full of eloquence.

I first met Hersey in Sicily, where he was a respected war correspondent, at the beginning of the Italian campaign in the Second World War. Hersey's intuition saw something beyond the battles: the encounter between young Americans and the Italian people after the downfall of fascism. Americans as military governors were a new experience; we were poor colonial masters. All this Hersey perceived the moment the guns were silenced on the Mediterranean island.

Out of that experience came his novel *A Bell for Adano*. What distinguished him from other correspondents was that he imagined the future role of the United States in an occupied Europe. His factual reporting provided the background for his perceptive fiction, perhaps a little romantic, but we were all romantics and idealists during those years.

Hersey was a writer on the side of the angels, fighting for civil and constitutional rights, advocating the rights of college students to be themselves—to enjoy freedom of protest—and protesting himself against the Vietnam War in the best possible way: by reading from *Hiroshima,* his brilliant report about the physical and human devastation caused by the atomic bomb upon a small group of Japanese civilians. It filled up a single issue of *The New Yorker* and remains one of the most lasting works of reportage by an American writer in this dying century.

"There are more tensions in freedom than in autocracy, and they are worth suffering for," Hersey said. But he was one of the most open-minded and tolerant persons I have ever known. He believed in building mutual trust and finding common ground. During a time of turmoil when he served as master of Pierson College at Yale, he called for a new concept of the worker-student relationship. "It will be based on a recognition that cops, hard hats, even southern racists are human," he said, "and therefore have the possibility of being led away from viciousness toward aspiration, courage, generosity."

For some forty years, up until the time of his death in 1993,

Hersey and I were in touch on matters affecting the rights and freedoms of American and foreign authors. He worked quietly and passionately as president of the Authors League of America for five years and as chairman of the Authors Guild contract committee for a decade. He found time to serve on the board of directors of the Authors League Fund, helping writers who were ill or down on their luck. We sat together during many a long meeting in New York. He felt a personal responsibility to the profession of letters and journalism. In our many exchanges he called his work for authors "our common labors."

In war and peace Hersey's large themes reflected his hope for mankind. Among his colleagues he was a shining example of courage and conscience, a beau ideal.

[SEPTEMBER 1994]

SAMUEL BECKETT

Paris

As he walked into the little café on the Boulevard St. Jacques in the Fourteenth Arrondissement, everything about Samuel Beckett seemed at once familiar and unexpected. The penetrating blue eyes, the furrowed brow, the strong beak, the lined face that seemed as if it had been carved in polished granite: They were all there. But the impression of hardness and diffidence acquired from remembered photographs and stories didn't match this man. For everything about him was softer and warmer by degrees: The pleasant voice, the ironic glint in his eyes, the cordial air he conveyed made a stranger in his beloved city feel like a guest.

Beckett does not grant interviews; that was understood. He had enough honors, including the Nobel Prize in literature, awarded in 1969 (which, of course, he did not accept in person), and worldwide acclaim. Public attention only distracted him from his writing and—what he gently intimated could be worse—only led to inaccurate "interpretations" of his life or what he "meant" to say in his works. And there are plenty of opportunities for misunderstanding: There is almost always a production of *Waiting for Godot* or *Happy Days* or *Endgame* on in Europe or in the United States.

And so no interview and no notes: *"Rien à faire"* ("Nothing to be done"), as the opening line of *Godot* goes.

Still, nothing forbade us from having a couple of cups of coffee, one long cigar and one short cigarillo, and a casual talk for an hour or so. He lit a Havanitos Planteros, saying that small cigars weren't as bad as smoking cigarettes. I had brought along a newspaper clipping noting that around the time of his seventy-fifth birthday on April 13, 1981, his one-character play *Rockaby*, would be put on at the State University of New York at Buffalo. He glanced at it, handed it back, and said he didn't save things written about him.

What matters to him, he indicated, is the integrity of his work. That is why he prefers such relatively small and attentive publishing houses as Grove in New York and Les Éditions de Minuit in Paris. He keeps a close watch on the staging of his plays; his American director, Alan Schneider, consults with him in Paris beforehand. He has directed his own plays in Düsseldorf; he says modestly that he knows enough German to make his ideas clear.

It was his interest in the Romance languages that first led him to France in 1926, when he was preparing for a career as a teacher at Trinity College, Dublin. What made him begin to write some of his works originally in French and then translate them into English?

Beckett says that he began to write in French because he wanted to get away from his mother tongue; writing in English somehow made it come too easy. The French language offered greater clarity and forced him to think more fundamentally, to write with greater economy. But instinct rather than a deliberate plan determined whether his plays were originally written in English or French. *Krapp's Last Tape* was first written in English; *En Attendant Godot* in French. Beckett's explanation about his bilingual writing is not as didactic as it may seem; listening to him, one gains new respect for ambiguity.

I wondered about his wartime experience during the Nazi occupation of France. When Paris was liberated, Beckett was awarded the Croix de Guerre for his clandestine activities. Denying that he had done anything unusual, he said that writing with economy and clarity was necessary when he worked inside a resistance group that conveyed information to the Allies. A French colleague carried certain details to him about German troop movements, and he translated them into English in as few words as possible for transmission to London.

He writes at home in his apartment in the Fourteenth Arrondissement, where he lives with his wife (the nameplate in the hallway of his building simply reads "BECKETT"). He has been writing fairly steadily, he said, hardly finding time to get away to his country place in the Marne region. He keeps up with his reading of old friends, such as Kay Boyle, admires the writings of Heinrich Böll and Saul Bellow, but doesn't follow current fashions in literature. In the small café where we sat, Samuel Beckett went unrecognized.

And so this is only an impression, with a few brushstrokes of fact added, of the author who bridges the century's literary history from James Joyce, his friend and fellow expatriate from Dublin, to the most avant-garde writers of our own day.

As we walked outside, I suggested to Beckett that his photographs always made him appear too somber and asked if he would allow me to take a few pictures. Relaxed, he stood in front of a street sign that read: "SORTIE DE SECOUR—*ne pas encombrer*" ("Emergency exit—do not block").

Beckett weighed the words aloud. "That's appropriate," he said, with a suggestion of a smile.

[JANUARY 25, 1981]

CZESLAW MILOSZ

When Czeslaw Milosz made his first appearance in New York on the platform of the 92d Street Y Poetry Center, both the writer and sponsor were ahead of their time. Since then the Polish poet from California has attained greater significance in the world of letters and political symbolism: he received the 1980 Nobel Prize in literature.

Milosz will open the Poetry Center's forty-third season, his first public reading in the United States since he received the Nobel.

"I shall read some of my poems in English—the shorter ones, because my accent causes some problems for the audience," he said with perfect clarity by telephone from Berkeley, where he has taught at the University of California since 1960. "I write only in Polish. Mostly, I translate the poems myself, with the help of students or colleagues.

"Then, for the sound, I plan to read a few of my poems in Polish. I'm much more secure in my own language. It's almost like having a personality change to switch from one language to another."

He will read from *Bells in Winter* and *Selected Poems,* which have been translated and are Ecco Press paperbacks, and several poems that have not been published in English.

Does he plan to read from his novels—or write any?

"No novels," Milosz insisted.

"I don't consider myself a novelist at all," he said. "There was a Polish writer in this century, Stanislaw Ignazy Witkiewicz, who described the novel as a bag to put in everything, and so I devote myself to poetry. Novels are not my best genre."

With due modesty, he said that he did not consider himself a professional reader of poetry. "I'm not like those Russian poets who act on the stage; that is not in the tradition of Polish poetry. We consider that somewhat arrogant. It's a special style that may be suitable elsewhere."

Milosz said that a friend, the poet Joseph Brodsky, chants on the platform. "But that's different from acting. I myself have a tendency to chant, too, but I repress myself."

Would he engage in political discussions in New York?

Somewhat cautiously, he replied: "No. I'd like to stick to my guns—poetry—and not comment on political affairs. Occasionally, of course, I provide brief information about the circumstances of my writing and themes, but that is something else." In some of his other works, such as *The Captive Mind,* he explained why he severed ties with the Polish government after World War II.

Milosz said that poetry—"unfortunately"—was not, as a rule, a political activity, "but in the twentieth century, whether or not we wish to, we must make options. A poet, like everyone else, is a human being, so in his work he, too, reacts in an emotional way."

He has returned to Poland for a visit, but he has not commented generally about the political situation.

"I received a good reception twice at the University of Lublin and twice in the shipyards from Lech Walesa, the leader of Solidarity, and from the workers. I found a peculiar situation—real harmony between the directors of the shipyard and the workers.

"I did not read my poetry there, but I gave a brief talk at a ceremony in front of a monument built by Solidarity honoring the workers killed by the police."

The monument, which stands in front of the shipyard gate, includes a fragment from one of his poems. He said it went:

> You who have harmed a simple
>   man,
> Don't feel secure because the poet
>   remembers,
> You can kill him,
> But a new one will be born.

Was he writing any particular poetry at the moment?

"Poetry isn't a steady business," he said. "I continue writing poetry because it is my main interest. I am against novels even though I've written two. I don't like using personal experiences and exposing them under the guise of characters.

"To be a good novelist, one must be shameless. That isn't quite true with poetry because a poem has such a strong element of form that guides its structure."

Milosz will occupy the Charles Eliot Norton Poetry Chair at Harvard, whose holders include T. S. Eliot and E. E. Cummings. His main obligation will be to deliver six lectures, but he has not decided the themes.

It is not unlikely that he will mention the significance of memory, as he did in his Nobel talk: "Our planet that gets smaller every year is witnessing a process that escapes definition, characterized by a refusal to remember."

[**September** 20, 1981]

DONALD BARTHELME

Donald Barthelme, whose short stories in *The New Yorker* and ten books (to name three tantalizing titles: *Snow White, Come Back, Dr. Caligari, Unspeakable Practices, Unnatural Acts*) have placed him on the summit of modern fictional invention, turned the tables on his critical interpreters the other night. He did what he has seldom done: interpreted himself—somewhat.

In a talk presented by the Writer at Work series of New York University's Gallatin Division in the Bobst Library, he offered a Rosetta stone for the meaning behind some of his demotic characters. If his interpretations weren't always a precise key to deciphering his work (now collected in *Sixty Stories*), at least his talk before some two hundred editors, publishers, authors, and students was received as a pyrotechnical performance in the use of the spoken word as literature.

Among the subjects he ribbed for nearly an hour were Sarah Lawrence seniors, Tiffany's, the Downtown Nursery, the Whitney Museum, Johns Hopkins, existentialism, Moonbeam McSwine, Alain Robbe-Grillet, the Bolivian Army, and the Internal Revenue Service. (In a fictional conceit in his talk, Barthelme invents Gaston, a literary critic, "who is a guard at the Whitney Museum, is in love with an IRS agent named Madeleine, the very IRS agent, in fact, who is auditing my return for the year 1979.")

By contrast, those who came off well were Stéphane Mallarmé, Upton Sinclair, Lewis Carroll, Samuel Beckett, the White Rock girl, Robert Rauschenberg, George Orwell, Louis Armstrong, and the pre-Hitler newspaper *Frankfurter Zeitung*. Especially Mallarmé, of whom the author said: He "shakes words loose from their attachments and bestows new meanings upon them, meanings which point not toward the external world but toward the Absolute, acts of poetic intuition."

At the core of his talk, which was serious despite its humorous, low-key delivery, was a defense of what he called "the alleged postmodernists" in literature. He placed himself in this category, plus, among other Americans, John Barth, John Hawkes, William Gass, Robert Coover, and Thomas Pynchon; in Germany, Peter Handke and Thomas Bernhard; in Italy, Italo Calvino.

He said, "The criticisms run roughly as follows: that this kind of writing has turned its back on the world, is in some sense not about the world but about its own processes, that it is masturbatory, certainly chilly, that it excludes readers by design, speaks only to the already tenured, or that it does not speak at all, but instead, like Frost's Secret, sits in the center of a ring and Knows."

Disputing such implied criticism of himself and other practitioners of avant-garde fiction, Barthelme explained: "Art is not difficult because it wishes to be difficult, rather because it wishes to be art. However much the writer might long to be, in his work, simple, honest, straightforward, these virtues are no longer available to him. He discovers that in being simple, honest, straightforward, nothing much happens: he speaks the unspeakable, whereas we are looking for the as-yet-unspeakable, the as-yet-unspoken."

Barthelme indicated that serious writing could not be simply charged on an American Express or Diners Club card, that it was really difficult for the creator to order up.

"Writing is a process of dealing with not-knowing, a forcing of what and how," he said. "We have all heard novelists testify to the fact that beginning a new book, they are utterly baffled as to how to proceed, what should be written, and how it might be written, even though they've done a dozen. At best there is a slender intuition, not much greater than an itch. The not-knowing is not simple, because it's hedged about with prohibitions, roads that may not be taken. The more serious the artist, the more problems he takes into account, the more considerations limit his possible initiatives."

Barthelme noted that changes had taken place in other forms of writing, including newspapers. Among other publications, he once worked on the *Houston Post*. He said: "The earlier newspaper culture, which once dealt in a certain amount of nuance and zestful, highly literate hurly-burly, has deteriorated shockingly. The newspaper I worked for as a raw youth, thirty years ago, is today a pallid imitation of its former self. Where once we could put spurious quotes in the paper and attribute them to Ambrose Bierce and be fairly sure that enough readers would get the joke to make the joke worthwhile, from the point of view of both reader and writer, no such common ground now exists."

He asked his audience to wonder with him if contaminated language could be considered a coconspirator in such "massive crimes" as "fascism, Stalinism, or" by implication "our own policies in Vietnam." And found that there was a "loss of reference" in the use of everyday language and citing Ernest Hemingway's observation, he noted that *honor, glory,* and *country* had become perjured words.

As Barthelme put it more lightly, we cannot "watch the wine of life turning into Gatorade."

[FEBRUARY 18, 1982]

RALPH ELLISON

Relaxing in his art- and book-lined apartment on Riverside Drive above the Hudson River, Ralph Ellison took time away from his electric typewriter to talk about his writing life.

"My approach is that I'm an American writer," he said. "I write out of the larger literary tradition—which, by the way, is part Negro—from Twain to Melville to Faulkner. Another element I'm aware of is American folklore. And then all of this is part of the great stream of literature.

"Americans didn't invent the novel. Negroes didn't invent poetry. Too much has been written about racial identity instead of what kind of literature is produced. Literature is colorblind, and it should be read and judged in a larger framework."

In 1952 Ellison's first novel, *Invisible Man,* was published, and Random House is bringing out a thirtieth anniversary edition, which is also being distributed by the Book-of-the-Month Club. Since 1952 *Invisible Man* has gone through twenty hardcover and seventeen Vintage Books paperback printings, and there has been a Modern Library edition.

The novel can also be read in Czech, Danish, Dutch, Finnish,

French, German, Hebrew, Hungarian, Italian, Japanese, Norwegian, Portuguese, Slovak, Spanish, and Swedish. The author's wife, Fanny, who magically finds just about everything he has written in their home files, says that a request came in for a Polish edition just before martial law was declared in Poland. He says that the Russians are aware of his writings, but that if a translation exists in Russian, he hasn't seen any edition.

What provides the greatest continuity for *Invisible Man* is that it is recognized as an essential twentieth-century American literary work in just about every high school and college in the country. Anne Freedgood, a Random House editor, enjoys telling the story of the seventeen-year-old student she knows who recently learned that Mr. Ellison had not written a second novel. "How could he?" the young woman said: "This novel has *everything* in it."

It won the National Book Award in 1953, and in 1965 two hundred authors, editors, and critics, polled by the *New York Herald Tribune,* picked *Invisible Man* as the most distinguished novel written by an American during the previous twenty years.

The novel, which defies easy summary because of its subtleties (a thumbnail description: It is about one nameless black man's dilemma about his position in the white world), builds from one of the most memorable opening paragraphs in modern American fiction:

"I am an invisible man. No, I am not a spook like those who haunted Edgar Allan Poe; nor am I one of your Hollywood-movie ectoplasms. I am a man of substance, of flesh and bone, fiber and liquids—and I might even be said to possess a mind. I am invisible, understand, simply because people refuse to see me."

Ellison revealed that he had meant to write a different novel—a war story rooted in some of his own experiences at sea and observations ashore as a merchant seaman in Europe in the 1940s—when he was seized by the notion of invisibility.

"I had come back on sick leave from my service in the merchant marine, and after a hospital stay, in the summer of 1945, my wife and I went to a friend's farm in Waitsfield, Vermont. Sitting in a lumberman's cabin, looking at the hills, I wrote the first line of the book: 'I am an invisible man.' "

Ellison said, "Once the book was done, it was suggested that the title would be confused with H. G. Wells's old novel *The Invisible Man,* but I fought to keep my title because that's what the book was about." His editor, Albert Erskine, recalled, "His novel doesn't have the article in its title, although the mistake keeps cropping up, and I've been telling people to drop the word *the* ever since the book came out."

The author was born in Oklahoma City, educated at Tuskegee Institute, worked as a researcher on the New York Federal Writers' Project before World War II, and hoped to enlist as a trumpeter (he still has a trumpet, but, he says, no lip anymore) in the navy, "but they were not taking any more musicians. So, instead, I became a second cook on a Liberty ship. I was in charge of making breakfast, and I also turned out cornbread, biscuits, and fried pies."

Inevitably a talk with Ellison turns to his long-awaited work in progress. It will be his third book. *Shadow and Act,* a book of essays, came out in 1964. It can be reported that his second novel is progressing, and apparently it is working; certainly, the author is, steadily, every day. He has given the novel his full attention since he retired in 1980 from his teaching duties as a Schweitzer Professor of Humanities at New York University.

Author and novel suffered a setback in the summer of 1967, when three hundred pages of manuscript were lost in a fire in Mr. Ellison's home in the Berkshires. "It was quite a traumatic experience watching the house burn and losing typewriters, cameras, and other personal property," he said. "The only thing we saved was our Labrador retriever. After that I tried to put together as much as I could, and I began to reconceive some of the characters. Now we have a photocopier at home, and I keep at least two copies of what I write."

Some Ellison fans, waiting so many years for his next novel, have wondered if he had writer's block.

"If so, it's a strange kind of thing, since I write all the time," Ellison replied. "The blockage is that I'm very careful about what I submit for publication. I learned long ago that it's better not to have something in print that you feel isn't ready. It's not a difficult thing to turn out more books. I had a hell of a lot more material that didn't get into *Invisible Man*. It may be a wasteful way of writing but I'm careful about what is published. There is a lot of formula writing today. I can't do certain things as a writer, but I enjoy the act of writing even if it isn't published immediately."

There is a strong metal file cabinet containing much of the manuscript of the untitled novel. He unlocked it for a visitor, pulled out the drawer, and measured the sections of manuscript with a tape measure: It came to nineteen inches.

"It looks long enough to be a trilogy," he said, smiling. "It all takes place in the twentieth century. I'm convinced that I'm working with abiding patterns. The style is somewhat different from *Invisible Man*. There are different riffs in it. Sections of it are publishable, and some parts have already appeared, in *American Review, Noble Savage, Partisan Review, Iowa Review,* the *Quarterly Review of Literature*.

"I'm dealing with a broader range of characters, playing with various linguistic styles. Quite a bit of the book is comic. The background is New York, the South, an imaginary Washington—not quite the world I used to encounter on the board of the Kennedy Center for the Performing Arts there."

He has seen Washington from on high, in public-service positions, such as membership on the Carnegie Commission for educational television. He was given the highest civilian honor, the Medal of Freedom, from President Lyndon B. Johnson, and he is a member of the American Academy-Institute of Arts and Letters, the ranking cultural body in the country.

"The novel has to be more than segments; it has to be a whole before it's ready for publication." He didn't say, nor was he asked, when. "But if I'm going to be remembered as a novelist, I'd better produce it soon," he said cheerfully.

[MARCH 1, 1982]

THEODORE H. WHITE

Theodore H. White places himself in the tradition of those journalists who follow what the French call *les choses vues*—observed
reality.

"It proliferated with my generation," the author says. "The
American literature of reality includes Walter Duranty on
Russia, John Gunther inside his U.S.A., Edgar Snow following
the Red Star over China, John Hersey reporting on Hiroshima.
I think I fit in that stream, and I'm proud of it; it's a thoroughly
American tradition."

In his most revealing work, *In Search of History: A Personal
Adventure,* White observes the reality of war and of the political
process, the unreality of the cold war at home and abroad, the
Camelot of the Kennedy presidency, and, as fascinating as anything about anyone else, the making of himself as a writer.

He recalled that he found himself telling a friend about his
"old neighborhood" in Boston, how it had changed, from poor
and middle-class Jewish to poor and middle-class black. In his
book he calls it the "ethnic ballet" affecting every city and its
politics. That conversation planted a thought in his mind.

During the 1976 presidential campaign, he found himself bewildered, a little tired of writing off his shoe leather, wanting to look back instead of go on. He thought that it was time to tell of the making of Theodore White instead of the making of another president, that somehow, he could embark on a personal adventure and tell the history of his time without hiding behind a reporter's objectivity.

"I discovered what I was writing about only after I had finished," he says. "The title is somewhat misleading. It implies that I can come up with the answer to what history is all about, but that's not so at all. The book is about the search, not the answers. In my next book I'll look harder for the answers, for the meanings."

White is an articulate man who speaks in commas and semicolons. "I realized after the book was finished that it was about people who knew how to take charge, from FDR to JFK. It's about watching guys who knew what they were doing. I cast my absentee ballot for Roosevelt in 1944 from a military hospital in Chungking after coming out of the East China retreat. Even someone like Ike could take charge; he sent an airborne division to Little Rock. Kennedy screwed up in the Bay of Pigs but was in control by the time of the missile crisis.

"So the big theme in the book is that America and its leaders were once in control at home and overseas, where reason and strength could be brought together for good purpose."

Writing *In Search of History,* White was helped as usual by his longtime friend and editor Simon Michael Bessie. "There are two kinds of editors, those who correct your copy and those who say it's wonderful. Mike Bessie is the best kind of editor. He'll tell me, 'This is wonderful, but not quite as wonderful as the rest of the chapter,' which means I've got to go back and redo it."

I asked White to comment on the charge made by some of his journalistic confrères that he treated political scoundrels too kindly in his *The Making of the President* books.

"Look. The only leaders I really hated were Hitler and Stalin. I've tried to see the different sides of people. I thought Spiro Agnew was a bum from the word *go*. Frankly, I liked Barry Goldwater, a nice guy who was unfit for the presidency. As for Richard Nixon, there are a lot of different Nixons. No one hated me more once, but we became friends when he came to New York. In *Breach of Faith,* I was as harsh on him as anyone. I've been called anti-Nixon and pro-Nixon. Just say I'm soft on the human race."

He was relaxing with a drink in his East Side brownstone, still groggy after appearing on programs in fifteen cities—with the familiar plaint: "If it's Tuesday, this can't be Dallas; it must be Fort Worth"—having four or five interviews a day, finding to his surprise that some of the interviewers had actually read his book before questioning him.

"Look, we are now fighting not for the buck but for attention," he said. "You are asking people to go into a bookstore because they've heard something about your book and then give five to ten hours of their time to reading it. It's a struggle to attract readers because of all the other distractions in the country. You're like a little child saying, 'Listen to me, Mommy.'

"In a way, it makes you feel slimy. You want your book to be discovered for itself, and instead you find yourself pleading for it. And you're competing for airtime with *Jane Fonda's Workout Book* or *No Bad Dogs* or *Thin Thighs in Thirty Days* and others publicizing their books, as well as entertainers and people selling products or viewpoints, sometimes on the same show.

"So you swallow your pride and say to yourself, 'I have twenty years of my professional life invested in this book, I can't let it go down the drain.' You wake up early, polish your anecdotes, catch the planes, sleep in the Atlanta hotel that doesn't have room service when you get there, not even a glass of milk, and start out all over again the next day.

"What's happened is that there is a dissolution of time in the United States; time has become very fragmented. You have to catch people where they are—listening to their car radios in the afternoon while they're driving home; after midnight, when they're calling in and asking you questions about the Kennedys or the budget or the Falkland Islands; in the morning, when they're brushing their teeth while you're trying to explain a presidential campaign."

The unshy author of *The Making of the President* series is something of a pioneer in promoting his books. In fact, his career almost spans the history of such efforts to reach more readers through broadcasting.

White found that interviewers ranged from those who had done their homework to hosts who simply billboarded the book and took off on tangents to the ingenues who would cover the microphone and whisper, "What should I ask you next?"

But not all authors are willing to subject themselves to a tour or be interviewed on the air. There are some authors who do not get asked by publishers to do so.

White offered his opinion of the promotional situation for an author: "Once the book could take care of you; now you have to take care of the book."

[JULY 24, 1982]

HENRY STEELE
COMMAGER

Amherst, Massachusetts

Taking the steps two at a time in his rubber-soled brown moccasins and trailing over a half century of professorial and literary
glory behind him, Henry Steele Commager, at eighty, bounded
into his seminar on the Bill of Rights at Amherst College, nodded to the sixteen freshmen and sophomores facing him around
the T-shaped table, and said without ceremony: "Our subject
today is symbolic freedom—demonstrations, boycotts, strikes,
and other legitimate forms of expression that do not usually fit
into the usual concepts of freedom of speech and of the press.
How far can you go without overstepping the bounds? Is carrying a Russian flag a violation when we're not at war with the
Soviet Union? How about waving the Confederate flag at a
football game? Isn't that the symbol of slavery and treason?
When does expression become incitement to action?"

Almost anyone in this country in our time—studying Commager's high school and college textbooks, enjoying his books
on American history, listening to his speeches, reading his steady
flow of articles in newspapers and magazines—knows where he
himself stands on the question of civil liberties. It is just about

where one of his idols, Thomas Jefferson, stood when he wrote the original documents of freedom.

Even so, conducting this class for twenty-year-olds, he seldom intruded his own views. Instead Commager kept challenging the students to look at freedom from a variety of viewpoints, to look up Supreme Court cases and citations, to disenthrall themselves, and to think anew.

Under his guidance the Bill of Rights suddenly turned into a living document. He asked tough questions: "Should anyone who shouts, 'Kill the umpire!' be arrested? Or does it depend on the listeners and circumstances? What about the California case where a draft resister carried a sign with an obscenity printed on it? Do you desecrate the American flag by sewing it on the bottom of your pants?"

Commager continued: "The Reagan administration believes nothing is complex, that it has easy solutions for everything. I prefer what Justice Holmes said: 'We should be ever receptive to loathsome ideas.' That is a noble way of putting it."

Before the seminar began, I met him at his spacious tree-fringed house on South Pleasant Street close to the campus. The house is lined with books—including several shelves holding the scores of books Commager has written and edited—and a thousand or so classical records. There is a piano in the living room that he no longer plays. "I like to listen while writing—some Brahms, the Haydn keyboard music, Bach, Beethoven, mostly the eighteenth-century crowd. I know every note that's coming."

Commager charged up a flight of stairs—he moves on his feet like a boxer—to show what his workroom looks like. It resembled a small factory whose main product is words: written and spoken. "I took out a picture window to make room for these extra bookshelves," he said. Two electric typewriters were set up on large tables that could hold research materials, and a third one was temporarily at rest on the ground.

"We have five typewriters in the household and one car,"

Commager said impishly. "I think that's about the right propor-
tion."

He added, "I'm not very organized, and I don't write as much
as I used to." The fact is, however, he is is working on three
books at the same time.

"I'm writing a book on Tocqueville today—short interpre-
tive essays. Then I'm writing a book on the invention of childhood, which I may call *The Discovery of Childhood*. And this cabinet holds research for *Foundations of American Nationalism;* it will
probably be two volumes. I've thrown in the sponge on a fourth
book I was doing, a documentary history of academic freedom,
because I didn't think I would get around to finishing such a big
subject."

To keep his restless mind at work in his eighty-first year, he
continues to serve as editor of *The Rise of the American Nation*
series of books, of which forty already are out. There are ten or
so volumes more to come—"if only I can get some of the lag-
gards to turn in their manuscripts," he said.

Commager explained that he teaches three seminars in the fall
term: two for freshmen on the Bill of Rights—"by the case
method, which is the best way, answering the question of what
should society do and what the Supreme Court has ruled it
should do"—and another for upperclassmen on Alexis de
Tocqueville today: "the problems that he raised and what has
happened to them since then; he feared military dangers and
inequality of wealth, which he called the manufacturing aristocracy."

Although professors usually retire at sixty-seven, an exception
has been made in Commager's case, and he can teach as long as
he wishes and on whatever subject he chooses to at Amherst. His
academic career began at the University of Chicago; he graduated in 1923 and received his doctorate there in 1928. He started
out as an instructor in history in 1926 at New York University,
became a full professor in 1931, served as professor at Columbia
University from 1939 to 1956, went on to Amherst from 1956

to 1972, and then eased up somewhat to his present role as a lecturer.

Although he has never received a Pulitzer Prize, his awards include a rare gold medal in history from the American Academy. Among his books are *Theodore Parker: Yankee Crusader*, *The American Mind*, *The Struggle for Racial Equality*, *Freedom, Loyalty, Dissent*, and *The Search for a Usable Past*.

For his eightieth birthday, he said that will be honored with awards from the American Civil Liberties Union, the National Unitarian Church, and the New England Teachers organization. "One or two other celebrations are planned," he said, "but I'm not supposed to know about them."

[OCTOBER 25, 1982]

IRWIN SHAW

Southampton, New York

When he was still in his early twenties and newly famous for his 1936 antiwar play *Bury the Dead,* Irwin Shaw was given some fatherly advice by the head of the RKO Studio in Hollywood: "Come out here; get married; get a house with a swimming pool. By the time you're thirty, you'll lose your ideals—and then you'll be happy."

He declined the advice and struck out on his own to become the author of twelve novels, a half dozen plays, eight collections of short stories, a couple of books of reportage, and a number of forgotten screenplays. Today he has a new young audience of readers who have seen the television series based on his novel *Rich Man, Poor Man* and have noticed the lengthening row of his titles on the bookshelves.

And he has a house with swimming pool here in Long Island's Southampton and another house in Klosters, Switzerland, where he and his wife, Marian, spend about five months of the year, and a grown son, Adam, also a writer, who lives in Spain, and he is fairly pleased writing about what interests him, and he did it all without being indentured to a movie studio.

Irwin Shaw's life and independent writing career coincide with just about half of this century's turbulence. He experienced some of its more extreme moments himself and put a lot of the experience down on paper. He lived in Brooklyn during the Depression and wrote a play, *The Gentle People*. In World War II he served as a private first class and later a warrant officer in the Signal Corps, which provided the background for his war novel *The Young Lions*. The Hollywood and television blacklisting period for writers and actors and directors in the 1950s has echoes in his novel *The Troubled Air* and his current novels and short stories about changing American lives here and abroad.

He was seated at his desk, casually dressed in a red polo shirt and blue sweater, red socks, and loafers, puffing on a Punch cigar after lunch. The light from a glorious winter sky over the Atlantic side of Long Island filled his orderly workroom, outlining his solid frame and brightening his gray hair and head. In a cheerful mood, he talked about some of the high moments he has experienced.

"There was the day I caught a winning pass at Brooklyn College," he said. "I started out as a tackle and then became a halfback and quarterback; I was the only one who could remember the signals." At one point he resigned as varsity quarterback to devote more time to his studies; in those years an athlete had to be a scholar, too. A listener, of course, was reminded of "The Eighty-Yard Run," one of his best-known short stories.

With a twinkle, he said, "I shouldn't have done it, but when *Bury the Dead* was put on in New York and the audience called, 'Author, author,' I went up onstage and joined the cast and felt great. Now, writing for the theater is such a hit-or-miss thing; you're supposed to bat a thousand. If a baseball player gets a hit one out of three times at bat, he's a star. It's almost an act of charity for a playwright. Imagine telling Sophocles or Shakespeare or O'Neill: 'One set and only three characters.'

"Now," he said, "I'm pretty much devoting myself to novels."

In the army, he recalled, there were two especially memorable days: "The greatest single public high moment was entering Paris with the Fourth Division and going up the Place de la Concorde with our helmets on, and capturing Germans, and heading for the Ritz Bar and the Dome, and drinking brandy when the city was free for the first time since the Nazi occupation. The other great private moment came a few months after the war ended, and I got out of the army and came home to my wife in the apartment we had on Seventy-fourth between Second and Third and shed my uniform and said, 'I'll never have to put it on again.' "

In the last two years, after an illness and time in the hospital, he felt intimations of mortality. He has recovered, but the old quarterback no longer can move to his left with the grown-up writer-jocks in the Hamptons or go sliding down a slope in Switzerland. He leaves that to his son, who is an all-round athlete. But every experience counts for a storyteller. He put aside one novel and wrote another, *Acceptable Losses,* which was touched off by his brush with death.

Its protagonist confronts a threat that forces him to look back upon incidents in his life, searches himself and imagines mysterious human forces, and presses on. Like his previous novel *Bread upon the Waters,* it is set in the United States, and several critics considered it more intense than some of his earlier popular fiction.

That word, *popular,* is something of a red flag for Shaw. "I cringe when critics say I'm a master of the popular novel," he said.

"I think I've become more generous in my views. When you're young, you look at things directly. Now I have peripheral vision. I'm still trying to write clearly and amusingly, without pretension, and avoiding rhetoric for its own sake, though I admire it in others when it comes off. You know, you get a little blasé, after the thrill of having your first stories published, and begin to carp at reviews or yell at your publisher.

"But then you begin to add it all up and feel right again. My books are published in twenty-five languages, including Icelandic and Macedonian. I'm about to begin on my next novel. I have the idea and the title, but I'm trying to work out the form. The last novel emptied out my reserve. I have the feeling that the reservoir fills up until it overflows and then you begin writing something."

Shaw pointed to the Olivetti 44 manual typewriter next to his writing chair.

"I keep one here and another just like it in Klosters," he said. "I like to hear the noise of the keys striking the paper. And sometimes the keys get jammed, and I have to stop; but I'm too old to change for any of the new machines. This one also has some keys with French accents on them for writing to friends in Europe and going over translations of my work. I'm also thinking of doing my memoirs—so much has happened—but first the reservoir has to fill up for the next novel."

[MARCH 6, 1983]

ALICE WALKER

Etched in Alice Walker's memory is that summer day in 1966 in Greenwood, Mississippi, when she was a civil rights worker. A man came up to her in the motel where she was staying—it hadn't been cleared as a safe place for blacks, and particularly for a black woman talking there with a white lawyer from New York—and warned her: "Don't you let the sun go down on you in this here town."

Recalling the incident now, Walker laughed, not so much at the fact that her life had been threatened—she took the hint and was escorted out of town by civil rights colleagues before sundown—as at the man's language.

"Such a cliché," she said, talking from her home in San Francisco, where for the last five years she has lived down the street from St. Mary's Cathedral in the neighborhood called Japantown.

For a born storyteller, the warning sounded like a line worth filing away, perhaps one that would turn up eventually as dialogue in a poem, short story, essay, or novel written by, well, Alice Walker.

Walker, originally from Eatonton, Georgia, had just learned that she had won the American Book Award in the hard-cover category for her novel *The Color Purple.*

Though she isn't a household name on the popularity charts, Walker's *Color Purple* was a modest best seller, and the novel is now expected to achieve a second wind because of the award.

Walker has been acclaimed critically for a decade. She is the author of a solid body of work: two previous novels, *The Third Life of Grange Copeland* and *Meridian;* two books of short stories, *You Can't Keep a Good Woman Down* and *In Love and Trouble;* a biography of Langston Hughes for children; three volumes of poetry, *Once, Revolutionary Petunias,* and *Good Night, Willie Lee, I'll See You in the Morning.*

"Willie Lee was my father's name," Walker said. "That was what my mother said at his funeral." The title poem also helped to explain her roots as a writer: "My parents were both storytellers. They always spoke with metaphorical richness."

In *The Color Purple,* Walker reached back into the era of her family's past more than of her own. The novel covers the period between the world wars, telling the story of two sisters, one a missionary in Africa, the other a child wife living in the South. They sustain each other, and themselves, through a series of letters.

"The novel ends about the time I was born," she said. "It's more like my grandparents' time in Georgia. Eatonton is still very much the same small farming town as when I grew up and went to public school there. At first the characters in the novel didn't want to come to life for me in San Francisco, so I went up to a little town in northern California, Boonville, and just sat there for a while, trying to discover the right voice.

"That's how I decided that the letter form would work best; women often write letters to each other. It was also a way of solving a technical problem of having characters in Georgia and Africa. They never actually get the letters, but that's beside the point. By writing, they drew closer. I suppose what I was saying is this: Although we don't get each other's messages, we can still have faith in each other."

Walker moved on from Eatonton to Spelman College in Atlanta, with a full scholarship. There she encountered two professors, Howard Zinn and Staughton Lynd, who encouraged her to pursue her studies. After a few years she moved north to attend Sarah Lawrence, meeting Lynd's mother, Helen, coauthor with her husband of the well-known sociological study of *Middletown*.

At Sarah Lawrence, also on scholarship, she was spotted by the poet Muriel Rukeyser as a writer of talent. Rukeyser passed on Walker's first book of poems, *Once*, to her own literary agent, Monica McCall. Hiram Haydn, an editor at Harcourt, Brace, accepted the book of poems in 1965, after Walker had graduated from Sarah Lawrence.

"Then I went to work for the New York City Welfare Department to support my writing," she said, "living on the Lower East Side between Avenue A and Avenue B in a building that had no front door. I'm not at all nostalgic for the place. I remained with the Welfare Department for four months, writing at night, but I couldn't stand it.

"In the summer of 1966 I went to Mississippi, to be in the heart of the civil rights movement, helping people who had been thrown off the farms or taken off the welfare roles for registering to vote. While working there, I met the civil rights lawyer I later married; we became an interracial couple. In New York, I worked as an editor at *Ms.* magazine, and he worked for the NAACP Legal Defense Fund. We're now divorced and share custody of our daughter."

After living in Brooklyn, Walker decided that the buildings in the city were too tall for her. "I realized I was a country person; I'm just not used to small spaces," she said, "so I moved to San Francisco. I also have a little cabin in Mendocino, where I've just planted a hundred trees."

Walker is now completing a book of essays, *In Search of Our*

Mothers' Gardens. It includes pieces from *Mother Jones, Ms., Black Scholar*, the *New York Times*, and the texts of her antinuclear rally speeches. What about her next novel? "I'm waiting for it to surface," she said.

[APRIL 16, 1983]

ITALO CALVINO

Italo Calvino, the Italian master of allegorical fantasy, was visiting and lecturing in Manhattan recently. "New York is a fabled city, a fabulous city," he said. "I feel that it's one of my cities—like San Remo, where I grew up, or Rome, where I now live, or Paris, where my wife and I keep a small apartment. I felt that way almost from my first visit here more than twenty years ago."

Enigmatically—almost like a Calvino story—he added, "I feel so at home in New York that I don't have the urge to write about it."

Calvino said that the American literary "experimenters" he admires, because they, too, venture into fable and allegory, are Donald Barthelme, Thomas Pynchon, John Barth, and Kurt Vonnegut, Jr. Without categorization, he added Vladimir Nabokov to the list of his most influential novelists. "Of course, I'm of the generation that grew up with Hemingway and Faulkner as strong influences. And to find out what is happening in America today, I read Gore Vidal, Saul Bellow, Mary McCarthy, and Norman Mailer."

Calvino's works include *The Baron in the Trees, The Castle of*

Crossed Destinies, Invisible Cities, Italian Folktales, Cosmicomics,
and most recently *If on a Winter's Night a Traveler.*

"A quiver of love runs through Italian folklore. Cupid and
Psyche are especially popular in Sicily and Tuscany. The Sicilian
tales are filled with local color, with many allusions to social
conditions. The Tuscan tales are more fantastic, closer to children's poems. The Venetian tales naturally have an aquatic influence. And there is a big difference between the Grimms' tales
and ours. Grimm can be brutal and cruel. The Italian folktales
also have their gory moments, but there is more redemption and
love."

How do his fantasies differ from science fiction?

"For a while after the war I tried to write realistic stories. My
first novel, *The Path to the Nest of Spiders,* was about my experience with the partisans fighting against the Nazis and Fascists in
the mountains of Liguria. Eventually I came to realize that the
only way for me to write was to invent. Straight science fiction
seems more remote. In *Cosmicomics* I came close to science fiction; I was inspired by cosmological subjects and the workings of
the universe and invented a character who was a sort of witness
to everything that was happening inside the solar system."

Now, Calvino said, he grapples with modern events in his
own way through fables that often crisscross time.

"I try to move inside what is happening around us. The world
of pure science doesn't provide me with enough of an ability to
see fully. If the reader looks, I think he will find plenty of moral
and political ideas in my stories. I suffer from everyday life.
When I'm depressed, I start with some euphoric image that
transmits itself.

"Anyway, I'm sure that I'm a man of my own times. The
problems of our time appear in any story I write. Knights and
chivalry—they are related to the wars of today. No, I'm not
writing in a vacuum. The fables just make use of a different
language. Politics is marginal, but literature moves along by in-
direction."

His views on modern writing—including commercial American novels, which often become European best sellers—were heard loud and satirically clear in *If on a Winter's Night a Traveler.* In it he invented a group called the "OEPHLW of New York (Organization for the Electronic Production of Homogenized Literary Works)."

Calvino smiled as he read his description of how the OEPHLW works: "In New York, in the control room, the reader is soldered to the chair at the wrists, her temples beneath their crown of hair held fast by the serpentine wires of the encephalogram that mark the intensity of her concentration and the frequency of stimuli. All our work depends on the sensitivity of the subject and it must, moreover, be a person of strong eyesight and nerves, to be subjected to the uninterrupted reading of novels and variants of novels as they are turned out by the computer. If reading attention reaches certain highs with a certain continuity, the product is viable and can be launched on the market; if attention relaxes and shifts, the combination is rejected and its elements are broken up and used again in other contexts."

It sounds like the marketing research conducted by the television networks and some publishers to weigh what the audience wants.

One of Calvino's books that definitely did not go through the computer process is *The Baron in the Trees,* which is about a young Italian nobleman in the eighteenth century who rebels against parental authority and lives for the rest of his life in "an ideal state in the trees." In a separate interview in New York, Louis Malle, the director, said that he has long dreamed of making the novel into a movie and hopes to do so soon.

Calvino, who was born in 1923, belongs to the generation of neorealist Italian writers and filmmakers that served in the underground during World War II and joined the Communist party: "It seemed to have the most realistic program for opposing a resurgence of fascism and rehabilitating Italy, but I left the party in 1957, and today I am apolitical."

To help preserve literary traditions and promote new writers, he edits a fiction series called *Cento Pagi* ("One Hundred Pages"), short novels that are published by Giulio Einaudi in Turin. "Italian literature today does not have any real school or current but only complex personalities of writers who are so different," Calvino said. "Difference is worth encouraging."

[MAY 1, 1983]

UMBERTO ECO

Speaking to Umberto Eco after reading his best-selling novel *The Name of the Rose* is like being in the presence of a Bolognese Roman candle. He illuminates his ideas with metaphysical fireworks. What Eco adds to Luigi Pirandello and Italo Calvino, no mean wits, is sly scholarship.

You cannot talk to Eco or read his ingenious novel about intrigues in a fourteenth-century Italian monastery without hearing about semiotics, a subject he has taught at U.S. universities from Yale to Berkeley as well as at the University of Bologna, where he holds the chair of semiotics. That specialty underlies his first novel without getting in the way of storytelling; half the time Eco seems to be kidding his own knowledge.

He must be a good teacher because he defines semiotics in a way that makes you think you understand what he is saying: "It's the study of the different sign systems from a unified point of view." He expands: "People communicate with each other by various means, from the clothing they wear to the houses they live in. Body language is one of the more obvious ways."

The other evening Eco and his friend Saul Steinberg, *The*

New Yorker magazine artist, who lived in Italy for many years, were talking about semiotics. Steinberg said, "I am interested in new visions. I do in drawings what Calvino and Eco do in words: take the familiar and see it in a new way. Like drawing streets and avenues in New York—I see changing biography on Lexington Avenue as much as geography."

Eco nodded. "Steinberg is the greatest semiotician because he uses the language of drawings. He doesn't need words."

On the surface, *The Name of the Rose* is a medieval detective story, and Eco doesn't mind if one reads the book as straightforward entertainment. The year is 1327; Franciscans in a wealthy Italian monastery are suspected of heresy; Brother William of Baskerville arrives to investigate, and suddenly several monks are killed in bizarre ways. The evidence and false leads include secret symbols and coded manuscripts: semiotics. Brother William's (or Eco's) tools are the logic of Aristotle and the theology of Aquinas. The centerpiece of the mystery is a manuscript of the lost second book of Aristotle's *Poetics,* which deals with the subject of laughter.

Eco invites us to join in the fun. To dispel any idea that *The Name of the Rose* is merely a professor's lecture, he notes that he used to believe that a writer wrote out of a desire to change the world. But he has changed his mind. Now he knows that "a man of letters can write out of pure love of writing."

No author likes to explain too much, but Eco doesn't deny that Shakespeare hovers behind the title of his novel. "A rose by any other name" comes, of course, from *Romeo and Juliet.* The Franciscan monk William of Baskerville is a sleuth out of Sherlock Holmes and *The Hound of the Baskervilles.* Brother William's Watson, named Adso, narrates the tale. The character Jorge of Burgos is blind and wise—who else but another literary game player Eco admires, the Argentine writer Jorge Luis Borges?

In person as well as in print, Eco fires off salutes to other men of letters, from James Joyce to Woody Allen. He has written extensively about Joyce, and he helped the late Cathy Berberian translate Allen for Bompiani, the Milan publishing house where Eco is a consulting editor. "We had a little trouble translating his Jewish jokes," Eco said.

Eco has been close to Anglo-American literature since his boyhood during the Fascist era and the German occupation of Italy. In those years, he recalls, "American literature was read as an anti–Fascist statement. The partisans and the left during and after the war reinforced their political statements with American works, from Hemingway to Steinbeck. American jazz was also a statement of resistance and defiance. I lived in the countryside and learned to escape the bombs when I was barely thirteen. If I ever write a second novel, I might turn to that exciting time in northern Italy."

In the meantime, Eco writes for the Italian weekly *L'Espresso* and lectures in the United States and Europe. As secretary-general of the International Association for Semiotic Studies, he organized its first congress in Milan. He contributes to the semiotic review *VS,* which he founded and edits. He spends a few days a week at the University of Bologna away from his home and family in Milan.

Does the fourteenth century hold signs for the twentieth century?

"It's impossible to write history without contemporary eyes. But I would not want my book read as a roman à clef. Instead I hope readers see the roots, that everything that existed then— from banks and the inflationary spiral to the burning of libraries—exists today. We are always approaching the time of the Antichrist. In the nuclear age we are never far from the Dark Ages."

[AUGUST 1, 1983]

ANTHONY BURGESS

Not for the first time, Anthony Burgess, best known for that controversial novel and film *A Clockwork Orange,* finds that he has to explain what he's up to creatively these days. Some of the critics were underwhelmed by his current novel, *The End of the World News,* wondering about its multimedia style. Divided into three parts, the novel includes a Broadway musical comedy about Leon Trotsky, a "televisualized" life of Sigmund Freud, and a science fiction tale of the planet Earth clobbered by an intruder from a distant galaxy.

And so Burgess chain-lighted Dutch Schimmelpennincks and explained himself.

"Modern fiction is a lying craft with no pretensions to exact knowledge. Plausibility is very nearly all. A novelist may check in a cheap encyclopedia objective data—details of the sinking of the *Titanic*—as he needs for his narrative, but his art is a very tentative one and depends largely on guesswork about how the human mind operates.

"Nothing could be less scholarly than the average novel, even where its basis is a historical fact. A number of twentieth-century novelists, copying Nabokov and Borges, make parodic scholarship an aspect of their artistic seriousness. The novelist is a confidence trickster, while it is the task of the scholar to abhor trickery and teach skepticism."

So much for his personal vision, but what about *The End of the World News*? He said: "The three stories in the novel are all the same story. They are all about the end of history as man has known it."

A key to Burgess's work generally can be found in that umbrella word *entertainment*. In fact, he subtitles this novel *An Entertainment*. By contrast, his British neighbor on the Riviera Graham Greene dropped the word *Entertainment* from the most recent listing of his books to describe his early thrillers. Burgess added that he had a right to label his books any way he wanted to. It is the only one of his twenty-six novels with that specific notice to the reader.

The theatricality of the novel derives from the author's own background as a serious, self-taught musician. His compositions include songs, concertos, sonatas, and incidental music for plays. In fact, Burgess is one of the few transatlantic triple-threat men of letters who move from one entertainment form to another—books, movies, symphonies—without missing a beat. In conversation, he talks like a musician about the music in writing and like a novelist about the writing in music.

He combines his two interests, writing and music, in an autobiography, *This Man and Music*. This book combines family anecdotes with his musical adventures—"the literary intentions of music and the musical intentions of literature."

Burgess recalls family parties around the piano at Christmastime in his youth in Manchester. "Everybody had his or her own song. I remember a priest singing 'Be Mine, My Marguerite' and even my stepmother giving out with 'We'll be merry, drinking whisky, wine and sherry, all be merry, on Coronation Day.'"

If Burgess could wish upon a star, his big work wouldn't be a book but an opera, preferably grand. He believes that there's nothing unliterary about entertaining (that word again) the reader or listener or viewer. And he talks of writing a Jane Austen novel in the form of a Mozart symphony.

Inevitably his music is more structured than his full-time business of inventing stories. He links words and music: a novel, he says, is like a symphony; a novella, a sonata.

"Christopher Marlowe was one of the few writers who could bring off blank verse," Burgess said. "There's music in his line 'Was this the face that launched a thousand ships?' A great man, Marlowe—dead at twenty-nine, stabbed to death in a tavern by double agents. Probably was one himself. Ben Jonson could also get the beat right in his prose: 'In Naples did I learn to poison flowers.' Jonson once killed a fellow actor in a duel. Writers in the old days brawled for their work."

But not now. Burgess offered an analogy from still another art form, the circus, to describe what's happening to writers today.

"We're all on a trapeze. You're with a publisher; the editor leaves; your book may or may not remain; suddenly you find your book swinging between two different houses. The situation in America for modern British authors calls for certain limited themes. Espionage. John Le Carré. Fiction about defecting diplomats, like my distant cousin Guy Burgess. We don't have many good British writers around. Henry James couldn't make it today."

Burgess believes that some of the old warhorses of grand opera ought to be brought up-to-date. He said that there are endless possibilities for rescuing opera from its tired, dated themes. "Oscar Hammerstein did it with *Carmen Jones,* and I myself have taken a new approach to *Rigoletto.*"

And how has he helped Verdi?

"Well, I've turned *Rigoletto* into a Mafia story."

Burgess relighted his cigar and declared, "Literature and

music depend totally on your sensibility. I find the sound of music in George Bernard Shaw, James Joyce, and Gerald Manley Hopkins. Unfortunately many writers today have music neither in their souls nor in their sentences."

[AUGUST 8, 1983]

ELMORE LEONARD

After writing twenty-three novels, Elmore Leonard has been discovered.

The critics are recognizing his work—including *LaBrava,* his latest book—as something special, moving him out of the category of mystery-suspense writer into that of novelist. It doesn't happen too often in times such as these, when a genre classification can brand a writer for life.

Hollywood, the paperback houses, and book clubs are also recognizing Leonard. And the reading public is finally catching up, too.

Leonard has been compared to Dashiell Hammett, Raymond Chandler, and Ross MacDonald but disclaims any literary kinship. "There's no similarity in style or subject matter," he says. "I was more influenced by Hemingway, Steinbeck, John O'Hara, and James Cain."

Of course, readers who have been following his recent books know it didn't happen overnight for this fifty-eight-year-old writer. Still, after making a living by his pen and wits for some three decades, Leonard says it's a nice feeling to be "discovered."

"I think that I'm really writing novels, not mysteries, but I don't want to sound pretentious," Leonard says. "I do like to read that I write clean prose and that my stuff is considered economical. Maybe I'm economical because I don't have that much to say." He pauses. "I'd love to have a real brilliant idea for my next book."

What makes Leonard's stories sound like the real thing compared to run-of-the-mill action stories? Critics and readers find that his writing is hard-edged and unsentimental, that while his characters are not heroic, their lives add up to social commentary, that their conversations sound absolutely authentic, and that his true-to-life characters and locales provide a look at ordinariness raised to the level of novelistic reality.

Leonard's fans are aware that he has the ability to fashion novels with narrative drive. He learned his craft by writing original paperback westerns for readers whose only demand was raw storytelling. In the last decade he has moved away from ordinary action stories; his professionalism has resulted in such novels as *Split Images, Cat Chaser, Stick,* and, now, *LaBrava.*

Like his other recent novels, *LaBrava* is set in southern Florida. That locale requires an explanation, because Leonard lives with his family in a house with swimming pool and vegetable garden in Birmingham, Michigan, a suburb of Detroit.

He says: "My mother runs a little motel in Pompano Beach that I bought sometime ago. Remarkable woman—she's eighty-eight. I visit her regularly. There's so much color in that part of Florida—retired people, Cubans, tourists, hustlers, and all sorts of crime. It's full of characters."

Leonard discloses a few tricks of his trade: "I try to get the right people assembled, give them right-sounding names, and then I'm off and running. The characters have to interact. Sometimes, when there's a confrontation, I don't know which way it's going to turn out—which character is going to come out of the house alive. Eventually the character has to tell *me.*

"The dialogue in my novels is mostly made up. It isn't the

words that are authentic but, rather, the rhythm of the way people talk. Only once in a while do I hear whole sentences spoken
when I'm listening for material. My wife picks up lines in the
ladies' room, which she repeats, and they sometimes find their
way into my stories."

Leonard was born in New Orleans and traveled in his youth
because his father worked around the country for General Mo-
tors. Eventually the family settled in Detroit. During World War
II Elmore Leonard served in the Seabees and then on a ship in
the Pacific. At the University of Detroit after the war he ma-
jored in English and graduated in 1950.

A few years later he made a deliberate decision to become a
free-lance and write either westerns or detective stories—
whichever would sell. Westerns won out after he had sold a
novelette to *Argosy* for one thousand dollars.

To support a growing family—he has five children—Leonard
worked in an advertising agency for several years. Getting up at
5:00 A.M. and writing until 7:00 before going to his job, he produced two pages a day and turned out five westerns.

For a few years he left the book field altogether and went to
work writing educational films for the *Encyclopaedia Britannica* as a
means of putting bread on the table. That film training, he said, has
served him well in fashioning screenplays from his own novels.

A half dozen of his westerns and thrillers have been sold to the
movies. Leonard was on a roll of contemporary action stories,
using realistic backgrounds in modern Florida, and he decided to
abandon the imaginary world of westerns.

Leonard says: "Now I work a normal nine-thirty to six P.M.
every day, first writing in longhand, then polishing on a typewriter, later turning over my book to a typist. No, I don't get up
at five in the morning any longer. But it was that early discipline
during the struggling years that enabled me to keep going."

[OCTOBER 29, 1983]

WILLIAM KENNEDY

There is a sentiment abroad that if you drop a good reporter, or novelist, into a place where nothing is happening, something will happen. The writer's very presence in an ordinary locale brings out the extraordinary. The instincts of an original writer serve as the stimulus for inventive reporting or storytelling; magically, an original sees things anew, bringing freshness to the familiar.

Many people in New York City consider Albany nowheresville. But wait a moment. There's an author who is making everybody eat his words. William Kennedy's street smarts and Irish characters would remind one of the late James T. Farrell and Chicago if only Farrell had been a smoother writer. Kennedy's trilogy of Albany novels—*Legs, Billy Phelan's Greatest Game,* and *Ironweed*—has put his native town on the literary map. Saul Bellow, who helped give the novels a boost, has called the trilogy "memorable."

Kennedy transports his readers back to the 1920s and 1930s, but the faraway time is unimportant because the dialogue, the politics, and the characters seem so current. The author invites us to wander along the characters' streets, drop into their saloons and gambling dens, watch them vote as the powerful Democratic machine boss tells them to (or else). In case anyone still doesn't get his fictional message, Kennedy will address a partly autobiographical paean to his city in *O Albany!* And for readers who want still more, Kennedy told me he is now working on a historical novel about Albany in 1849, using some of the ancestors of the families in his novels and possibly carrying them up to the present.

Recently Kennedy spent some time in Manhattan, inhaling the sweet smell of successful used air around his hotel on Central Park South. He is working with Francis Coppola on the script of an original film about Harlem's old Cotton Club, complete with the kind of gangsters he has written about so effectively in his novels. Kennedy appears the least likely person to know about the underworld. He comes across as rather formal, friendly but reserved, like one of the priests in mufti of the Albany stories who are aware of what's going on in both their parishes and their wards.

Albany's own novelist knows about newspaper life and death. He started out as a sportswriter for the *Glens Falls Post-Star,* worked for the *Albany Times Union* on general assignment, left New York State for several years to work for the *San Juan Star* and then the *Miami Herald.* At the last paper, he first began writing fiction.

In 1975 the first part of Kennedy's Albany cycle, *Legs,* appeared. It was a fictional account of Jack ("Legs") Diamond, the 1920s gangster who had the foresight to be gunned down in Albany. "I wrote *Legs* eight times," Kennedy recalled. "I spent a lot of time researching the gangster era, but it's the last time I ever intend to research a novel. It's a self-propelling thing to sit in a library and go down so many false trails. Too much research can overburden the imagination."

Billy Phelan's Greatest Game, based on the 1930s kidnapping of the nephew of Albany's political boss Dan O'Connell, came out three years later, and *Ironweed,* about the homecoming of the fictional character Billy Phelan's Depression-era hobo father and much else, was published to acclaim.

Speaking like an author with a long memory, Kennedy said, "None of my first three novels was reviewed in the *New York Times.* When *Ironweed* came out, the good response to the other books was as if they never had been published before." It was Corliss M. ("Cork") Smith, his editor at Viking, who took on *Ironweed* after it had been turned down by several houses. This led to a revival of interest in the other Albany novels, which had gone out of print. All three have now been published as trade paperbacks.

Albany is Kennedy's Paris, Tangier, and Manhattan. As he puts it, "Albany became an inexhaustible context for the stories I planned to write, as abundant in mythic qualities as it was in political ambition, remarkably consequential greed, and genuine fear of the Lord. I saw it as being as various as the American psyche itself, of which it was truly a crucible. It was always a melting pot for immigrants as was New York or Boston, and it epitomizes today the transfer of power from the Dutch to the English to the ethnic coalitions."

Kennedy says that he came to realize that a novelist has to write about what he knows best. And so he discovered an old truth: The greatest fictional riches can live in the characters and neighborhoods of your own home place.

[NOVEMBER 13, 1983]

STEPHEN SPENDER

London

Stephen Spender is writing seven days a week. "Now, more than ever, I realize that I don't have much time," he said when I called on him at his house—a modest one in St. John's Wood, in London—shortly before his seventy-fifth birthday. He is assembling a new edition of his collected poems, preparing a book that is based on his translation of Sophocles' three Oedipus plays, staged in Cambridge last year; and working on his memoirs. "I'd like to reduce the book reviews and journalism," he said, "but I always seem on the point of having two articles to write before I can get around to writing poetry." Yet Spender appeared happy to be working steadily; pleased to be living by his pen instead of off his name.

Wearing an open-throated blue shirt and a brown sweater, he looked casually elegant. His blue eyes shone softly beneath the familiar shock of silver hair. Even today he could probably be recognized from Christopher Isherwood's description of him during his university days, over half a century ago, when he and Isherwood and W. H. Auden became friends: "He burst in upon us, blushing, sniggering loudly, contriving to trip over the edge of the carpet—an immensely tall, shambling boy of nineteen, with a great scarlet poppy-face, wild frizzy hair, and eyes the violent colour of bluebells."

Between the two great wars, Auden, Isherwood, and Spender, together with Louis MacNeice and C. Day Lewis, influenced an entire generation of poets and other writers. Spender, in particular, remains a symbol of the effort to balance art and political engagement—a struggle that continues for many writers in the Western world, who are seeking to demonstrate in print against the nuclear arms race. His turning point was the Spanish Civil War. In Spain he spent some time at the front, but his poetry was concerned more with the horrors of war than with its politics. "No poet of my generation wanted to be political," he told me. "We recognized the need to defeat fascism, but we also saw that the threat was to our literature. Later Auden tried to remove anything political from his poems, but I never tried to edit out my past, even when my past stuck to me.

"I've had funny experiences with immigration officers in New York because of my left-wing affiliations and the Spanish Civil War. The first time, when I came to the States to teach at Sarah Lawrence, I was questioned about my passport by an immigration officer and got a pleasant shock. 'Are you Stephen Spender, the poet?' he asked. I confessed that I was, and he let me through. Another time I carried an old passport, and the immigration officer said there was something wrong with it— something arcane from my past. There were two little dots on the passport, indicating some sort of radical affiliation. Then the officer surprised me. He asked, 'Do you know Auden?' I said that I did, so he admitted me without further questioning."

Spender and Auden frequently debated the role of the writer in wartime. "Auden thought that writers had no influence on politics, but that was nonsense," Spender said. He fetched two wineglasses, set them down, filled them, and went on. "Shakespeare, Goethe, and Dante all influenced ideas and events. By deciding to write in the vernacular, Dante helped to achieve

Italian unification. The same could be said about Goethe in Germany. It was Shakespeare's language that created the political inspiration to resist the Nazis during the Battle of Britain. Even though these writers were not political figures, their words counted. Don't you think that writers like Tolstoy and Brecht gave shape to events? Brecht was always trying to align himself with Stalin, because of his own anti-Fascist and anti-Nazi views, but he was basically concerned with human aspirations, and that is why his work endures."

Spender served in the London fire service during the Second World War. Later he wrote that London acquired "a regal dignity" under the flames. One of his fireman poems, "Epilogue to a Human Drama," celebrated that time:

> London burned with unsentimental dignity
> Of resigned kingship: those stores and
>   Churches
> Which had glittered century-long in dusty
>   gold
> Stood near the throne of domed St. Paul's
> Like courtiers round the Royal sainted
>   martyr.

At the end of the war Spender volunteered to serve in the British-occupied zone of Germany. He knew Berlin well, having observed it in the company of Isherwood during the early 1930s. "After the war ended, I was responsible for reopening the libraries and at the same time denazifying them," he said. "I remember one librarian who worked with me summing up my work in her own words: 'I must take all the books by Nazis off the shelves and put them in the cellars, Herr Spender, and bring up from the cellars all the books by Jews and put them on the shelves.' It was a fairly accurate job description."

Spender is still involved in the concerns of writers and their freedom around the world. His main activity in this sphere is serving as a director and on the editorial board of *Index on Censorship,* a bimonthly, published in Great Britain, that is partly subsidized by the British Arts Council and by the Fund for Free Expression, in New York. He was one of its founders, in 1972, and had earlier enlisted the support of friends, among them Auden, Henry Moore, Bertrand Russell, and Igor Stravinsky, to help get the magazine off the ground. Every issue contains a country-by-country survey of censored writers and banned books in the East, the West, and the third world. No nation is immune from exposure, he pointed out. A recent issue reported abuses by the Reagan administration, including the withholding of historical documents "under stringent new declassification rules." He helped to raise money for the magazine by giving poetry readings in the United States last year.

Although Spender takes no direct part in political affairs, he is very much aware of the trends in his own country and elsewhere. "If Reagan and the Politburo listened to humanity, they would not do what they are doing on armaments," he said. "Politics is too closely caught in the net of physical power today—as in the Falklands, where Mrs. Thatcher had to go out and defend them. Power may run contrary to the interests of ordinary people, and it can result in national paranoia. Toward each other, America and Russia display a hysterical paranoia."

Since many British authors and journalists support the activities of the Campaign for Nuclear Disarmament and the remarkable group of women demonstrating season after season against the missile base at Greenham Common, I asked Spender if their actions engaged his support.

"I am not a participant in the work of the CND," he said. "It appears to be old-style proletarian. I wish the writers in it would grapple with other things as well as with nuclear disaster—for example, attack poverty wherever it exists. The CND has a negative view—against the arms buildup—but it ought also to be concerned with improving the lot of people in the third world and with antipoverty programs generally. I'm sure the members hold those views as well, but it is not their main expression. I'm glad that the CND exists— it would be a scandal if it did not— but such actions need participation by both sides. As long as the Russians have their terrific military arms, I don't think the demonstrations will have a real effect."

As Spender stood up, I noticed a drawing of him by Henry Moore on a wall. He explained that it was made in the 1920s for a magazine to illustrate some of his poems, when both he and Moore were at the beginning of their careers.

"In any event, I could not help CND by joining them," he said. "I'm too much associated with the views of fifty years ago. As I get older, life comes to be like fiction: One sees terrible things happening to people one knows, to old friends. But I have no complaints. Auden and I rather belonged to a generation that did not complain. I have been very lucky. I am still earning my keep, making a living by writing. Touch wood."

[FEBRUARY 27, 1984]

DORIS LESSING

Doris Lessing, who is in the front rank of internationally acclaimed novelists, recently gave two talks in New York on literature, women and men, and similar puzzling matters.

The 92d Street Y Poetry Center was the first stop on her tour of this country and Canada. Since she is regarded by many of her readers as one of the high priestesses of the feminist movement, the women in the audience who questioned her after she had read two of her short stories clearly desired a strong statement to carry off into the night. Instead, politely but firmly, Lessing declared that women had missed a great opportunity since the 1960s to propel their rights forward more practically and less emotionally.

"I'm not disappointed because I didn't expect much to change," she said. "It was a violently emotional time then, but I would have liked to see a much cooler movement. An effort should have been made to work with men. How can you expect things to change if you're talking to yourself? I've never agreed that progress can be achieved by being separated from men; some of the greatest and most useful feminists were men. I suppose that things have improved for a certain limited class of women in the United States, England, and Europe, but others in the third world have not been touched."

Lessing, who has been mentioned as a contender for the Nobel Prize in literature, was pressed to identify herself with the characters in *The Golden Notebook* or *The Four-Gated City* or *Briefing for a Descent into Hell* or *The Memoirs of a Survivor.*

"If I were all of them, I would have had a fairly full life," she said. "I get cross with those who identify me—me, personally—with my characters. I finally discovered the right response. I say that I am totally and absolutely *all* of the characters in my books. It's a useful device even though the reaction I get is often instant indignation."

Lessing is frequently asked what she regards as another obvious, uninspiring question: Is your writing specifically related to women?

And she answers, "Not at all. I naturally wrote *The Golden Notebook* from the viewpoint of a woman because I am one. I tried to write a book that was a kind of map of the human mind. We tend to label and pigeonhole things. If men write books— I'm now going to strike a feminist and plaintive note—nobody dreams of saying that they're written from a male perspective or are antiwoman. But if a woman writes a book about the despair of human relationships, she is regarded as a kind of Mrs. Pankhurst the Fourth," referring to Emmeline Pankhurst, the turn-of-the-century British suffragist leader, and her daughters.

Lessing can draw on several worlds for her short stories and novels, and recently she has ventured into a self-created fictional world of planetary space. She was born in Persia in 1919, grew up in Southern Rhodesia, and remained there until 1949. Since then she has lived in London but occasionally travels abroad because she is published in many countries. Her African background has resulted in a number of stories deploring the color bar, touching on social reform, and advocating individual freedom. While her fiction can be hortatory, she follows traditional storytelling methods.

Today, in private conversation, Lessing seems much cooler

about politics—which still fascinates her—but she no longer considers her political bearings "leftist," as she once described herself and as some characters in her early fiction appeared to be. She seems now as independent in her political thinking as she is on the women's movement.

Lessing has gone from the realistic to the fantastic in a strange series of controversial novels, *Canopus in Argos,* that are space fiction narratives. These include *Shikasta, The Marriages between Zones Three, Four, and Five,* and *The Sirian Experiments.*

Why did she decide to leave the earth for these distant realms?

"What is happening in the world is so fantastic that it needs fantasy—a rebirth of the imagination," Lessing said. "It was inevitable that with the development of science would come a new literature. Technology has provided the basis for cosmic influence. But my books are not simply science fiction. They are related to the fantasy fiction of the past. I am going back to the origins of storytelling twelve thousand years ago, the way it all began, with fables, parables, legends, and fairy tales. Thomas More's *Utopia* more than four hundred years ago was in the tradition, describing an ideal state. Some of the works of H. G. Wells in this century continued fantasy writing.

"There have been dreams and fantastic ventures even in realistic fiction, as in *Jane Eyre,* where there are apparitions and she hears voices. In Thomas Mann's *The Magic Mountain,* the hero has dreams and even tries to pull back his brother from the other side of the grave. Mann himself was a realistic novelist, and he seemed uncomfortable writing these scenes. Today, because of the emphasis on realism, the novel has suffered severe impoverishment. I think that one writer can contain two worlds—the realistic and the fantastic—sometimes in the same story. I don't think my new books are either the pits or the greatest; the critics must be off the mark if they can't find a middle ground. The truth about my fantasy novels lies somewhere in between.

"Everybody is different—even writers. You have to learn how to use your energy and not squander it. In the writing process, the more a story cooks, the better. The brain works for you even when you are at rest. I find dreams particularly useful. I myself think a great deal before I go to sleep, and the details sometimes unfold in the dream."

She does not suffer fools gladly, only cordially.

"Beginners who are first starting out sometimes try to write a novel, but they won't do enough work on it. You only learn to be a better writer by actually writing. I don't know much about creative writing programs. But they're not telling the truth if they don't teach, one, that writing is hard work and, two, that you have to give up a great deal of life, your *personal* life, to be a writer."

[APRIL 22, 1984]

To the SS official who branded his left arm a few inches above the wrist at Auschwitz, he was No. 174517. Forty-one years afterward, he folds back his cuff and stares at his wristwatch to see what time it is. Above, the numbers on his hand never change. The time always reads: Auschwitz 1944.

No. 174517—Primo Levi, a major Italian essayist and novelist, author of the current and highly acclaimed books *The Periodic Table* and *If Not Now, When?*—was quietly talking about the SS and the camps, about memory and the need to bear witness to central experiences: life in the underground during the German occupation of Italy; life in a concentration camp; life as a wanderer in the wilderness of Europe during the postwar years.

If Not Now, When?, which won the Viareggio and Campiello prizes in Italy, chronicles the adventures of Jewish partisans as they fight back in the closing months of World War II in Eastern Europe and dream of finding freedom in Palestine. In *The Periodic Table,* the author uses his knowledge as a professional chemist to show the ironies of normal life after the concentration camp experience, including the discovery that a German businessman with whom he corresponds had been chief of a laboratory in Auschwitz.

What distinguishes Levi's work is his straightforward yet elegant writing; emotion is drained, overpowering truths surface. Saul Bellow says that in Levi's books "nothing is superfluous and everything is essential," and Italo Calvino says that his countryman and friend "bridges the two cultures of science and the arts."

Levi was born in Turin in 1919 and worked as a chemist specializing in paints and varnishes. In 1943, in German-occupied Italy, he joined a partisan band in his native Piedmont. "I was not a very good partisan," he says modestly. "The racial laws excluded Jews from carrying firearms. When my unit was betrayed by an informer, I was interrogated by Italian Fascists and handed over to the Germans. I was put on a train with hundreds of other Jews and sent to Monowitz-Auschwitz, the factory part of the camp that used slave labor. It belonged to I. G. Farben."

How did one survive the SS selection system that filled the daily death quotas?

"In my own case, three things enabled me to survive," Levi says. "First of all, luck. I did not get sick. It was very dangerous to have a disease. In the last days before the camp was liberated by the Soviet Army, I did contract a fever when other inmates had to march and die from freezing and starvation. Because I was sick at the right time, I was left behind and managed to recover.

"Then my profession. In November 1944 the Germans needed chemists. They asked who was one and actually gave me a chemistry examination while I was a slave. So I was given a job in the synthetic-rubber factory. In this way I became a specialist. Before then I had been an unskilled laborer.

"Finally, in the factory I met an Italian bricklayer who also was from the Piedmont region. I was assigned to a squad erecting a wall. The bricklayer, who was not Jewish, had been working in France and then was transferred to Germany. When he noticed that I was an Italian, without speaking, he brought me bread and soup. Not only me but others, too."

Levi shakes his head, remembering. "The bricklayer who saved me was a strange, sad man. He was affected by the slavery and slaughter. After the war he went back to Italy in despair and began to drink. I tried to rescue him, but he slept in the snow and died. He felt a compulsion to help someone in the death camps. I named my son, Renzo, after him."

After the war Levi returned to his profession again. He married, and his wife, Lucia, helped to bring him back to normal life. Today their son is a physicist, and their daughter a biologist. In a state of depression when he first came home to Italy, Levi decided to free himself of the memories. This led to his book *If This Is a Man*. He turned to writing full-time ten years ago. How could he remember all the details after so long?

"I write from memory," he said. "It would have meant instant death to be caught with a pencil and piece of paper in the camp. But I have not forgotten. My mind is like a mine that has yet to be mined out. I remember phrases uttered by Hungarian friends. I remember Polish phrases. I don't know Hungarian or Polish, but dying words are fixed, like a tape recording."

Levi, who is now writing more about the overwhelming experience of life under the SS, says, "There is a Yiddish proverb that goes 'Troubles overcome are good to tell.' Life is a texture of victories and defeats. If you haven't experienced at least a victory and a defeat, you are not a full-grown man."

[MAY 27, 1985]

ISAAC BASHEVIS SINGER

A cup of coffee and one fried egg with Isaac Bashevis Singer urging, "Eat, eat," like a character in a Singer tale. He was talking about his latest collection, *The Image and Other Stories,* at his favorite table overlooking the street scene in a neighborhood restaurant (the sign advertises "Home Cooking") on Manhattan's Upper West Side. It seemed like a perfect background for a Nobel laureate.

What makes for a good story?

"Tension, meaning suspense. Good writing is rare—rare among Jews, rare among Gentiles. Storytelling to me is the very essence of writing. When I read Genesis, I think how beautifully it is written: full of suspense. Take the story of Joseph."

Are all your stories set in the old country?

"Quite a number take place in the United States. But the characters speak Yiddish. I came here when I was already thirty-one, so my characters have deep roots in Polish life. Of course, the modern Jew has all the problems of man generally."

Do you translate your own stories?

"I usually work closely with a collaborator to put them into better English. At the end they read, 'Translated by the author and someone else.' The English translations are very important to me because they are used for other languages. My son, who lives in Israel and is a journalist, translates the stories into Hebrew. Translation is always a problem but always a pleasure."

How do you dream up such an endless number of stories?

"There are powers who take care of you. If you're a doctor, you get sick people; if you're a lawyer, you get cases; if you're a writer, the Almighty sends you stories, sometimes too many."

When do you do your writing?

"Lately, since I got the Nobel Prize, between telephone calls. I write in Yiddish with a leaky pen on lined paper. Now that I am eighty, it is becoming harder to write, but I love it."

Where do your stories usually appear?

"I am happy that this morning two of my stories were accepted by *The New Yorker* and will probably run there soon. Every Friday they give me a page in the Yiddish-language weekly the *Forward*. I worked there as a journalist for many years, and it did not hurt me. If Moses had been paid newspaper rates for the Ten Commandments, he might have written the Two Thousand Commandments."

Do you have a chance to read other writers?

"For me, the greatest American writer is Edgar Allan Poe. I first read him in Polish. Some professors here know him but don't appreciate him. I think he was a genius. Jack London, when he was good, he was excellent. I read *Call of the Wild,* in Yiddish; the translator could not spoil it."

What will happen after Yiddish disappears as a language?

"I said in my Nobel talk that Yiddish has been in trouble for the last five hundred years and it will still be in trouble for the next thousand."

[JUNE 30, 1985]

ANATOLY N. RYBAKOV

Anatoly N. Rybakov, who is speaking on campuses across the United States, has completed a major new novel that is set in a time of turbulence in Stalin's Moscow before the war. To students of Soviet literature and nuance, both his book and his visit are noteworthy.

For Rybakov is a popular author in the Soviet Union; his books are regularly turned into television plays and movies. In the West what he writes is considered a mirror of life in his country—and a reflection of what sensitive subjects authors can expect to be published.

Rybakov and his wife, Tatyana, a former magazine editor who regularly edits his work—"She's tough, we argue, and then make up in the kitchen," he said as she looked on, smiling, during a talk in New York—are in this country together for the first time. Five years ago, when his wife was denied permission by Soviet officials to accompany him to London for the British publication of *Heavy Sand,* his best-known novel in English, he refused to go without her.

Lecturing in the United States, Rybakov is discovering that a

Russian writer need not be a dissident or in exile to be appreciated by American readers. Faculty and students in Russian-language and European literature courses are familiar with *Heavy Sand,* a story about the courage and resistance of a Jewish family in the Ukraine during the Nazi occupation.

"I invented nothing at all in that book," he said. The author grew up in Moscow in an assimilated Jewish family. Russian and French were spoken in his home; he knows no Yiddish or Hebrew. *Heavy Sand* is his only book that has not been turned into a film or television play. It is also his only book whose predominant characters are Jewish. Otherwise, he said, "my work can be seen on large and small screens."

Rybakov came here at the invitation of Oklahoma State University and a dozen other colleges. He sees his presence here with his wife as symbolic of a more liberal attitude toward the arts and literature in the Soviet Union—an optimism commonly voiced these days by visiting Soviet artists, but one that has proved unwarranted in the past.

Rybakov is built low to the ground—not unlike the armored vehicles he commanded as a major in the Soviet Army during World War II. His wife, a dark-haired, stylish-looking woman with an artistic air, spent her first day in New York going through the Museum of Modern Art.

Just before leaving for the West Coast, Rybakov said that his new novel, *Children of the Arbat,* was autobiographical and derived its title from the Moscow neighborhood where he grew up. The protagonist is a college student, Sasha. According to reports by editors and writers in Moscow who are familiar with the book, it covers a whole era, blending actual and fictional characters, in the manner of Herman Wouk's *Winds of War.*

The long, complex novel examines aspects of Soviet life in 1934, a time when the first postrevolutionary generation of Russians reached maturity. Rybakov said the novel looks at the idealism, and the realities, of Soviet life. It ends with the assassination of Sergei M. Kirov, the party boss in Leningrad, for which many historians blame Stalin; the murder was the signal for the worst of the Soviet purges.

Rybakov said that the characters in *Children of the Arbat* dealt with different layers of society and reached the very top.

Including Stalin?

"Da!"

The book has not yet been published in the Soviet Union.

"Its fate is being determined as we speak," Rybakov said. "I think the signs are favorable. I believe it can have a strong impact among readers in Russia. I'm convinced the outcome will be positive for publication."

If for some reason the novel was not brought out by one of the publishing houses in his own country, would he allow it to be published first in the West?

"My people need this novel; *my country* needs this novel," he said. "It should be published at home first.

"For a professional writer in the Soviet Union, it works this way," he explained. "First, you have to have something to say; that's the main thing. Second, it's a matter of who publishes you. If your book has real stuff in it, readers will ferret it out, even in a Siberian journal. But if it isn't real, it doesn't matter whether or not it's first published in *Novy Mir,* it won't help.

"For example, *Heavy Sand* was first serialized in *Oktyabr,* a less well-known literary monthly than *Novy Mir,* which had printed two of my previous books. But they turned down *Heavy Sand.* Since it first came out in 1978, it has been published twice by Soviet Writer, the Writers Union publishing house, in a mass-market edition by Friendship among Nations publishing house, and again in a special belles-lettres edition last year."

Rybakov, who graduated from the Moscow Institute of Transport Engineering in 1934, joined the army in 1941 and remained in uniform for the next five years, fighting all the way to Berlin. He was thirty-seven before beginning to write full-time. Since then he has received several state honors for his writing, including the 1951 Stalin Prize for the novel *Drivers.* His first book, *The Knife,* published in 1948, has been printed in thirty-nine languages. It is an adventure story that relates how children lived in the early 1920s, after the Bolshevik Revolution. "All my books are adventures," he said, "but they also have a social viewpoint."

His ten books have given him and his family a comfortable life. He has two cars and an apartment in Moscow, and he occupies a country house in the Writers Union colony at Peredelkino, outside Moscow.

"The comforts come from my movie and television writing," he said. "It is unusual to live this well simply from books."

As for *Children of the Arbat,* Rybakov is confident it will be published in the Soviet Union—sooner or later. [It was published a year after our talk.]

[APRIL 26, 1986]

LEONARDO SCIASCIA

Racalmuto, Sicily

Leonardo Sciascia's farmhouse sits half hidden on a hillside over-looking a landscape of vineyards and olive groves deep in south-central Sicily, near the town where he was born. But he does not have a telephone or keep a car, and his house has no address. To visit the writer regarded by European critics as one of Italy's most distinguished novelists, it's almost necessary to make a wrong turn or two first. One such turnoff near Racalmuto led me to a cul-de-sac named Via Pirandello—a symbolic accident.

"I don't want to explain too much in my novels," Sciascia said, and a similar answer might have come from Pirandello or some of the artists on his walls who practiced the art of leaving out, thereby forcing the imagination to fill in.

Sciascia's metaphor for his reality as a regional writer employs art. "I write of an imaginary country which you can think of as being Sicily, but only in the sense in which an artist friend of mine explains when he says, 'Even if I paint an apple, Sicily is there.'" With a tiny smile, Sciascia adds, "And the worm that is eating the apple from within."

"At the moment I'm working on a book about Pirandello,"

Sciascia says. "A dictionary that will include everything about him and his work: the names of his characters, his stories and dramas, biographical details, and the personalities in his life. I've written one book about Pirandello and Sicily. I'm also thinking about my next article for *L'Espresso*. I write a monthly essay for the magazine on almost anything—literature, politics, history."

He reaches into the bookshelves in his living room—which hold editions of works by Shakespeare, Borges, and Pirandello—and finds a copy of his latest novel, *La Strega e il Capitano* ("The Sorceress and the Captain"). The eighty-eight-page book was published in Milan; it might be a few years before it appears in English.

"After I collect my material, I write very quickly," Sciascia says. "When I begin a novel, I know everything about it—including the actual words and sentences. I outline rather carefully. That means I make very few changes—*pochissimo*—when I get down to the actual writing. This novel was first serialized in a Milan newspaper, but I didn't like the way they did it. They broke it into sections just for the sake of suspense, like a cliff-hanger. A book has to be read straight through."

Readers who look forward to his books sometimes wonder if he writes too slowly. "I type with only one finger of one hand, my right index finger," he says. "I keep one typewriter here in the country and another just like it at the apartment that my wife and I share in Palermo. I type about four pages a day. After every page I take one cup of coffee. Three pages, three cups. Sometimes a fourth page is the one that I've written the day before."

He has a ready response to the occasional criticism that some of his novels, at least in length, are more in the nature of novellas, that he does not go the long distance. He puffs on his English cigarette. After a moment: "Well, there are thick writers and thin writers. Stendhal was the first thin writer. I share with the late prince of Lampedusa, the Sicilian author of *The Leopard,* a love for Stendhal, though his writing greatly differs from mine. You can categorize most novelists in one way or another. Stylistically I think of novelists as baroque or not baroque. Faulkner was baroque. Hemingway, despite appearances, was also baroque. Lampedusa, part baroque, part not. Conrad, not baroque. Thoreau, baroque. Whitman, baroque. Saroyan, baroque."

And himself? "Not baroque."

How does he know so much about many of the major American authors? Sciascia says he educated himself by reading whatever he could get his hands on that had been translated. He is not a university graduate, and when offered an honorary degree from the University of Palermo several years ago, he turned it down. With a half wink he says, "So far I've managed to write without one." For most of his working life, he served as a schoolteacher in Caltanissetta, not far from Racalmuto. He became a full-time writer only at the age of forty-six.

Two distinguished names in modern Italian literature—Elio Vittorini and Italo Calvino, both no longer living—are linked to his career. Vittorini edited an anthology of American literature that originally was suggested by Sciascia. And Calvino became the first editor to accept Sciascia's stories.

Sciascia thinks very little of the popular American writers who have turned out commercial books about the Mafia. He did not finish *The Godfather* because he found it "tawdry." In several of his own novels and essays mafiosi appear in an evil light. "The Mafia here is rooted in Sicilian ideology," he says. "Mafiosi have a sense of superiority. It's an attitude that contributes to their criminality. Lampedusa once wrote that the Sicilians regard themselves as the salt of the earth."

Isn't he afraid that the Mafia will harm him because he has exposed them in his writings? "The mafiosi aren't interested in literature," he says. "Normally the Mafia confines itself only to a very well-defined danger." Sciascia smiles. "They're not worried about me. Who knows? The Mafia might even be proud that I'm a Sicilian writer."

[AUGUST 26, 1986]

AHARON APPELFELD

Jerusalem

Aharon Appelfeld, author of *To the Land of the Cattails,* posed his own rhetorical question: "Is there a danger of the Holocaust being overtold in literature?"

Without pausing, he responded: "The answer is no. The Holocaust is a central event in many people's lives, but it also has become a metaphor for our century. There cannot be an end to speaking and writing about it. Besides, in Israel everyone carries a biography deep inside him, including myself. I write about individuals more than about the Holocaust."

Appelfeld, who lives in Nevasseret Zion, a small municipality of two-family houses on the outskirts of Jerusalem, is one of his country's internationally recognized novelists. He was talking about his latest book to appear in English. Among his other novels that have brought him a growing readership in the United States and Britain are *Badenheim 1939, The Age of Wonders,* and *The Retreat.*

"Mainly I write Jewish stories, but I don't accept the label 'Holocaust writer,' " he said. "My themes are the uprooted, orphans, the war. I write about the Holocaust because I grew up in that time. Of my twenty books, perhaps one-third are on the Holocaust period, one-third on Israel, and one-third on Jewish life in general. One of my interests is the Jewish intelligentsia, the Jews who lost their culture in Eastern Europe and became vulgarized. I am not a politically oriented writer. I have my say in fiction, and I think I say a lot. I find that fiction is more permanent than other forms of writing. Literature is endangered when it becomes only a trumpet."

He described *To the Land of the Cattails* as a story about the relationship between a thirty-four-year-old mother and her adolescent son on the eve of World War II.

"In a sense it's a love story," he said. "People who lose their parents when young are permanently in love with them." The two main characters wander on a Kafkaesque journey of innocence and fear through the author's native Bukovina, in the region between Romania and the Ukraine that is now part of the Soviet Union.

The novel is partly autobiographical, but Appelfeld said he has no desire to go back. "First of all, there are no Jews there now," he said. "It's border Russia, and I'm an Israeli." The "land of cattails" in the title stands for the area he came from—"a place of water and trees with all kinds of water plants," he said. "In Freudian terms, it symbolizes the yearning to go home. But as Thomas Wolfe said about going home again . . ."

Although the characters in *To the Land of the Cattails* are fictional, their feelings are rooted in the reality of his experience and the wandering of his imagination.

"I am writing from memory, like Proust," Appelfeld said. "A writer can invent, but if it's not inside you, you cannot invent. My mother was killed by the Nazis when I was eight years old. My father was sent to a work camp and then deported to the Ukraine. I escaped from a concentration camp and spent three years in hiding, wandering and eventually becoming attached to the Russian Army as a kitchen boy.

"I was in permanent danger. The Ukrainians were the worst

because they helped to round up the Jews. I survived in the fields and forests. Sometimes I worked as a shepherd or taking care of broken-down horses. I lived with marginal people during the war—prostitutes, horse thieves, witches, fortune tellers. They gave me my real education.

"Things became better toward the end of the war when I lived with the Russian Army, peeling potatoes and working as a junior cook. It was a drunken cavalry unit, very wild, but they treated me as a human being. I was lucky; some of the Russian officers were Jewish and sympathetic. I worked my way to refugee camps in Yugoslavia and Italy. When I was sixteen, in 1948, I went to the new state of Israel. Then, when I was twenty-eight, I discovered that my father had survived, and we were reunited in Israel."

Appelfeld learned Hebrew before going to Israel; it was the first language he had ever studied.

"I suppose it makes a difference to use words that are acquired and not your original language," he said. "It probably causes me to simplify my narrative voice."

He first began teaching at a kibbutz, where one of his students was Amos Oz. Married and with three children, Appelfeld is now a professor of literature at Ben-Gurion University.

Appelfeld said: "A wise man once observed, 'I learned what I know.' And it's true: You cannot learn what you don't know. I lived through the Holocaust as a young boy. I'm very happy to be a Jewish writer and to write in Israel. For me, it's the essence of humanity."

[NOVEMBER 15, 1986]

THOMAS FLANAGAN

In fiction rooted in history, a novelist uses but transcends fact. This is what happens in a hefty novel (size: 824 pages; number of real and fictional characters: 107) that was preceded by trumpets of critical acclaim.

The Tenants of Time, a second novel, is written by Thomas Flanagan, who lives in a frame house built in 1754 in Setauket, Long Island, and who was born across the Sound, in Greenwich, Connecticut. Around the campus of the State University at Stony Brook, Long Island, where he has taught English and American literature since 1979, he is better known as Professor Flanagan.

Flanagan's first novel, *The Year of the French,* which won the National Book Critics Circle fiction award in 1979, took him about five years to write and came to 512 pages. *The Tenants of Time* took eight years, or, put another way, about 100 printed pages a year.

Right from the opening paragraph of *The Tenants of Time,* the reader is given a sense that the novel has grandeur and spaciousness and mystery. Through a character's perspective, the last line of that first paragraph also plants the author's historical notion about events in Ireland: "He had fallen in love with the past, a profitless love."

Flanagan told me: "I think that in a serious novel of this genre, history itself becomes one of the subjects. And Ireland could be considered a character in the novel."

The Tenants of Time begins in 1867, the year of the Fenian Rising, which was intended to establish an Irish republic, and continues through the downfall of Charles Stewart Parnell, the nationalist leader, in 1891. There are multiple narrators, each following different destinies, and action that embraces the aristocracy and the peasantry, in Dublin, London, Venice, and immigrant New York and Chicago.

Flanagan goes to Ireland every summer with his wife, Jean, and often does his historical research in the archives of the National Library in Dublin. "Joyce used to work there, too," he said, letting that thought sink in. "As you remember, he set one of the scenes in *Portrait of the Artist* in the library."

Flanagan talked about technique in historical fiction. For example, speaking of a major battle scene in the novel, he said: "I invented it, but every detail is based on something that happened that day, fused into a single event. I also made up three or four ballads, but they are typical of a real style. One kind of ballad that still exists is called a come-you-all because it typically begins, 'Come all you gallant Irishmen.' I also invented newspaper articles after spending many hours going through contemporary newspapers here and in Ireland—all allowed in the novel form."

Early in his story, Flanagan boldly makes reference to 1904, Joyce's Bloomsday year in *Ulysses*.

"I picked 1904 purely for plot reasons, because I wanted my narrator to come on the scene," the author said. "Then, about halfway through the book, I said to myself, 'Hey, the novel opens in 1904!' Joyce's Stephen Dedalus went to Clongowes Wood College, an excellent Jesuit school in County Kildare. Joyce himself didn't graduate from there because his family had to remove him for lack of funds but my character, Patrick Prentiss, stays the course.

"Then I thought, 'Why not the Bloomsday parallel?' I even had an idea of having an *unnamed* novelist come on the scene and saying, 'I'm thinking of writing a novel that takes place during a single week.' And having my character reply, 'Why not a single *day?*' But that would have been pretty corny."

About his dual life as teacher and novelist, Flanagan said: "I bumped into a poet friend of mine and I told him that it was funny but for the first twenty-five years that I was teaching, I didn't write any fiction. And he said that during that time I was probably thinking about the story, working it out, writing the novel without knowing it.

"I remember the morning I started *The Year of the French*. I was sitting in my office at the University of California at Berkeley, where I taught between 1960 and 1978. Suddenly I picked up a piece of paper and began writing in longhand and that night typed out what I had written at home. Eventually that became the prologue of the novel."

"When I teach," he said, "I'm a professor, not a creative writer. The gears simply get changed. I go into my study upstairs and work on the novel. Different parts of the brain are involved in the two processes. Sometimes when I'm writing fiction I think, 'My God, this is the easiest job I've ever done. Why didn't I get started on it earlier?' "

[JANUARY 10, 1988]

TONI MORRISON

Responding to my early call informing her that she had won the Pulitzer Prize for fiction, Toni Morrison caught her breath, asked for a few minutes to form her thoughts, then said: "I think I know what I feel. It's true that I had no doubt about the value of the book and that it was really worth serious recognition. But I had some dark thoughts about whether the book's merits would be allowed to be the only consideration of the Pulitzer committee. The book had begun to take on a responsibility, an extraliterary responsibility that it was never designed for."

By "extraliterary responsibility," Morrison was referring to the controversy surrounding a statement on her behalf, signed by forty-eight black writers and published in the *New York Times Book Review*. The statement, prompted by Morrison's having not won the 1987 National Book Award, for which she had been a finalist, decried the fact that she had never won the Book Award or the Pulitzer Prize. Some authors thought that this goodwill gesture might not have served her best interests, but the award made that question moot.

Literary figures agreed that *Beloved* had won the Pulitzer Prize on its own much-deserved merits as a novel. Morrison herself said she believed that the award was made despite "gossip and speculation."

"In the end I feel as though I have served the characters in the book well, and I have served the readers well, and I hope the Pulitzer people are as proud of me as I am of them," Morrison said.

At the center of *Beloved,* is Sethe, a runaway slave who kills her daughter, rather than have the child captured and raised as a slave. The novel is very close to Morrison's life and feelings. It begins before the Civil War and continues into the Reconstruction era. She said that her grandfather was born a few years before Lincoln's Emancipation Proclamation and therefore was a slave in Alabama.

Asked about the statement the writers published in her behalf, Morrison said: "That was a kind of blessing for me—to know that irrespective of the formal recognition that is available to a writer, they appreciated the worth of my work to them. They redeemed me, but I am certain they played no significant role in the judgment. If anything, it was in the teeth of speculation and gossip that the Pulitzer committee was forced to operate. They apparently resisted it."

For the first time Morrison revealed that she did not know anything about the statement before its publication. Only afterward did she suspect that some of her friends were doing something as a consolation prize for her not winning the National Book Award, which had been won by Larry Heineman for his novel *Paco's Story.*

Beloved was also a finalist for the National Book Critics Circle Award, which was won by Philip Roth for *The Counterlife.* (Morrison received the Critics Circle Award for *Song of Solomon,* published in 1977.) And she was one of the three contenders for the Ritz Hemingway Prize in Paris.

Paula Giddings, a journalist and historian who was one of the signers of the statement for Morrison, said: "It's wonderful and very important because the prize acknowledges not only a great American novelist and intellectual but a vision of the American experience in this country. The great American novels have to deal with the meaning of oppression and love, and black women are at the eye of that storm. *Beloved* is a great American novel."

Ralph Ellison, author of *Invisible Man,* which received the National Book Award in 1953, did not sign the statement. Ellison said: "Good for Toni. I was pretty annoyed with some of the stuff that's been boiling about her not getting recognition. Toni didn't need that kind of support even though it was well intentioned. Sometimes it's a matter of luck. Look how long Hemingway and Faulkner had to wait to get their just rewards. I never won a Pulitzer. I think that an artist like Toni who has talent leaves it to the book. This proves that Toni could get the prize, and she will get others in the future."

[APRIL 1, 1988]

[ELLISON'S PREDICTION CAME TRUE. TONI MORRISON WON THE NOBEL PRIZE IN LITERATURE IN 1992.]

ROBERTSON DAVIES

Robertson Davies was asked if there was a particular quality that
distinguished the Canadian novel from those written in England
or the United States, where his books grow increasingly popular.

"Ah, that is a very tricky question," the Toronto author told
me. "What used to be called a Canadian novel was a kind of
prairie frontier story, but it was phony. In the plot, people came
to the land; the land loved them; they worked and struggled and
had lots of children. There was a Frenchman who talked funny
and a greenhorn from England who was a fancy pants but when
it came to the crunch, he was all courage. Those novels would
make you retch.

"I remember one novel years ago, which I won't identify,
that was hailed as the great Canadian novel," he continued.
"There was a rather strong girl in it from northern Europe. She
loved the land so much she used to go out in the spring, open
her blouse, root in the soft loam, and get closer to the Canadian
earth. With so many people living in towns and cities now,
those country dweller novels are no longer representative. The

Canadian novel today is a more introverted novel without that pure outlook on life."

Davies was in New York to talk about *The Lyre of Orpheus,* which is the concluding novel in his third trilogy. His novels have been acclaimed in his own country, the United States, and Europe. He said that Canadian writing has more of an affinity with that of the Scandinavian countries than with the works of its close North American neighbor.

"I like to think that Canada's greatest writers are Ibsen and Chekhov," he said, laughing. "When I go to Scandinavia and step off the plane, I ask myself if I've really left home. There is that very powerful sunlight and the wind-torn pine trees. The real Canadian is a northerner. I'm a great believer in the influence of the climate and the land in plays and novels. Even though I've been coming to the States for many years, I don't write about New York. The city alarms me."

Davies's works have been grouped into trilogies: the Salterton trilogy *(Tempest-Tost, Leaven of Malice,* and *A Mixture of Frailties);* the Deptford trilogy *(Fifth Business, The Manticore,* and *World of Wonders);* and, now, with the addition of *The Lyre of Orpheus* to *The Rebel Angels* and *What's Bred in the Bone,* what will be known as the Cornish trilogy.

"It's nonsense to call them trilogies, but that's how they're put together for the convenience of the reader," he said. "They cover the same locale, and in some cases the same characters recur; but they're all independent novels. The second, the Deptford, is much more of a trilogy because it follows three boys whose fates are bound together. The mainspring of my last three novels is the Cornish family fortune. But I always think of a trilogy as more of a story where the same theme runs through from one book to the next."

Davies said that in *The Lyre of Orpheus,* the third Cornish generation is trying to dispose of some of its money by giving to the arts. The Cornish Foundation wants to do good works, which provides a takeoff point for the author to satirize foundations, operatic music, and a cast of self-seeking characters that includes gypsies, blackmailers, and cuckolds—and all on the author's Ontario home ground, too.

The musical, theatrical, and scholarly background of *The Lyre of Orpheus* enabled Davies to draw from his own experience. The author has been a journalist, actor, playwright, drama and literary critic, advocate of Canadian authors' rights, and master of Massey College at the University of Toronto. He is the first Canadian writer to become an honorary member of the American Academy and Institute of Arts and Letters.

"I might have been a musician, but I didn't have a crumb of talent," he said. "Some people are stagestruck. I was music-struck. Both my parents were journalists and keen musical people. I had a very good musical education and played several instruments—the clarinet, flute, anything I could blow."

Now that he devotes himself to the novel, did understanding music help his writing? "Yes," he replied, "the composition of music makes you aware of the composition of sentences; it gives you a sense of form and economy and tells you when to continue and when to shut up. Music is elegant structure. Writing can be, too, as in Thomas Mann's novels *Buddenbrooks* and *The Magic Mountain,* which greatly influenced me."

Did he detect any new theme breaking through in the Canadian novel?

"I don't see one," he said. "Of course, every author pursues his or her own theme in fiction. Margaret Atwood, Mavis Gallant, Alice Munro, Mordecai Richler—they all go their own way. There's no central theme in the Canadian novel because there is no unifying Canadian problem. Government can influence themes. You can see it in the nineteenth-century Russian writers who had to suffer under oppressive regimes.

"Canada doesn't have an oppressive government. It's hard for people in the States to recognize this, but Canada is a socialist monarchy, like Sweden, Denmark, and Norway. We have a leg in both camps, a limited welfare state and also a monarchy that causes a kind of clinging to the past. Canadian writers are different from the Americans, who have an optimism in their writing that we don't have."

Did his own novels have a central theme?

"I do have one," Davies said, "but I hesitate to mention it because it's so ordinary: the growth of a life, of a spirit, from innocence to experience. But isn't that the theme of every serious novel?" He paused. "I have a favorite motto that I sometimes inscribe for friends in Celtic. It goes: 'A man must be obedient to the promptings of his innermost heart.' "

[DECEMBER 29, 1988]

E. L. DOCTOROW

E. L. Doctorow, author of *Billy Bathgate,* was reflecting about the colorful characters who populate his novels.

"You know, for years people have told me, every book of mine is different—and I've always known that to be not entirely true. I told Jason Epstein, my editor, to whom I dedicate the book, that I have a repertory of souls who appear in different bodies and different situations in my work. But *I* recognize them."

Once again, as in his 1975 novel and movie *Ragtime,* the author is blending real and imaginary characters. The fictional Billy Bathgate takes his name from Bathgate Avenue in the Bronx, a lively market street in the mid-1930s, the time of the novel. The plot centers on Billy's involvement with the real-life gangster Dutch Schultz, whose name is also an alias; his real name is Arthur Flegenheimer.

Doctorow noted that from one novel to the next, there were echoes that a close reader of his work could discover.

How close is the fictional Billy Bathgate to the young E. L. Doctorow, who also once lived in the Bronx?

"Only in the sense that every book encodes your life am I in this one, too," Doctorow said. "My criminal career as a boy was nonexistent. If I claimed any firsthand knowledge about crime as a way of life, it just wouldn't be true."

We were talking on a pier in the shadow of the Brooklyn Bridge, watching the sea gulls soar above the tugboats chugging along. It seemed an appropriate place to capture the mood of his new novel because in its dramatic opening scene the dapper Bo Weinberg, a double-dealing associate of Dutch Schultz, is being carefully fitted for a pair of cement shoes on a tugboat in the darkness of New York Harbor.

"I don't know if you remember that when Edgar in *World's Fair* goes to the library in the East Bronx, he's nervous because this is a dangerous precinct," Doctorow said. "There are a lot of tough boys around, and this is where Dutch Schultz used to live. So that novel actually mentioned him in passing."

In the tugboat scene, as Billy Bathgate looks on, a beautiful woman in a white evening gown comes up from belowdeck to see her doomed gangster lover for the last time. Was there a kinship here to *Loon Lake,* his 1980 novel about a young man cast adrift during the Depression?

"Yes, there's a woman in a white dress in *Loon Lake,* too," Doctorow said. "As a private train passes by, the young man sees her holding a satin dress up to her shoulders. That image stays with him as the train goes through the woods."

But there the resemblance to *Loon Lake* ends, he said. "Here, I'm concerned with Billy, a personable young man, bright, energetic, enterprising, but he has this attraction for the disreputable. He's receiving a sentimental education in matters of the underworld. He has all the best instincts and virtues, but the result is a kind of inverse Horatio Alger, because his mentor, Dutch Schultz, has high audacity."

Doctorow said he had no intention of writing a 1930s gangster novel in *Billy Bathgate,* but Dutch Schultz's career in the old neighborhood did fascinate him.

"I liked the sound of the name Dutch Schultz, and I was

intrigued by his activities," he said. "You know, he was given that name as an award by his fellow juvenile delinquents. The first Dutch was the leader of the old Frog Hollow gang, so when he got it, he was proud. Dutch was a loner who was reluctant to affiliate himself with the downtown mobs, with a cartel, and that interested me. I liked that independence even though eventually it led to his destruction. Gangsters lead tribal lives, bonding among themselves. That tribalism underlies all criminal enterprise to this very day."

Did he have in mind that the old mobs like the one run by Dutch Schultz extend to other criminal activities, such as today's white-collar criminals?

"Well, when you write a book, you must stay within its system," he said. "However, one of the great gifts a book can give you are metaphoric possibilities. The resonances and references expand the system that you've constructed, and the meaning grows larger and larger. You write the book, and if you write it well, it begins to reward you.

"There's a certain ethos abroad in the land today in which there's no strict demarcation between evil and good. The most surprising people have been caught in dubious activities in the last ten years, all the way up to the level of our national life. I mean, writers don't exist in vacuums. I've written this book at this time, so there's some kind of music going back and forth between me and what I find. There are perfectly reasonable and proper individuals whose business it is to pollute the atmosphere and to make atomic weapons and to keep secrets from the public.

"I take a light pass at it in the book, but I would rather the reader discover things for himself," Doctorow said. "I'm ready to be instructed as much as anyone. What you see in the book is thievery, extortion, voracious sex, murder." He paused. "All the major components of our spiritual life today."

How much research was necessary to establish the world of Dutch Schultz for the novel?

"I learned just enough to write about him," he said. "I don't like documentary fiction. There is a transforming thing that happens to some of the facts you learn. When I reach that point, that's where the book starts. Where mythology and history converge, that's where I begin my novels."

Doctorow watched the striving tugboats move along the East River. Then he laughed and said, "First you write a book, and then you invent a way to talk about it."

[MARCH 9, 1989]

OCTAVIO PAZ

Octavio Paz, poet-diplomat, won the Nobel Prize in literature in 1990—the first Mexican writer to achieve the high honor. Since many authors and civilians consider the Nobel political and geographical, I thought it would not be impolite to ask him if the prize was for him or for his country. He didn't seem surprised, and his answer was philosophical: "To me, a poet represents not only a region but the universe. Writers are the servants of language. Language is the common property of society, and writers are the guardians of language. A writer has two loyalties. First, he belongs to the special tribe of writers. Then he also belongs to a culture, to his own country. Mine is Mexico."

I asked him what made a poet a poet and a person a human being.

"We are all born alone. There is a need for human communication, and a poet writes about the human condition. A poet has to write well, and a writer is also a critic of society. But I am only one voice among many voices. A writer is a descendant of other writers. When I was very young and later in life, I read foreign poetry by Eliot, Breton, Montale, Ungaretti, Calvino, the

French surrealists. Surrealism is dead, but surrealism lives in different form."

Paz, who has represented Mexico as an ambassador in France, Japan, and India, has found time to write more than twenty-five books of poetry and prose, including *Sunstone, The Labyrinth of Solitude, The Double Flame: Love and Eroticism,* and *The Collected Poems of Octavio Paz.* His poetry usually stands apart from politics.

Should poets play a role in the political life of their countries?

"Sometimes poets do mix in politics, not always with great intelligence. Don't forget, the greatest poet of all, Dante, had a lot of political ideas in his poetry." Many writers have been diplomats. For example, Pablo Neruda and St.-John Perse. I believe in the need to be an *homme engagé* at certain times. This has been a very cruel century. I speak for the generation of the 1930s, which has suffered from fascism, Marxism, and revolution. Think of the Nazis, with their concentration camps where millions of Jews and other innocent people were put to death systematically. Think of the poets who died in Stalinist prisons and the oppression visited upon so many men, women, and children by Latin American dictators. Now we are seeing a return to freedom in many corners of the world."

I wondered what poetry can contribute to the making of a new political order.

"Not new ideas, but something more precious and fragile: memory. In each generation the poets rediscover the terrible antiquity, and the no less terrible youth, of passions. In the schools and universities, where the so-called political sciences are taught, the reading of Aeschylus and Shakespeare should be obligatory. Poets nourished the thought of Hobbes and Locke, Marx and Tocqueville. Through the mouth of the poets there speaks—I emphasize *speaks,* not *writes*—the other voice, the voice of the tragic poet and the buffoon, the voice of solitary melancholy and of joy, of laughter and of sighs, the voice of the lovers' embrace and of Hamlet contemplating the skull, the voice of tumult and silence, mad wisdom and wise madness, the intimate murmur in the bedroom and the surging crowd in the square. To hear that voice is to hear time itself, the time that passes and comes back still, transformed into a few crystalline syllables and sentences."

Whether using Spanish, French, or English, Paz employs a polished prose characterized by the balanced phrasing of a diplomat. In this respect, his spoken and written voices are almost indistinguishable. When writing in Spanish, he uses a classical meter without rhymes. "Blank verse," he says, "like Wordsworth or Milton. But I use rhythm in my poetry and calculate everything."

Of his poetic laurels, Paz says, "The Nobel Prize is not a passport to immortality. But it does give a poet the possibility of a wider audience, and all writers need to broaden their readership. The Nobel is a kind of challenge. I hope to continue to be self-critical. I've been around too long—after all, I was born in 1914—either to stop writing or to be the sole judge of my own work."

As for his view of the state at the end of the twentieth century, Paz says: "Our democratic capitalist society has converted Eros into an employee of Mammon. Profit, gain, and the materialism of our society are weakening the human condition. Democratic capitalism applied to literature is mass production. Stores are filled with novels with big titles; they sell huge amounts for three months, then disappear. In a sense, clandestine poetry is a critique of the consumer society."

And where does he stand politically today?

Paz smiled, then said: "Disillusioned leftist."

[OCTOBER 1990]

ERIC AMBLER

London

Eric Ambler is hard at work on his next book. Repeat: Eric Ambler, author of a succession of classic thrillers, beginning in the mid-1930s, that blazed a trail for two generations of writers of political suspense novels, right up to the present moment.

"Not long ago, while I was doing a program for the BBC overseas service, one of the bright young broadcasters mentioned my writing, and then he said, 'That book is by Mr. Eric Ambler, and incredible as it may seem, he's still alive.' "

Recalling the remark, Ambler cocked an eyebrow above his pale blue eyes and somehow looked more amused than chagrined that anyone seemed surprised at the news he was still aboveground. "I suppose there are some young people around . . ." he said, but then didn't bother to finish the thought.

Ambler makes you realize that a seasoned writer doesn't retire. He continues to write, in his head, if not on paper, even if he's in his eighty-sixth year.

We were dining in a pricey restaurant five minutes by taxi from his home in London's W1 country. Rather than talk about longevity, Ambler preferred to talk about literature, with emphasis on the future: his novel in progress. He looked elegant in his blazer, white shirt with widespread collar, pink-and-blue-striped tie, and brown suede shoes. A walking stick ("it was the arthritis thing that got me"), parked next to our banquette, was his only visible concession to age.

Obviously the BBC broadcaster was unfamiliar with the internal-combustion engine that drives a professional writer's life. And he probably didn't know much about Ambler's score of books, including—to name only one handful—*Background for Danger, Epitaph for a Spy, A Coffin for Dimitrios, The Intercom Conspiracy,* and *Doctor Frigo.* These thrillers led Graham Greene to call himself one of Ambler's "disciples" and John Le Carré to say that Ambler's novels were "the well into which everybody had dipped."

I asked him why he continued hitting the keys of his typewriter every day instead of resting on his laurels and royalties.

"Why do I write? Because I enjoy it. I don't really need the money," Ambler said matter-of-factly. For a decade after World War II he was a multithousand-dollar-a-week screenwriter in Hollywood. Among his screenplays were *A Night to Remember, The Wreck of the Mary Deare,* and *The Cruel Sea,* for which he received an Academy Award nomination. "I did a lot of film work, including fourteen drafts of *Mutiny on the Bounty* for Marlon Brando, but I got off the credit," he said.

The provisional title of his novel in progress is *The Scapegoat.* Ambler said: "It takes place during the last thirty years in Austria, Italy, England, and America. One of the characters deals with a firm in the States that handles commodities futures in St. Petersburg. With all its retirees, Florida is as good a place as any for losing your money. Nearly all the characters are lawyers. What's unusual for me is that it's mainly about women. I've never before written a book in which the women are dominant." He thought for a moment. "No, there are no intelligence people in it. There are civil servants, but no spies. My books always start out as straight novels. But then they move on."

His explanation sounded deliberately vague and circuitous, as if Ambler were acting as a double agent to conceal the contents of *The Scapegoat* from his imitators in a crowded field. If so, he was entitled.

In the past his thrillers were praised for their backgrounds as well as for their endangered characters. As a matter of technique did he spend much time researching his material in various locales?

"No, I don't visit the countries I write about for the purposes of research; that's fatal for a novelist. It's like taking a camera along. When you do, you're worried about what the camera is seeing. It becomes a filter between you and the story. If you go to a place and say to yourself, 'I'll get material here,' you're not really receptive to stories; you're not likely to digest. I know of writers who make a lot of notes. The trouble later is that nearly all the notes go into a book. The better way is to write the story and then go to see if the research is right!"

Although a sense of irony ran through our conversation, Ambler didn't speak in the dark tone that characterized the dialogue of some of his early protagonists. "I don't consider myself a political person," he said. "I don't really like politics very much. I don't admire the democratic process; it's not very uplifting."

If not democracy, what system did he like? His reply surprised me: "I admired the New Deal in America. I lived in the States for eleven years and in Switzerland for sixteen years, but I remained a British citizen. A lot of Americans hated Franklin D. Roosevelt, but he was an ideal president."

The Roosevelt era called to mind Ambler's five years of wartime service, beginning as a private in the Royal Artillery and ending as a lieutenant colonel with the War Office, writing and producing training and documentary films in England and Italy. Captain John Huston borrowed Captain Eric Ambler to work on the famous American documentary *The Battle of San Pietro,* an experience that included getting bombed and strafed on the

Italian front, but he received no credit for his contribution. The film was suppressed during the war because it showed a burial detail; the army told the uniformed filmmakers that it was not the business of the War Department to make antiwar movies. Did he work on any other films with Huston in wartime or later in Hollywood? "No," Ambler diffidently said, "once was enough with John."

He remembered that after the war, when he was living in Dover, his neighbor Noël Coward offered him some advice: "Forget all this film nonsense. Write more books. You think that you will always be able to go back to the well. That may be so, but remember this, if you stay away too long, there will come a day when you will go back and find the well dry."

Ambler did manage to balance some novel writing with screenwriting for several years, but his reputation remains with his books. I asked him what he thought about his prolific career and if (as with most dedicated popular writers) it included any regrets.

Without hesitating—or throwing me a sharp elbow—he replied: "I've never looked at myself from the outside. I have enough to do to look from the inside. I'm still writing every day. I don't see myself as a portentous figure; in 1979 or 1980 I received an OBE from the queen, an Order of the British Empire, as if there were a British Empire. If you don't have ambitions, you don't have disappointments. The object of the exercise is to entertain. I'm really not kidding. Mark you, I do not argue that means being a stand-up comedian and going for belly laughs. In my writing I'm not trying to reach for intelligent scholars but for people who read books and people who go to the movies. Of course, most serious novels have some relevance in a social context."

Ambler rose slowly, reached for his walking stick, straightened his shoulders, and, in the style of an enigmatic Ambler character, said: "I'm a moderate elitist—or an elitist moderate. I dislike modesty; it's unbecoming." Ambler paused for a moment, then smiled and added, "He said with becoming modesty."

[SEPTEMBER 1994]

JOHN UPDIKE

John Updike said something challenging and surprisingly controversial about the United States mails during a PEN assembly in New York a few years ago that has lingered in my mind. It seemed to tell something about his origins in small-town America and, by a stretch of the imagination, about the yearnings of the characters in his *Rabbit* and other novels. So when we connected after he returned from the golf course near his home in Beverly Farms, Massachusetts, I asked him if he still felt the same way about those blue government mailboxes down the street from where we all live.

He did. Updike reminded me that his talk was given during the Reagan era, when anti-intellectualism hovered in the air around the White House. The theme of the PEN assembly was built around a peculiar question: How does the state imagine? Inevitably many of the speeches by the writers were political attacks on Washington, but Updike responded to the question in an antipodal, long-range way.

"My talk caused a lot of criticism of me personally," Updike recalled. "Do you want to hear exactly what I said?" He repeated the part that struck some PEN members at that time as politically evasive. It went: "I thought about the romance of the mails when I was a child. Later in life I would send a manuscript away, and I sometimes would get praise and money in return. It is the United States mails, with the myriad routes and mechanisms the service implies, not to mention the basic honesty and efficiency and noninterference of its thousands of employees, that enable me to live as I do and to do what I do. I never see a blue mailbox without a spark of warmth and wonder and gratitude that this intricate service is maintained for my benefit."

Updike's words sounded apolitical, yet they emphasized individuality and freedom of opportunity. "Politically I've always been a Democrat, like my parents," he said, "and I was a member of my Democratic town committee. That doesn't prevent me from following my own instincts. Similarly, I've been a churchgoer most of my life, but I try to write the truth whether it pleases the churchgoing side of me or not."

Updike's novels, short stories, poems, and essays have often drawn blood from the veins of striving middle-class America. Writing about main street in the eastern United States, he comes across as a more tolerant Sinclair Lewis, but without the biting Babbittry. Updike was born in 1932 in Shillington, Pennsylvania, a suburb of Reading, and has frequently tapped into that background for his fictional characters.

In his early stories Updike was a chronicler of American boyhood and of the nostalgia of loss. His later work is a commentary on the country's social mores, particularly the complex relationship between morality and sexuality. The Updike canon includes suburban adultery, the crises of religious alienation, and the encroaching shadow of death.

I wondered if there was some unifying theme that bound all his books together.

"I'm not sure that's for an author to say," Updike replied. He thought for a moment. "I think I've tried to seek out the corners of human experience. The adventures of ordinary middle-class life. The tensions between our need for safety as against our need for freedom. Outward and inward tenderness. Love, certainly . . ."

How did he strike a balance among his novels, poems, and other forms of writing?

"Poetry is an impulse. I haven't written many poems lately. But a novel is monopolistic and greedy. Once I begin a novel, I usually don't write short stories because the characters can get mixed up. But I tend to violate my own rule. You can write short stories in the middle of the night.

"Book reviews? I have one or two at *The New Yorker*. Book reviews are afternoon work. I take book review assignments when some author excites me and I want to share the good news, or when I want to write an essay, or when a book compels me to read and learn. But I try to give priority to a work of fiction."

We talked about research and fiction writing. He said that for *Brazil,* his 1994 novel, he did go there for a week, but it was travel for the imagination, not a grand tour. "So many books are praised for their research, but research in itself doesn't make a novel," he said. "There has to be some authentic truth at the center."

Updike, who studied at the Ruskin School of Drawing and Fine Art in England after graduating from Harvard, still keeps his paints around the house. "But I'm too lazy to paint," he said. "Painting is great training for a writer. It makes you more visually alert and forces you to compose. A book has to have a shape. It settles in a reader's mind. I think of my books as canvases. I paint with words."

Unlike many heat-seeking authors who close like missiles on targets of opportunity in the tabloids, Updike doesn't promote himself in the gossip columns. You won't find him at the famous watering holes of literary New York or at the publicity-driven softball games played by aging scribes in the Hamptons. After serving as a "Talk of the Town" writer for *The New Yorker* for a few years in the mid-1950s, he left Manhattan in 1957 and moved to a small town not far from Boston.

"New York was not going to help me unpack my shadowy message," Updike said.

For whom does he think he's writing?

"In the past I've said that I aim in my mind not toward New York but to a vague spot to the east of Kansas. I think of the books on library shelves, without their jackets, years old, and a countryish teenaged boy finding them and having them speak to him. The reviews, the stacks in Brentano's are just hurdles to get over, to place the books on that shelf.

"Now I'd say I write for some teenage boy who is like I was during my reading days—that kind of innocence. I would go to the library and read a whole shelf of Wodehouse and Bernard Shaw. As you get older, your audience diminishes. I could say I write for my editor, Judith Jones, to please her. She believes that bookmaking is special, that there is a sort of childlike impulse behind the arts. I generally don't think of my books and what they do. I hope they stir up, move the reader, because books are also an act of seduction."

Updike said that he was now writing a "multicultural" novel that begins in 1910 and moves onward. Aware that Updike is one of the country's most prolific authors and time is a writer's most precious asset, the interviewer closed his notebook.

"Back to the novel," Updike said.

[MARCH 1995]

LITERARY

LANDSCAPES

PALERMO:

LAMPEDUSA'S LEOPARD

Palermo, Sicily

If, at dusk, you walk along Via Butera, stalking the literary heritage of *The Leopard* in Palermo, this old area along the depressing waterfront appears at first glance incompatible with the elegance of the prince of Lampedusa's classic Italian novel. Architecturally, it is a mixture of Baroque and Bombed. At set-out tables rugged workers and their women sit on ice-cream chairs before the dinner hour, sipping fruit crush and sugared espresso; behind them the flaked stone buildings come almost to the edge of the cobbled streets.

Before a stranger can find the street number for himself, a knot of residents in a narrow alleyway guesses his mission. They thumb toward a dark doorway within a dark courtyard, saying: *"Il Gattopardo, Il Gattopardo. . . ."* The Leopard, The Leopard. A character, in an international best seller, bearing his nickname, has become an address in modern Sicily.

This venerable building is the Palazzo Lampedusa. Here a manservant, with Quasimodo-like gestures, greeted me and quickly pulled a handbell with two sharp rings of warning. Lights suddenly illuminated a grand double staircase. At its head, in black silk and austerely statuesque, stood the author's widow, the principessa di Lampedusa. An anachronism: The cultivated princess is a psychoanalyst, former president of the Italian Psychoanalysts' Association, who practices her profession in an office below these stairs.

In the high-ceilinged library the walls are lined with literary works in French, Italian, and English, acquired by her husband and herself over a period of fifty years. Leather-bound volumes on one wall are from the library of the original "Gattopardo," the author's great-grandfather, the model for the prince of Salina in the novel. And editions of *The Leopard* from many countries are stacked on a table. "I can see what interests the Japanese in the Gattopardo," the princess says, "but why cowboys from Texas?"

This fading room from another era—where Lampedusa wrote a good part of his novel in longhand "sitting in the chair in which you are sitting"; this ghostly palace—once owned by his ancestor a hundred years ago and reacquired after the original Palazzo Lampedusa was destroyed (a bitter note here) by bombs aimed at the German headquarters; even the teeming street below the palace windows—with its still-encrusted emphasis on a titled aristocracy despite a striving lower-class mobility: All seemed appropriate background for the literary mysteries of *The Leopard*.

With the publication in the United States of Lampedusa's second posthumous book, *Two Stories and a Memory,* much of the mystery behind the Italian grandee's novel, talent, and life is uncovered. Here are descriptions of the actual places that served as fictional inspiration for *The Leopard,* with photographs of how they are today. Here is proof, in two short stories, that Lampedusa was an artist of the highest order—a more exclusive aristocracy. There is a foreword by E. M. Forster. "Leopards do not hang on every bush," says Forster, but he is grateful for the "personal legacy" Lampedusa has left him as a reader. In a few telling sentences, Forster makes us understand why Sicily, this passed-by island and prince, captures our fancy: "Will Man succeed in poisoning the solar system? It is possible: generals are already likely to meet on the moon. What Man probably won't effect— and here I am getting back to *The Leopard*—is the disintegration of the outer galaxies. How soothing, in that grand novel, are the astronomical passages where the hero, who has wasted his Sicilian day, repairs to his telescope, and looks up through the Sicilian night at the stars. What a release to the human spirit in its struggle against human possessiveness!"

The brightest jewel in the new book is "The Professor and the Mermaid," a fantasy revealing Lampedusa's learning and powers of imagination. The heroine, Lighea, is the daughter of Calliope, a voluptuous sixteen-year-old mermaid. She is, like Angelica in *The Leopard,* timeless. In a hidden bay near Mount Etna, she emerges from the water, speaking Greek. She and a young Greek scholar begin idyllic days together, and her voice and magical love are so pure that never again can he look at a mortal woman. The construction of this short story is so natural that it puts to shame all the fashionably effortless short stories. And its language, in this exquisite translation, soars with such phrases as "the candor of the dawn sea" that are part of the spell cast by the author.

"The Blind Kittens," the second fictional piece, is the first chapter of an uncompleted novel that might have been a sequel to *The Leopard.* It is almost enough, but would (as hinted) the nineteenth-century villains have turned into twentieth-century *fascisti?* We shall never know. Here the emphasis is on a rapacious family of peasants building a dynasty—the opposite of the angle of narration of *The Leopard.* Here, too, Lampedusa is preoccupied with "the tragic jerking of a class which was seeing the end of its own landowning supremacy, that is, of its own reason for existence and its own social continuity."

Most of *Two Stories and a Memory* is concerned with a memoir called "Places of My Infancy." This nostalgic recollection of the palaces, high style of living, seeming respect of the peasants (un-

questioned by the author) for their baronial keepers, corresponding noblesse oblige, and evocations of places and manners
of semifeudal Sicily serves as a pony to the creative processes
behind *The Leopard*. The places can be recognized, and it is a rare
experience for the reader to be let behind fictional scenes in this
way. Even in these samples of travel and sociological writing,
one feels in the presence of a man of letters.

Lampedusa died before *The Leopard* was published. He lived
and worked in Palermo, following his walk from Palazzo Lampedusa on Via Butera past the bombed ruins of his boyhood
palace and toward the literary cafés and Flaccovio's clublike
bookstore. One also learns—so that was why!—that the hand-
bells rung by the bent porter to the princess at the top of the
stairway are in code: "twice for a man, once for a woman, and
one and a half times for a priest."

The principessa di Lampedusa told me, as we sat in the library
of the Gattopardo, that there is a third and last work by her
husband: a series of literary discussions, or lessons, on sixteenth-
century and seventeenth-century French literature, which she
calls *Invitation to Read French Letters*. After he had written these,
he began to write *The Leopard* and "Places of My Infancy." She
encouraged him to do so to lift him from the despair of seeing
the rubbled Palazzo Lampedusa. The stone palaces crumble; the
books survive.

[NOVEMBER 25, 1962]

SAIGON: GREENE'S AMERICANS

Saigon, South Vietnam

Now that it's all over but the writing, I wonder if the bearded Hindu who owned the Salamath Book Center, toward the waterfront at the end of Rue Catinat in Saigon, will be able to stock Graham Greene's *The Quiet American* again. When I casually asked him for a copy one steaming night, during the height of the war's fury nearly a decade ago, a look of terror crossed his face. I tried to reassure him that my interest was only literary, and no, I didn't work for any American intelligence agencies. With a smile of doubt he said that he did not carry any books written by Mr. Greene—"especially not that one."

Would I be interested, perhaps, in another book he had in great quantity? It was also about Vietnam and came highly recommended. I noticed that it was a study subsidized by the military-oriented Rand Corporation and the Michigan State University Advisory Group, which was linked to the CIA. He admitted that books in his store, some of which he imported directly from American publishers, were subject to censorship; he did not wish to offend the South Vietnamese authorities or their allies. I bought a pre–Dien Bien Phu copy of Booth Tarkington's *Alice Adams* stuck away in the back shelves and bade the wise bookseller good evening.

About twenty years ago, in 1955, Greene finished his novel, which is set in Saigon during the Eisenhower-Dulles era, when the United States began to substitute its zeal for French colonialism's dying gasp. At the time Americans were there as advisers instead of combatants, but Greene's "Economic Aid Mission" diplomat, Alden Pyle, was already spoiling for a fight to save the Vietnamese from communism and themselves. In the story Pyle talks about the old colonial powers, England and France, to two of their fictional representatives: "You two couldn't expect to win the confidence of the Asiatics. That was where America came in now with clean hands."

Other prescient observations in the novel were a blueprint for the sixties and seventies: "What a lot of money it costs, I thought as the pain receded, to kill a few human beings—you can kill horses so much cheaper." "One shouldn't fight a war with children." "What I detest is napalm bombing. From three thousand feet, in safety. You see the forest catching fire. The poor devils are burned alive." "I'm not fighting a colonial war. We are fighting all of your wars, but you leave us the guilt."

A few days after not buying *The Quiet American* in Saigon, I learned that the character after whom Pyle supposedly was patterned still served as an adviser on matters of pacification to the United States ambassador. And so, on another evening, I went to an anonymous villa in a wealthy area of Saigon to have a *rhum et citronnade* with retired General Edward Lansdale. In the fifties he had played a visible role here as an expert on counterinsurgency and intelligence. Now the tall, graying ex-CIA man lived more quietly, trying to establish links to the various factions in South Vietnam. A half dozen civilian aides worked with him; one, whose name meant nothing to me then, was a pleasant chap introduced as Daniel Ellsberg [of later *Pentagon Papers* fame].

"In those days I used to see Greene sitting around the Rue Catinat," General Lansdale said. "He was writing for French and

British newspapers. Once he became offended because I was greeted by a husband-and-wife team of American correspondents, and for some reason he banged the table. I had the feeling that Greene was anti-American."

With some trepidation, I refilled my glass and asked Lansdale if he thought that Greene had conceived his naïve, villainous character after observing him.

"Greene knocked him off in the first chapter," Lansdale said, amused.

The novel begins with the discovery of the American's body by a Greene-like character ("God save us always," the English correspondent remarks, "from the innocent and good") and then proceeds with the story.

"No, it couldn't have been me. I'm alive and well."

After dinner I strolled on Tu Do Street (Rue Catinat had been changed to a Vietnamese name when the French departed), following the course of Greene's own character in the novel: "One trishaw driver pedalled slowly by towards the river front, and I could see lamps burning where they had disembarked the new American planes." The scene was not merely similar; it was practically identical a decade later.

Twenty years after *The Quiet American* said in fiction what took so long for others to discover in fact, Greene's epigraph in the novel, quoting Lord Byron, still cuts to the heart of the matter: "This is the patent age of new inventions/For killing bodies, and for saving souls,/All propagated with the best intentions."

[JUNE 8, 1975]

[BASED ON A JOURNEY TO WARTIME VIETNAM IN
MARCH 1966.]

WEST EGG:
FITZGERALD'S GATSBY

∞

West Egg

"The scene is the Long Island that hangs precariously on the edges of the New York City ash dumps—the Long Island of gaudy villas and bawdy house parties," wrote H. L. Mencken of Scott Fitzgerald's *The Great Gatsby* when it came out in the mid-twenties.

Well, not quite, old sport.

The valley of ashes? Changed, something like Robert Moses's reputation, into a park in Flushing, hard by a potholed boulevard celebrating the fast-food franchised way of life: the Colonel's chicken delight, towers of pizza, fish-and-chipperies, Big Macs and Burger Kings in Queens. The overbred lady golfer in the novel who cheated to win? Possibly—in one of the towns up the North Shore around Republican Oyster Bay, where the family heirlooms include white and brown spectator pumps inherited along with the choker of pearls.

And Doctor T. J. Eckleburg's yellow spectacles staring down godlike on an advertising billboard? Definitely—at last count, there were a half dozen competing optometrists along the main drag in West Egg, which nonliterary maps show as Great Neck, Long Island.

The tantalizing Fitzgerald quest involves places rather than people. Surprisingly, one well-known biographer misplaced the Gatsby house, and predictably, real estate agents sell it often. I determined to see if I could find where Scott and Zelda had lived and to track down the real places only hinted at in the novel. Some conglomerate made a movie of *The Great Gatsby* a few years ago or, rather, a fashion show and house tour disguised as a movie. The trouble was that they filmed it in Newport, and anybody who consults the Port Washington timetable should know that there's no stop called Newport on the Long Island Railroad. You can't even get there on the expressway. It is true that Newport is more pretentious—it still calls a forty-room place a cottage—but then there is a catering establishment at the Northern Boulevard entrance to West Egg that looks like the Taj Mahal built on a mound of chopped chicken liver.

It is not just localism that makes me think that Scott Fitzgerald would have preferred the original West Egg for authenticity, even a half century after he rented here. The geography is pretty much unchanged (neither polluted waters nor apartment house builders on greensward have altered the outlines) since the time he called Great Neck West Egg and Manhasset across the bay East Egg in stunning description:

> Twenty miles from the city a pair of enormous eggs, identical in contour and separated only by a courtesy bay, jut out into the most domesticated body of salt water in the Western Hemisphere, the great wet barnyard of Long Island Sound. . . . I lived at West Egg, the—well, the less fashionable of the two, though this is a most superficial tag to express the bizarre and not a little sinister contrast between them. My house was at the very tip of the egg, only fifty yards from the Sound, and squeezed between two huge places that rented for twelve to fifteen thousand a season. The one on my right was a colossal affair by any standard— it was a factual imitation of some Hôtel de Ville in Normandy, with a tower on one side, spanking new under a thin beard of

raw ivy, and a marble swimming pool, and more than forty acres of lawn and garden. It was Gatsby's mansion.

For a long time, I had been curious about the actual location of these fictional houses. I was less interested in the personal artifacts of Fitzgerald's existence than in his creative process as a novelist: how he transplanted characters and emotions and even houses for the sake of verisimilitude.

The first part of the mystery was fairly simple: finding out where the Fitzgerald's rented between the autumn of 1922 and the spring of 1924. The address turned up in Andrew Turnbull's biography and letters: 6 Gateway Drive in the incorporated village of Great Neck Estates. "You must come stay with us in our nifty little Babbit-home at Great Neck," Fitzgerald wrote to a friend, adding that they were equipping the place with "very interesting flour sieves and cocktail-shakers." In his driveway was a secondhand Rolls.

The main focus of interest is the room over the detached garage where Fitzgerald wrote the opening chapters of *The Great Gatsby*. It is drab and surprisingly small, with a naked dangling bulb, two windows, and a bathroom—a place for a writer to describe wealth without living it.

The next piece in the puzzle—the site of the narrator's house in the novel—was easy to solve. It did not exist, except to serve as a locale for voyeurism. It was an amalgam of all the little gatehouses and boathouses and gardener's cottages of a crumbling era that still dot the undivided properties on both sides of the courtesy bay.

Nick Carraway rented it for eighty dollars a month, a bargain even then, because of its "consoling proximity of millionaires." The actual house that Fitzgerald-Carraway rented in Great Neck Estates is a few miles from the waterview of the unattainable that is essential geographically in *The Great Gatsby*. The real rent was three hundred dollars a month.

That left the most tantalizing and difficult question: Where was Jay Gatsby's house in West Egg?

I drove slowly along East Shore Road, the only area on the bay that looks directly across to East Egg. The Gatsby mansion had to be along winding East Shore Road, in an area little more than a mile in length. It was time to bracket my artillery. I knew that Ring Lardner, the great sports and short-story writer, had lived along the enchanted road, with his family of talented children. And so I got in touch with Ring Lardner, Jr., the distinguished (and blacklisted) screenwriter, for clues. He provided the details of Fitzgerald's creation in the 1920s and the facts.

"My recollection is that our house in Great Neck didn't have a street number, but it was easily recognizable by the fact that it was the first house inside the village of Kings Point coming from Manhasset," he said. "There was a road called, I think, Ravine Road, at right angles to East Shore Road, then an empty lot, which may not be empty now, and then our house, with a sharply terraced lawn in front and a steep driveway."

Check. The house still sits on a rise, overlooking East Egg, painted fading white and with an old-fashioned warmth. Next to it is the empty lot, turned into a play area with swings and seesaws. I spoke to a woman walking her dog, and she said that Ring Lardner's initials were carved in a tree on the property.

"The next house, second in a row of rather grand mansions overlooking the bay," Lardner recalled, "was the Herbert Bayard Swopes', where weekend activity was something like that at Gatsby's. My father and Scott spent a good deal of drinking time on our north porch watching this activity, and I believe this led to the concept of Gatsby.

"There wasn't, of course, much resemblance between Swope and Gatsby, though I do consider it significant that H. B. Swope, Jr., with whom I later roomed at Princeton, referred to Arnold Rothstein's widow as Aunt Caroline."

A few days later I invited myself into the former Lardner house and walked out on its windy north porch. I looked toward the area where the Swope place stood. It was no longer standing. The rather grand mansions overlooking the bay had been replaced by the usual zoned-for-an-acre ranch houses.

Yet peering eastward, through the screened porch, I could see the same view that Lardner and Fitzgerald and "Gatsby" had seen: the bay dividing West Egg and East Egg, dividing the new and old strivers, and the docks on the far, fictional side of paradise.

The rambling Victorian mansion had served the aims of literature. Its inspired location and storied parties, far more than its real and imagined towers, had captured the shimmering glitter of the glamorous twenties. Herbert Bayard Swope *père*, the fabled executive editor of the *New York World,* who preferred independence to objectivity, had rented it from Lottie Blair Parker, author of *Way Down East,* a pre–turn-of-the-century melodrama. Swope's son and namesake, a television producer, later told me that Clifton Webb's house had stood on the other side of his family's place. The Parker-Swope-"Gatsby" house, he recalled, had burned down at the beginning of World War II.

"Mr. Swope lives across the way," Ring Lardner once remarked, "and he conducts an almost continuous house party. It's almost impossible to work at times and still more difficult to sleep." But Lardner and Fitzgerald, tinkling glasses and pressing their noses against the windows of the rich who were different, were indeed working, making mental notes for their stories.

The old house is gone, but its dream survives.

On this bend in the waters of Long Island Sound, Fitzgerald's long vision saw something that transcended the elegance of the past and the size of the mansions and the manicured lawns: people who could smash things and retreat back into their money or their vast carelessness and—are there environmental echoes here?—then let other people clean up the mess. Standing for a moment along East Shore Road and looking across the courtesy bay, you can envision that green light turning to a warning yellow and wonder about "the dark fields of the republic," the orgiastic future.

[FEBRUARY 22, 1976]

NEW YORK:
MELVILLE'S MANHATTAN

A troop of intrepid scholars braved the cold the other afternoon to put up a bronze plaque on the side of a nondescript Manhattan office building just east of Park Avenue South. It reads:

HERMAN MELVILLE
The American Author
Resided from 1863–1891 at This Site
104 East 26th Street
Where He Wrote
BILLY BUDD
Among Other Works

They were members of the Melville Society, keepers of the flame for the great American novelist. Spouting white whales, imprinted in the design of the blue ties worn by several of the thirty-five men and women present, added a touch of color to the street scene. After searching detective work, the society, which has five hundred members and reaches devotees as far away as Japan, had finally pinned down the exact place where

Melville lived during one of his most productive periods.

Melville was a New Yorker, not a New Englander. There is another plaque for him on the site of a garage in downtown Manhattan, at 6 Pearl Street, where he was born in 1819.

As a young man he sailed out of Massachusetts and gathered material in the South Seas for *Typee;* he wrote the first draft of *Moby-Dick* while living in Pittsfield, Massachusetts, and then returned to New York, a sardonic, somewhat embittered family man, struggling for recognition as a writer. When *Moby-Dick* was published in 1851, it had received disappointing notices.

During the last twenty-eight years of his life, Melville lived in the one-family brick house on East Twenty-sixth Street. Here, while supporting himself as a customs inspector, he wrote his first volume of poetry, *Battle-Pieces,* and other poems and stories, but nothing that won as much fame in his own time as *Typee.*

"What about the best thing he ever wrote—his eighteen-thousand-word poem *Clarel?*" asked Professor Hershel Parker of the University of Delaware, one of the academics who had gathered on the sidewalk for the event. "He wrote it in 1876 in his house here. Why isn't *Clarel* on the plaque?"

"Because we couldn't include *everything,*" said Donald Yannella, chairman of the English department at the University of Southern Mississippi, who is secretary-treasurer of the society. "For the general public, we thought that *Billy Budd* would be his most familiar work."

"Fellow Melvillians," said Edward H. Rosenberry, an emeritus professor of the University of Delaware, the outgoing president of the thirty-six-year-old society. "As you know, *Billy Budd, Sailor,* was not published while he was alive."

"It didn't come out until 1924," explained the incoming president, Thomas Tanselle of the Guggenheim Foundation to a non-Melvillian.

Someone asked about Melville's working routine here, and Louis Zara, who is writing a biography, pointed to Professor Stanton Garner of the University of Texas at Arlington. In the branches of Melvilliana, Professor Garner is considered "the customhouse expert."

"Melville was a district inspector in the customhouse service," said Professor Garner. "He walked from his house west to the Hudson River. In later years his post was moved uptown along the East River. He probably took the Third Avenue el to work; it was already in existence in the 1880s. It's strange to think of this man, who once sailed in square-rigged ships, riding the el.

"He got into the customhouse right after the Civil War, one of the few men who obtained such a post without a political sponsor. The job he held was one of the lowest in the service—a thousand dollars a year. And he never got a raise; he still made the same thousand when he resigned in 1885. But he used his idle hours near the piers to write on little scraps of paper."

How did Professor Garner unearth these vital details?

"I've been spending a lot of time in Bayonne, New Jersey, where the federal records are kept," he said. "There's not too much. Melville was an expert on keeping his name out, which probably helped him to escape the perils of the civil service. Later in his career he had to wear a uniform while inspecting cargo. It's mind-boggling—Melville wearing a uniform that was just like a city policeman's."

Melville lived here with his wife, two daughters, and two sons (both died while the author occupied the residence). Paul Metcalf, whose mother was a Melville granddaughter, sent a postcard from Becket, Massachusetts, to Charles Neumeier, who teaches at Stuyvesant High School, approving where the Melville plaque was being placed: "Much better he should be a delivery entrance than an armory!"

The 104 East Twenty-sixth Street address today is the delivery entrance to the office building at 357 Park Avenue South. Right next to the plaque is the rear of the Sixty-ninth Regiment Armory building on Lexington Avenue. For many years, until research by Neumeier and Professor Yannella proved otherwise, many people thought that the armory rather than a business building had replaced the Melville house.

In tracking down the exact site, the Messrs. Neumeier and Yannella examined tax records in the Municipal Archives and old atlases. There was a certain amount of confusion caused by renumbering in the records; the 104 address had earlier been designated as 60 East Twenty-sixth Street.

Then the tax records unfolded the clues: The Melville home was in the city's Eighteenth Ward on Block No. 881. It occupied Lot No. 82. The listing for 1882 reads: "Owner, Elizabeth S. Melville; Size of Lot, 20 × 98; Size of House, 20 × 45; Stories, 3; Value of Real Estate, $6,500." At the time of Melville's death, the value of the property had gone up to seven thousand dollars. It was replaced in 1902 by a seven-story structure.

In 1890 Melville could look up from the stoop of his home and see a nude golden Diana, the mythical huntress, poised on one foot, aiming her arrow in his direction from her tower crown on Stanford White's gleaming new Madison Square Garden.

The Garden site on the northwest corner of Park Avenue South and East Twenty-sixth Street is the location of the New York Life Insurance building. The old Garden was razed in 1928, but Augustus Saint-Gaudens's *Diana* survives atop a grand staircase in the Philadelphia Museum of Art. And a movie Diana appears in the film *Ragtime,* in which Norman Mailer plays the role of Stanford White.

Melville, who had once lectured on the marbles of ancient Rome, may have approved of Saint-Gaudens's thirteen-foot *Diana,* mounted on a revolving base like a weather vane, hovering over his neighborhood. The scholars are not sure. However, one incensed newspaper, the *Philadelphia Times,* denounced the sculpture as representing "the depraved artistic taste of New York."

Among the scholars at a later meeting of the Melville Society at Baruch College was Jay Leyda, professor of film studies at

New York University and author of the two-volume work that Melvillians consider an essential research tool, *The Melville Log.* Professor Leyda said: "I've included every document I could find about Melville, and I've had to add material recently; there's always some new detail turning up. He was probably the best read of any American writer. Of course, questions have been raised about Melville's sanity."

Was the great novelist, whom fame eluded in his own lifetime, not sane?

"Well, insanity was a very broad diagnosis in those days," Professor Leyda replied. "He had family problems, and he couldn't make a living, and his work wasn't fully recognized. Let's put it this way: It was a miracle that he held on to his sanity."

On September 29, 1891, a day after the man who today stands in the front rank of American novelists died, the *World* wrote a short notice. The first sentence began: "Herman Melville, formerly a well-known author."

[JANUARY 19, 1982]

SANTA FE:
CATHER'S ARCHBISHOP

Santa Fe, New Mexico

For some travelers, there is a literary rhythm to their wanderlust: First, reading in advance about the places on an itinerary to heighten the anticipation as well as to gain what might be called "impractical" knowledge; next, with book in hand on the scene, looking up from the printed page and seeing how closely the words match the actual places; finally—and sometimes this can occur months after the trip is only a memory—reading about where they've been to deepen their knowledge and preserve the afterglow.

The annual guidebooks are fine for practical information, but travel literature, including fiction, serves to spark the imagination: Good literature isn't perishable.

On a recent visit to Santa Fe, New Mexico, instead of simply perusing the chamber of commerce material and the road maps, I prepared myself by closely rereading Willa Cather's *Death Comes for the Archbishop*. The 1927 novel turned out to be just the right literary-historical-geographical guide I was looking for.

The sun had set now, the yellow rocks were turning grey, down in the pueblo the light of the cook fires made red patches of the glassless windows, and the smell of piñon smoke came softly through the still air. The whole western sky was the color of golden ashes. . . .

Driving toward one of the pueblos surrounding Santa Fe, you discover how accurate an observer Cather was. Certainly the natural sites, the piñon trees and snow-fringed mountains and sunsets, are unchanged, and the old missionary churches, a central theme in the novel, are preserved and in use in the pueblos. The author's apprentice years included reporting; she had written for and served as managing editor of *McClure's,* the muckraking magazine, before the First World War.

You can envision why Cather, while first traveling on horseback in New Mexico in 1912 and during later visits, was captivated by the story of the Roman Catholic prelate—Archbishop Jean Marie Latour in the novel, Archbishop Jean Baptiste Lamy in fact—who came from France and had to accommodate the religion of Rome to the different lifestyles and spiritual search of Spanish pioneers and Indians. His story became the unifying metaphor for her that portrayed the historic Southwest fictionally.

In 1925, while staying at La Fonda Hotel (it has not changed too much in appearance, especially in its old part; the fine French bakery and croissant breakfast shop on the street level may well be an improvement) in the center of Santa Fe, Cather turned her mind to the novel. The idea supposedly came to her in a rush one evening at the hotel, but it probably had deeper roots. She gathered reminiscences from Spanish settlers and handed-down Indian tales in the pueblos, researched the church biographies, and traveled through the countryside that had once been the archbishop's domain.

"The longer I stayed in the Southwest," she wrote in a letter after the novel appeared, "the more I felt that the story of the Catholic Church in that country was the most interesting of all its stories. The old mission churches, even those which were abandoned and in ruins, had a moving reality about them; the handcarved beams and joists, the utterly unconventional frescoes, the countless fanciful figures of the saints, no two of them alike, seemed a direct expression of some very real and lively human feeling."

These sights and feelings are still there—in the novel and in fact.

D. H. and Frieda Lawrence had persuaded Cather to return to New Mexico after a ten-year absence. Alfred A. Knopf, Cather's publisher, had brought the three together for tea one afternoon in New York. The Lawrences invited her to visit their ranch. In 1922 the British novelist himself had been lured to Taos, a village of artists and writers that is a short drive northeast of Santa Fe, by Mabel Dodge Luhan. The New York heiress had moved to the desert, established a literary salon there, and taken as her fourth husband an Indian. Cather also lodged with the Luhans for a time.

In New Mexico Lawrence hoped to recapture the primitive "blood-consciousness" of man to combat materialism. A visitor can still see the much-photographed Taos pueblo with its "apartment house" levels, river running through it, and mission church that enchanted the novelists. The Taos ranch that Frieda Lawrence willed to the University of New Mexico is not far away.

"I never passed the life-size bronze of Archbishop Lamy which stands under a locust tree before the Cathedral in Santa Fe without wishing that I could learn more about a pioneer churchman," Cather wrote later, noting that his countenance expressed "something fearless and fine and very, very well-bred . . ."

One can find the cathedral in the pages of the novel. The archbishop speaks:

> I have an old friend in Toulouse who is a very fine architect. He cannot come himself; he is afraid of the long sea voyage, and not used to horseback travel. But he has a young son, still at his studies, who is eager to undertake the work. Indeed, his father

writes me that it has become the young man's dearest ambition to build the first Romanesque church in the New World.

A few blocks from La Fonda stands the cathedral—its Midi-Romanesque style incongruous against an almost uninterrupted landscape of mission and adobe-style architecture—that is a tribute to Archbishop Lamy. It was built by workmen brought from Italy and France to do the masonry and soaring interior construction. The cornerstone was laid in 1869, and the statue of the archbishop stands before the cathedral.

In the final chapter of *Death Comes for the Archbishop,* Cather wrote:

> This period of reflection the Archbishop spent on his little country estate, some four miles north of Santa Fe. Long before his retirement from the cares of the diocese, Father Latour bought these few acres in the red sandhills near the Tesuque pueblo, and set out an orchard which would be bearing when the time came for him to rest. He chose this place in the red hills spotted with juniper against the advice of his friends, because he believed it to be admirably suited for the growing of fruit. . . .
>
> Some years afterward he built a little adobe house, with a chapel, high up on the hillside overlooking the orchard. Thither he used to go for rest and at seasons of special devotion. After his retirement, he went there to live, though he always kept his study unchanged in the house of the new Archbishop.

The archbishop's "little country estate" is very much a part of the life of Santa Fe. It is now a fairly quiet resort called the Bishop's Lodge, with walking trails, horses, a swimming pool, orchards, and the same small chapel on the hillside. The archbishop's retreat was purchased by Joseph Pulitzer, the newspaper publisher, who preserved it. With the addition of two new houses the hacienda became a summer home for his family. In 1918 James R. Thorpe of Denver bought the property and turned it into the resort.

The little chapel is just as the archbishop left it, with a high vaulted ceiling and painted glass windows in frontier simulation of the stained glass in French cathedrals. The desk clerk at the lodge lends you the old key to open the door to the chapel. There is one modern touch: Weddings are held there now and then by special arrangement with the lodge and the archdiocese. Archbishop Latour (or Lamy) might well have approved the chapel's continuous use. So, too, might Willa Cather (1873–1947), who immortalized the archbishop and his Santa Fe surroundings in her remarkable novel.

[FEBRUARY 20, 1983]

TOKYO:
MURAKAMI'S MAJIME

Tokyo

As a new generation of Japanese novelists achieves cult status in Japan, with books frequently selling millions of copies in hardcover editions alone, publishers in New York and Tokyo are making a fresh effort to internationalize the market for Japanese fiction. Already some of the Japanese publishing houses have employed bilingual editors from New York and London to make sure that the translations do justice to the authors.

To be sure, Americans have been reading fine Japanese literature for some time now, but they have never before had access to such a broad range of Japanese fiction—romances, sagas, mysteries, feminist novels, business novels, and, yes, even American-style hard-boiled detective fiction.

It's too soon to tell whether the new Japanese writers will have the staying power of some of their renowned literary predecessors: Kobo Abe, the author of *The Woman in the Dunes;* Yukio Mishima, the author of *The Sailor Who Fell from Grace with the Sea;* Junichiro Tanizaki, the author of *Some Prefer Nettles;* and Japan's only Nobel laureate in literature (1968), Yasunari Kawabata, the author of *Snow Country* and *Thousand Cranes.*

Their novels found audiences abroad because they were widely translated and, in some cases, turned into films.

Whatever the ultimate fate of the current generation of Japanese novelists, their works are now being read, talked about, and translated for an international audience: Haruki Murakami, the author of the acclaimed novel *A Wild Sheep Chase,* will have his next two novellas, *The End of the World* and *Hard-Boiled Wonderland,* translated for publication in the United States; Ryu Murakami (no relation to Haruki), the author of *Almost Transparent Blue,* will see his *Coin-Locker Babies* published in the United States, and American and European publishers are reportedly bidding for the translation rights to the works of a woman named Banana Yoshimoto, whose five novels (including *Kitchen,* her first) each have sold roughly a million copies in Japan, according to her publisher.

Editors here use terms like "Banana fever" and "Murakami madness" to describe the success of the new fiction. But what makes it distinctive? Reading these writers in English translations and seeing summaries of forthcoming translations of their work, I am struck by how dramatically different the characters in this fiction are from those in the classic Japanese literature of the recent past. The writers have been obviously influenced by the fast-paced action, racy language, casual sex, and laid-back attitudes of contemporary American novelists.

While these writers take many cues from American culture, they often worry about their reputations in Japan. When I visited Haruki Murakami, who had just returned to Tokyo from a three-year stint in Rome, he emphasized that he is a serious novelist despite his popularity. Dressed like one of his fictional characters—in jeans, a sweater, sneakers, and a Felix the Cat wristwatch (Felix is one of the most popular comic book characters in Japan)—and speaking in a low-key voice, occasionally accented by a raised eyebrow, Murakami said: "In Japan many people did not take *A Wild Sheep Chase* seriously. They didn't think I was *majime*—that's a word meaning 'earnest' or 'sober.'

Writers like Kobe, and Mishima are considered *majime* because
of what they wrote. Some of the older writers were also public
personalities. I stay out of the public eye because I want to be
free to move around and get on a train without being recognized. I don't go on television or to book parties, and I don't
socialize very much. I like to travel with my wife, listen to
music, and read." He paused. "But I think that I am *majime*,
too."

In *A Wild Sheep Chase,* the third of Murakami's six novels and
the first to be translated into English (by Alfred Birnbaum, an
American who grew up in Tokyo), a mysterious mutant sheep is
pursued by a middle-class protagonist who, in turn, is pitted
against powerful businessmen with political clout. Readers
looking for symbolism in the novel are free to imagine a clash
between modern and traditional forces in Japan. But Murakami
describes it in American fictional metaphors: "Melville and Fitzgerald both had the same thing in mind—the vain search for
something beyond reach."

Murakami, who grew up in Kobe, an international port city,
learned English by reading paperbacks left there by American
sailors. When he was in his mid-teens, he haunted secondhand
bookstores for cheap editions of American fiction. And eventually he turned to the business of writing and translating fiction
from English into Japanese. "I've translated Tim O'Brien, John
Irving, Raymond Carver, Tobias Wolff, and some of the short
stories of F. Scott Fitzgerald, he said. "I like translating very
much. When I work on a novel—and I'm at my Fuji-Two word
processor from six in the morning till ten at night when I'm
writing—I use one part of my brain." He tapped his head.
"When translating, I use another part of my brain. Translation
makes me escape from my regular work. I become transported,
relaxed."

Much as he enjoys translating, Murakami, who once studied
film and writing plays in hopes of becoming a director, refuses to
adapt his own works for film. "I don't allow any of my novels to

be made into movies," he says. "I've been asked to write screenplays of my books many times, but I've always declined. It's enough for a book to be a book."

Ryu Murakami, on the other hand, is more of a celebrity. He grew up in the port city of Sasebo in western Japan, studied at a college of art in Tokyo and submitted his novel *Almost Transparent Blue,* to a competition for new authors that was conducted by the literary monthly *Gunzo.* This free-wheeling novel, full of violence, sex, and casual mentions of Marlon Brando movies and Rolling Stones records, won the Akutagawa literary prize, a major award, and catapulted him to fame. While Murakami continued writing, he also worked as a radio disc jockey and interviewer. His latest novel, *Raffles Hotel,* is adapted from a screenplay he wrote about the famous old British hotel in Singapore.

In Japan, women authors who write about feminist themes and offbeat characters are also in demand. Banana Yoshimoto, the daughter of a well-known literary critic, is one. Although her work has yet to be translated, she has had three different publishers in Japan. And *Kitchen,* which is about an orphaned college student and her friendship with a transvestite, has already been filmed and is now is now being considered by American and European publishers.

Harumi Setouchi is another writer exploring unconventional domestic themes. Her autobiographical novel *The End of Summer,* which was translated by Janine Beichman and received the Women's Literary Award of Japan, tells of Tomoko, a woman in her late thirties, who is a married man's mistress. When an old lover of hers appears, she is forced to reexamine the emotional direction of her life.

Of all the current authors, though, Sawako Ariyoshi is regarded as the leading feminist writer of her generation. Several years ago she committed suicide, while still in her fifties, but not before leaving an impressive body of fiction (some of which has been translated) on such themes as pollution, the problems of caring for old people in contemporary society, and racial segregation.

One of Ariyoshi's books, *The Doctor's Wife,* translated by Wakako Hironaka and Ann Siller Kostant, is about the first doctor to perform surgery for breast cancer and the sacrifices his wife and mother make as they compete to promote his career. *The River Ki,* translated by Mildred Tahara, is the story of an arranged marriage that unites two families, one of wealth and position, the other of more modest means. The river Ki follows the course of the plot, which covers three generations of the families. Before the war, the river is a lovely jade green color; in the industrialized postwar period, the riverbanks are lined with smokestacks and the waters filled with chemicals.

There is plenty of serious Japanese fiction, but Japanese readers also have a taste for genre stories—from shopgirl romances to science fiction to business novels to murder mysteries. Mystery travels well across the ocean. One of the most popular Japanese mystery writers is Shizuko Natsuki, whose *Innocent Journey,* translated by Robert B. Rohner, centers on a double suicide pact. The young woman in the story, who is bored with college and her job as a Tokyo bar hostess, plans to join her lover, the president of a failing business, in death. Their plan fails. Instead of a double death, there is a murder that must be solved.

The most venerable mystery writer of them all, though, is Seicho Matsumoto, the author of some 450 novels, histories, and nonfiction works, who has won, among other honors, the Mystery Writers of Japan Prize. One of his most popular works, *Inspector Imanishi Investigates,* translated by Beth Cary, is a police procedural that features a wise, slightly jaded inspector who could pass as the first cousin of Georges Simenon's Inspector Maigret if he did not have one quirk that identifies him most definitely as Japanese. Inspector Imanishi does not puff on a pipe while he's pondering the murder of a disfigured man whose body was found in a Tokyo rail yard. No. Inspector Imanishi writes haiku.

[JANUARY 20, 1990]

PRAGUE:
FREEDOM'S VOICES

Prague

After decades of censorship and imprisonment, Czechoslovakia's writers are mounting a literary revolution after the political revolution that ended Communist rule. Nearly every author, editor, and samizdat publisher in the country has a story to tell.

There is something real and earnest about an author who has been jailed for his works and beliefs, especially here, where one such writer, the playwright Vaclav Havel, is now the nation's president.

Three cases illustrate the sordid past and the hope for the future of books in this corner of Europe: Jiri Stransky, an author who spent nine years in jail; Vladimir Pistorius, an editor who published illegal samizdat under the noses of the authorities; and Bohumil Hrabal, one of Czechoslovakia's most popular authors, whose novels were published uncensored in Europe and the United States but who was forced to change them at home.

To authors sentenced to the coal mines for writing or signing something that offends a government apparatchik, Stransky offered half-serious advice: Given the choice, it's better to dig for coal than uranium. The uranium mines are harder on the muscles, and the uranium may not be used for peaceful purposes. Writers like Stransky are too old to be called new. Stransky remembers first the Nazi and then the Soviet domination of his country. Yet in a real sense he and other Czechoslovak authors are starting anew because they are finally seeing their forbidden works published.

Stransky came from from a well-known family in the first Czechoslovak Republic in 1918; his grandfather was president of Parliament, and his father, a lawyer, survived a German concentration camp. The author said he was jailed for seven years, beginning in 1952, after a friend gave his name to the authorities. The friend had been caught leaving Czechoslovakia without official permission. The authorities told his friend they would shoot him unless he gave them the names of his friends. "So he did, but I didn't blame him," Stransky said. "That's the way things were then. Later my friend turned up in the same prison I was in. He was so embarrassed when he saw me there that he jumped out a window."

In prison someone gave him an English edition of Jack Schaefer's *Shane,* which he loved. "I pledged to myself that if I ever got out alive, I would translate it into Czech. And in 1965 I did, and it was published. I also translated Francis Parkman's *Oregon Trail.* I learned a lot about the American West that way."

After he got out, he worked in the building industry for three years. In 1963 his first short story was published; that led to invitations to write films. Two years later he was driven out of the film business because he had been a political prisoner. For the next seven years the author worked in a filling station pumping gas.

In 1969, a year after the Prague Spring of liberalization ended with the Soviet-led Warsaw Pact invasion of Czechoslovakia, Stransky's first book, *Happiness,* was published. Five days after the novel appeared, it was suppressed and all copies were ordered destroyed. The title story was linked to his prison experience. In 1970 he was sent to prison again for two years as an unrepentent dissident. The manuscript of his longest novel, *The Land That Got Wild,* which he describes as "the first Eastern Western," was banned.

More than twenty years after its suppression, Stransky finally saw *Happiness* published by Panorama, one of the newly free publishing houses. He gave President Havel one of the first copies.

Vladimir Pistorius is a former samizdat publisher in Prague who managed to elude the authorities and stay out of jail during more than a decade of illegal publishing. He's now forty and the new editor in chief of Mlada Fronta, a publishing house.

Pistorius published his books secretly in his home under the imprint "KE,78," which stands for Krameriova Expedice, a famous eighteenth-century bookseller. The 78 is for 1978, the year he began.

Among some thirty samizdat works that Pistorius brought out—each book in typed editions of a half dozen or so copies—were *Alcools* by Guillaume Apollinaire, the French poet; Isaac Bashevis Singer's novel *Shosha,* about ghetto life in Poland before World War II; *The Professional Fault,* a work by Tom Stoppard, the British dramatist who was born in Zlin, Czechoslovakia, now called Gottwaldov, and both parts of Shakespeare's *Henry IV.* The Shakespeare play had to appear in samizdat form because its translator, Zdenek Urbanck, had once signed a dissident statement advocating freedom to publish.

Pistorius, a physicist, first got into trouble with the authorities while performing his army service in 1975. The political commissar in his brigade called for a show of hands in favor of Gustav Husak, the Communist party leader with close ties to the Soviet Union, for president of Czechoslovakia. Nobody liked Mr. Husak, yet everyone raised his hand—everyone, that is, except Sergeant Pistorius.

"After that, I had a black mark on my record," he said. "The brigade commissar invented a fable that I was in favor of war and other stupid stories like that. The army sent a letter to the Communist party in Prague when I finished my service, reporting my political misconduct. So I couldn't get a job as a physicist. But I managed to earn a living as a computer programmer."

Over the next ten years Pistorius edited about 125 typed books, plays, novels, political tracts, and poetry that added up to some 2,000 copies.

"I typed some of the books myself, and sometimes I paid a typist out of my own pocket," he said. "I count that the time we spent on these copies came to ten thousand hours, meaning five years of work."

How did he avoid getting caught?

"Well, I lived by certain rules," he said. "I never spoke on the telephone. My colleagues did not know each other. Nobody knew anybody else. We did not use state office machines but worked at home. I tried to minimize my contacts. And my wife and I cautioned our son never to talk about what we did at home to any of the other children at school. We were proud that he never did."

Bohumil Hrabal, who is seventy-six, is known in the United States and Europe as the author of *Closely Watched Trains,* which became a film; *I Served the King of England;* and a novella, *Too Loud a Solitude.* It is about the indestructability of books and also a parable about the effort to maintain a semblance of sanity despite the presence of Nazi jackboots and Soviet tanks in Prague.

In Prague, shortly after three in the afternoon, when the church bell at the far end of the square first rings—a signal that his favorite beer hall, the Golden Tiger, has opened—Hrabal strolled in, wearing a backpack imprinted "University of Chicago." He walked past the crowded tables of beer drinkers and headed straight for the small back room. There he held court at his table, surrounded by a half dozen of his drinking buddies.

At first Hrabal seemed the least talkative, but then, after the good Czechoslovak Pilsner had taken effect, he glanced at an American review of *Too Loud a Solitude* that I handed to him, raised his glass in acknowledgment, and said: "*Solitude* is my favorite book. It's the only one that I can reread."

One reason, a friend who translated for him explained, is that the hero of the book is a baler of wastepaper. It's one of many nonwriting jobs Hrabal once had.

Hrabal's samizdat publisher, Vaclav Kadlec, pulled out three copies of his books. "The first was done in 1971 on a typewriter," Kadlec said, "with its pages held together by nails, the second some years later by making photocopies, the third in 1988 by word processor." Kadlec, now the editor of Prazke Imaginace, another free publishing house, said he used state-owned machines to type and copy Hrabal's books.

"I invented a false name for a publishing house: Carnation," he said. "The police were never able to find who was behind Carnation or where it was located because it didn't exist."

During the same period Hrabal's books were officially published in censored editions in Czechoslovakia but published abroad in translation from the uncensored samizdat. All of his books are now expected to be published in uncensored editions in Prague.

The authorities obviously knew he was publishing illegal editions of his books abroad. Why wasn't he stopped or imprisoned?

"Because, like Jaroslav Seifert, the Czech who received the Nobel Prize in literature in 1984, Hrabal was too popular," Kadlec said. "It would have caused too much of a scandal."

Hrabal's samizdat publisher added: "The police did interrogate Hrabal. He recently wrote an essay called 'The Total Fears,' confessing and apologizing for the fact that he was afraid of the Communist government in Prague and the Russian presence. But one thing he did not do was blame others for allowing his books to be published in censored editions. He did not name names."

Freedom—for our pens and persons—is what it's all about, everywhere.

[JANUARY 7, 1991]

INDEX